MISSING

More true stories from families of Australian missing persons

NICOLE MORRIS

Big Sky Publishing Pty Ltd
PO Box 303, Newport, NSW 2106, Australia
Phone: 1300 364 611
Fax: (61 2) 9918 2396
Email: info@bigskypublishing.com.au
Web: www.bigskypublishing.com.au

Cover design and typesetting: Think Productions

 A catalogue record for this
book is available from the
National Library of Australia

Title: Missing. More true stories from families of Australian missing persons
ISBN: 978-1-923144-48-4

MISSING

More true stories from families of Australian missing persons

BIG SKY PUBLISHING
www.bigskypublishing.com.au

NICOLE MORRIS

Contents

TESTIMONIALS

Life for a missing person's family is a harrowing experience, a journey of ambiguous loss quite incomprehensible for those who have never travelled this path. Too often when we read of missing persons in the media, they are portrayed in quite a dispassionate way. Nicole's empathy to understand the feelings and emotions of families, allows her to be objective and rational, whilst at the same time allowing the reader to truly "know" the missing – humanising them. These stories are gut-wrenching, frustrating, an emotional roller-coaster, triggering. You'll feel despair and hopeful. May these loved ones be brought home to their families.

Suzie Ratcliffe, sister of missing child Joanne Ratcliffe, founder of "Leave a Light On Inc."

Reading Sandrine's chapter, I'm lost for words, as I'm overwhelmed by emotion! Throughout reading it I feel each emotion they feel. The frustration, confusion, heartbreak, and the hope! I was able to hold back tears until Jessie's letter. From a daughter to a daughter; you feel and relate to it so much more. Perhaps also because there's so many similarities, not just with our parents' health and lifestyle, but the handling of their cases. Even down to incorrect spelling of family names! All missing persons need to be treated as homicides until proven otherwise! Certainly not just written off as suicide, especially if there is mental health present. It's always comforting to hear you are not alone in the way you feel.

Susie Stoodley, daughter of missing Billy Steffen (featured in "Vanished")

Of all the haunting stories in this book, the mysterious disappearance of doting South Australian dad, Steven Lockey is by far the most unfathomable and unsettling. Nicole meticulously highlights the many troubling twists in this tragic story – from numerous unconfirmed sightings of the missing man spanning twenty years, to the more disturbing prospect that he may be yet another victim of the notorious Snowtown Serial Killers. Most puzzling of all, is the recent refusal of SA police to release Steven's missing person's file to his grieving family - because they believe it may hold crucial clues in what remains, an active investigation.

Megan Norris, award-winning true crime author, journalist and freelance writer

FOREWORD
Julie Hand

Nicole Morris is the Director of the Australian Missing Persons Register (AMPR), which she founded in 2005. She is a voice for voiceless missing persons, tirelessly making appeals for them, and raising awareness. She has provided comfort and guidance to countless families and friends of missing persons as they undertake their journeys to find their missing loved ones.

The Australian Missing Persons Register Facebook page has 181,000 followers; these are people in the community who want to help reunite the missing with their families and help families find their missing loved ones, and send care and hope to families of the missing. Sadly, some missing persons are found deceased.

My own daughter Jody Galante was listed on the AMPR Facebook page when she went missing in January 2006 and thousands of people shared the information, commented and looked for her. Unfortunately, our Jody was found murdered, and Nicole Morris reached out to me in a way that only she can, and we have become good friends. I have followed her passionate pleas for the missing ever since.

Nicole is such a comfort to hundreds of family members and friends both here at home and abroad. She leaves no stone unturned in the search for answers for the families and has made many lasting friendships along the way.

Nicole has gained the respect of law enforcement and government agencies both in Australia and around the world and works closely with them. She has participated in many podcasts about missing persons, appeared on radio programs, magazines articles and news stories, wherever she can bring awareness to missing persons and highlight the trauma their families go through, sometimes for decades.

In 2012, Nicole won the Queensland Pride of Australia award for Community Spirit, then in the same year went on to win the National Gold Medal. She has been nominated twice for Australian of the Year. She has appeared many times on radio and television and in newsprint.

In 2023, Nicole finished writing her first book titled *Vanished*, sharing the stories from families of Australian missing persons. The book covers ten missing persons cases and the families' stories; two of those families are Queenslanders. *Vanished* launched in June 2023 and is further testament to Nicole's tireless efforts in raising awareness of missing persons in this country and giving families hope that their loved ones are not forgotten.

As a footnote, I will add that Nicole Morris has never experienced having a loved one or friend go missing, but in 2005 she watched a news article about missing persons and, as a caring human being, knew she had to help.

Unlike other deaths, homicide has a special insidiousness

which bores away at families, it never ends, really.

There has been such a good response to *Vanished*, and everyone is eager for book two. Nicole and AMPR deserve every bit of recognition.

INTRODUCTION

I think for a moment of the cold earth around the pale bones and I feel the same cold creep inside me, and if I had known I would willingly have curled into that wooden chest and kept her company for seventy years.

So wrote the brilliant Emma Healey in her novel *Elizabeth is Missing*. I wrote to Emma and told her how incredibly she managed to capture the feelings of those who are missing a loved one, and she said she'd be honoured for me to include this passage in my book. For it is rare for us, who have never experienced having a lost loved one, to understand what these families go through.

In the introduction of my last book, I told you that 53,000 people a year go missing in Australia. Sadly, I must now update that number, as the new statistics have been released by police. In 2022, 55,000 people went missing. That works out to be 150 people a day. However, over 99 per cent of those people are located; not always alive, but at least the families who love and miss them know what happened. That isn't always the case, as you will see with the missing people featured here in the sequel to *Vanished* which features more true stories from families of Australian missing persons.

Once again you will get to hear first-hand from the brothers and sisters of these missing persons as they describe their painful journeys, which often last for decades. In the missing persons world, you hear catchphrases like 'ambiguous loss', and 'lived experience'. I have not had that lived experience, but I try to help the families describe what they're feeling, what they live with. It's the simplest of phrases that truly sums up for me what it's like having a person you love go missing: 'Wish you were here, Jess,' says Nickylee, sister of missing person Jessica Gaudie, who will forever be 16, but should have turned 40 the day Nickylee wrote that on the Australian Missing Persons Register (AMPR) page.

I am grateful and humbled by the success of *Vanished – True stories from families of Australian missing persons*. The ten cases in that book struck a chord with readers, and had a profound impact on people who follow Australian Missing Persons Register, and people who have never heard of me and the register before. People don't always think about missing persons unless it's someone they know, or there's a high-profile case on TV, like the Chris Dawson trial, or the anniversary of William Tyrrell's disappearance. So, I deeply appreciate those who picked up my book, knowing nothing about missing persons, and read it. I had such a positive and heartfelt response from the public, and I love hearing from people, particularly those who said they haven't read a book in years, but read mine.

The families who featured in the first book were so thankful and relieved that so many more people were learning about their missing loved ones. There are a couple of updates from the stories in the first book. As I finish this second book, we are still waiting for identification of human remains that were found in Hobart, Tasmania, quite close to where Billy Steffen went missing. As soon as I heard about the find, I messaged Billy's daughter Susie, as I knew she'd want to know immediately. She contacted Tasmania Police, but unlike Hollywood TV shows, the wheels of DNA testing and identification of remains move very slowly. This can be more difficult when remains have been exposed to the elements, and this is the case with the Clifton Beach remains.

Susie told me the police had not yet DNA-tested the remains when she called them. 'The detective certainly didn't dismiss me, which means they haven't ruled Dad out,' she says. The remains were found on 6 July 2023, and police say they had been there for between five to at least thirty years. Billy went missing in 1985, so a little longer than thirty years, but it can be hard to be exact with skeletal remains. They know the remains are of an adult male. They were found on a farm property above cliffs, halfway between Clifton Beach and Goats Beach.

The ABC reported Inspector Andrew Keane as saying: 'Preliminary forensic analysis determined the remains belong to a man of Caucasian or Indian sub-continental descent, most likely to be middle aged.'

Billy Steffen was in his mid-thirties when he went missing. Inspector Keane said a pair of black dress shoes, a short-sleeved top and a plastic bag containing two keys on a keychain, a cigarette lighter and two possible ID cards were also located. Oddly, just the right shoe had several orthotics in the heel, the kind purchased from a chemist. These last items are puzzling; his family say Billy didn't have any issues with his feet, but we know he had been living rough for a while before he went missing and did not have a car, so he would have walked a lot. It's possible Billy may have developed a foot problem such as plantar fasciitis, or an Achilles tendon issue, which might have been alleviated with orthotics.

Daughter Susie wonders if the shoes were too big, as perhaps they were donated or found or purchased second hand, and he may have used the orthotics to make them fit better. Billy was a smoker, so the cigarette lighter fits. Susie said: 'I could see Dad having that type of lighter.' Police released a photo of a T-shirt found with the skeleton, and when I look at it, I see an almost identical shirt to the ones Billy is wearing in just about every single photo I have of him. Billy had been living on the beach at Saltwater River. By road that's an hour and a half between the two, but Billy didn't have a car. If you look at a map, the two peninsulas face each other. If Billy wanted to keep living in an isolated coastal area, Goat's Beach would be an ideal place to choose.

Readers may also recall that in the story of Kay Docherty and Toni Cavanagh, there was a witness, himself a victim of abuse, who was willing to take police to a site on a beach where he believes Kay and Toni's bodies are buried. Tragically, that man recently died. We will never know what he wanted to show police.

After the publication of *Vanished*, I was thrilled to finally meet some of the people I spoke with in my book when they came to the book launches. I met both of Richard Leape's sisters, Annette and Mandy, and Mandy's husband. I met Susie, Billy Steffen's daughter, and her family, as well as Billy's sister

Susanne, who I also interviewed for the book. It was a proud moment when, as we all went to dinner together after the book launch, I saw the Leape sisters, Susie and her aunt all chatting together, sharing their experiences. They told me they'd never met another family of a missing person. It's a club no-one wants to belong to, but if there are positives to come from their experiences, it is surely the friendships, connections and support that they can give one another, as they alone uniquely know what it feels like to have a missing family member.

Later that year I went to Melbourne to record the audiobook version of *Vanished*, and I was so excited to finally meet the amazing Leicester sisters, Ali and Bron, whose story in the final chapter of *Vanished* broke everyone's hearts.

I loved meeting Jess Mazurek during the writing of *Vanished* – we caught up for lunch one day – and I have plans to soon meet with Marcia Ryan's brother Tony. I have been online friends with all these people for many, many years.

Thanks for coming back into the world of missing persons with me and learning about another 12 people. My last book was not an emotionally easy read, and neither is this … but this book does end with a story that will restore your faith in the world.

CHAPTER ONE
Steven Lockey

Steven Lockey was last seen on 11 August 1994, near Broadmeadows Railway Station in Elizabeth North, Adelaide, South Australia. He was 30 years old.

Is Steven Lockey still alive? The deeper I dug into his story, the more confused I became, and the more questions I had.

Steven and his family emigrated to Australia from the UK, arriving in 1973. The six Lockey siblings were Patricia, Brenda, Gloria, Steven, Sonia and Sylvia. The newly arrived family settled in Prospect, a northern suburb of Adelaide, South Australia, then moved around to various other locations. The family came to Australia with almost nothing and had to build their life here from scratch.

'We made the most of what we had,' says Sonia. 'We'd get out and do things together; play sport, cricket and soccer, go swimming, build go-karts together. Steven liked outdoor things. He liked goldfish; that's something he and Dad did together. I remember he and Dad were cleaning out the tank one day, and one of the fish got too close to the hose and was sucked up. Steven got really upset about that.'

When I asked the sisters what their relationship with Steven was like as children, they had identical answers: 'We used to fight all the time,' says Sonia. 'He used to try to push my buttons, like a normal brother. He was a bully. Having five sisters, he had to be the man.' Sylvia agrees. 'We fought like cat and dog,' she says. 'Although we were very close. I was very young, but we used to punch on, you know? My sisters would get dolls, but me and my brother would get Evel Knievel figures. There were three or four years between us in age.' Gloria remembers Steven as being spoiled by their mother. 'Me and my brother were very close, as we were almost the same age,' she says. 'He always used to stick up for me.' Brenda remembers a normal, happy childhood where they all played together and had fun outside.

When he was about 13 or 14 Steven started to get into trouble. He stopped going to school, telling his mother he was simply not going anymore. 'She couldn't really make him go; she was powerless,' says Sonia. Instead of going to school, Steven spent his time at home, doing very little. His father had little to do with his family after he left in about 1977. 'Dad was seeing someone when we were children, and I was so angry,' says Gloria. 'He said he was leaving, and he just went to Queensland.' Brenda remembers the reason her father left. 'He gave my mum an ultimatum,' she says. 'He said, "It's either me or the kids". He wanted Mum to give up all of us kids, and just live her life with him. Mum chose all of us. Dad used to hit us; he used to give our sister, Patricia, black eyes, he used to thump her. He drank every weekend. Before we moved to Australia, in Cypress, my father stabbed my mother. She went to hospital, but no charges were made.' The family stayed together and moved to Australia, and the violence continued throughout their childhood.

Sonia thinks the breakdown of their parents' marriage had a negative impact on Steven. 'He took it really hard,' she says. Steven started rebelling. He was about 13 when he started to get into trouble, after previously being a pretty good kid. He mixed with a crowd of other boys, and they started breaking into houses and stealing.' Sylvia doesn't think he was the leader in this group, but instead went along with the others. 'It was because of who he was associating with,' she says. 'It was a group decision, to do the crimes.' Around this time, Steven also started sniffing glue. 'He had a few mates who would do it with him,' says Sonia. 'I think he was rebelling. He wasn't coping after Dad left.'

Brenda recalls Steven would also chew the dried glue. Sylvia's former partner, Rick, was a friend of Steven's, and says the glue-sniffing lasted at least 10 years. Steven's pain was also manifesting itself in self-harm. 'He used to cut himself, across the chest,' says Sonia, 'and on his wrists. He did a lot of things in his life, to hurt himself. He was definitely depressed. It grew on him.' Sylvia remembers the glue-sniffing and slashed wrists. She says she thinks Steven wanted attention, but also says: 'It was just the way he was. He was probably crying out for help, but we didn't know back then, did we? Today's a bit different to when we were growing up. I didn't think there was anything wrong with him.' Steven's wife Tammy believed these were suicide attempts, which occurred when his first relationship ended.

The substance abuse had a serious effect on Steven's mental health. 'His personality went from bad to worse,' says Sonia. 'When Dad left, Steven tried to walk in Dad's footsteps; he tried to take over as head of the house, but we said nah, this isn't going to happen. We stood up to him, but when he couldn't get his own way, he'd hit us. He tried to tell us what to do, acting like our father instead of our brother.' Sylvia, being the youngest, doesn't remember seeing Steven's angry side. 'He did drink a lot. That's what our parents did back then, and *monkey see, monkey do*, but other than that I thought he was fine.'

Gloria remembers one Easter, when a group including Steven went camping together. Steven was about 15. Apparently, it was too cold for Steven's liking. 'Steven said: "I know where I can go that's nice and warm ..." and he shot himself in the hand, and went to hospital,' says Gloria. 'He had a BB gun, or something.' At some point Steven was jailed, in Adelaide Prison, but the sisters can't recall when this was, or what it was for. Daughter Jodie was told her dad was a larrikin, who did get into trouble at times.

In his late teens Steven met a girl, and together they became parents. 'That was a good thing for him,' says Gloria. 'It made him wake up to himself. He matured. She turned his life around.' Sylvia agrees. She doesn't think Steven was too young to become a father. 'He loved all his kids,' she says. 'It was just unfortunate that it didn't work out with his first girlfriend. She moved to New Zealand, but when they came back over, he did see his daughter. His girlfriend and me were best friends. We all hung out together, went out.' Steven had moved out of the family home to be with his girlfriend, living in a flat in North Adelaide, but the pressure of being teen parents was too great, and the relationship broke down. Steven was 17 when his daughter was born, and his girlfriend only 15. Steven moved back home.

When his daughter and her mother moved back to Australia, he started to see daughter Jodie regularly, and these were very happy memories for her. 'He used to ride his pushbike to Nanna's house,' she says. 'I remember he'd dinky me back to his house. He dropped off a T-shirt to the house one day, when we weren't home; it said, "Daddy's Little Girl". I always felt like he wanted a lot to do with me and wanted to see me. He was very quick to make contact when we came back to Australia and set up the visits. He'd ask me, jokingly, if I had a boyfriend yet and I'd say, "No Dad!" And he'd say: "Well, you'll have to let me know when you do … so I can kill him!" He was a gentle, kind dad.'

Steven met Tammy and together they had three more children. Along with Tammy's son, Steven now had five children. He was working and taking care of his family. Steven's daughter Samantha was happy to speak to me in the hope of finding some answers about what's happened to her dad. She knew very little about the situation before our conversation and has been very surprised at what she's learned. She was not even aware that her father had been living with her aunt in the week prior to his disappearance. 'I didn't know my parents weren't living together when my dad went missing,' she says. 'The family is very fractured. I was only three when Dad went missing, so I only have two or three memories of him. I have a memory of walking my brother to kindy; I was riding on Dad's shoulders. I've been told he was a very hands-on, great dad.'

When Jodie spent time with her dad, he took her fishing, and these are very happy memories for her. 'We used to go to Second Valley, fishing and squidding. He would wake me up in the night and whisper, "Hey, do you want to go fishing?" I'd say yeah! We'd take off in the night, and we'd go fishing as the sun was coming up.'

The greatest pain in his life was still his father leaving, but Steven's father did come back into his life, and when Steven married, his dad gave the couple $1000. They didn't have many family get-togethers, however, really only coming together at Christmas. 'We had our own families to look after,' says Gloria. 'We didn't really stay close after we all had kids.' Six days after their wedding Steven and Tammy's family home burned to the ground. Tragically, their dogs were later found under one of the children's beds. 'He worked his arse off to get us out of the house,' says daughter Samantha. 'But he couldn't get the dogs out.' The only thing the couple managed to save, apart from their family, was the $1000 given to them by Steven's dad. Samantha didn't know that story. The police and fire brigade did investigate the fire as a possible arson, but concluded it was an electrical fault. The young family moved into a new house.

'We just stuck together and moved forward,' says Tammy. They had been living at Kilburn. Gloria says Steven didn't want to live in Elizabeth, where his sisters lived. 'He thought it was a dump,' says Gloria. Steven had given up the glue-sniffing, but did drink heavily. 'Something else happened that really affected Steven,' says Sonia. 'We had a brother-in-law, David, who was Brenda's husband. Steven and David were close drinking buddies. On Christmas Eve 1991, David was in a car accident and was killed.' Sonia says this tragedy added to Steven's ongoing pain and trauma. Around this time, Steven was working in carpentry, constructing sewing machine cabinets, but had recently been retrenched.

'He started to become withdrawn and depressed, and relied on the drink,' says Tammy. She doesn't know the reasons behind Steven's unhappiness, other than being abandoned by his dad. She says Steven was easy-going and happy when they first got together, but as the years went on he became a closed book and did not talk about how he was feeling. 'He just wasn't there,' says Tammy. 'He was on antidepressants when he left. I was never allowed to go to any of his doctor's appointments with him.' Steven's youngest child was almost one at this stage. There were four children in the home, and Steven also had his daughter from his first relationship. He made it clear he was not in a position to add any more children to the family. This caused conflict between Steven and Tammy.

In August 1994 Steven had a serious argument with his wife. Tammy, herself, is candid about this incident, telling me how she got into the car and drove over Steven's foot. Six months after Steven disappeared Tammy told her story to *That's Life* magazine, including this fight. The story in this article is a little different to the recollections of today. Tammy told the magazine that Steven's brother-in-law John, husband to Brenda, had offered the couple a $10,000 loan. Tammy refused the loan, but Steven wanted to take it. The article says Steven had been retrenched from his machinist's job, and the family had no money. A close friend of Steven's has said this would have been a very strange thing to happen, as Steven hated borrowing money and almost never did. Even his first car was paid for with cash and not a loan.

On the day of this fight, Steven and Tammy had friends over, and were drinking with them. In the article, Tammy says Steven got into her car, and when she tried to stop him, *he* ran over *her* foot while reversing out of the driveway. The police were called, and they asked Steven to leave the home. The next morning at 6 am Steven returned to the house and again tried to take her car. Tammy shut the gates to stop him leaving and Steven threw her car keys onto the roof. She then told the magazine that Steven 'ran off'. Not mentioned in the article, but also occurring that day, is a very serious incident that Tammy told me about. 'The last time Steven and I saw each other, we had a major fight and I beat him up,' says Tammy. 'The police have still got my cricket bat. They won't give my cricket bat back until his body is found. Apparently, I went to town on him. I don't have any recollection of it, but I have to believe my best friend and the police, and when I went home, I had to clean up the blood.'

After this incident Steven left the house. 'I believe he'd had enough of family life, and just wanted his own,' says Tammy. 'I still hold onto that belief.' I asked Tammy if she thought Steven could just do that, walk away from his kids, and she replies, 'Absolutely. Because of the way he was, mentally.'

Steven went to stay with his sister Sylvia, and was there for about a week. 'He was living with me, at my house,' she says. 'I was at work one day, and came home to find a note from Steven. It was 11 August 1994. The note said, 'Tell my kids I love them.'

I have seen a copy of the note and it reads in full:

Rick Sylvia It's time to leave. Thanks for everything. P.S. Love all of you. Tammy – Life's a bitch then you marry one. P.S Hope you and Trina are happy together. Love all my kids. Signed Steven Lockey.

Samantha didn't know about the note. I was able to tell her about it when we spoke, and the thought that her Dad's last written words were about her and her siblings leaves her very emotional. 'That breaks my heart,' she says. Her sister Jodie had a similar reaction. Sylvia's former husband, Rick, was able to fill in some of the blanks of what happened next, telling a story even Sylvia didn't know until I interviewed her in 2023.

Rick was home when Steven decided to leave. 'He just turned around and said: "I'm out of here, I'm gone." He said he was pissed off with everything. I said, "What do you mean? You're not coming back?" And he said no. I said, "What do you want to do with your stuff?" And he said, "Keep it." I did ask him where he was going, and he said he didn't know. He left the house, and someone was waiting outside to pick him up, and they left in their car. That was in the morning sometime, about 10 o'clock. I thought the person was dropping him off at the train station.' Rick was under the impression that the person who picked Steven up was one of his brothers-in-law. Brenda does not know who picked Steven up, but is certain it was not her husband. 'We lived in Kilburn, and Sylvia lived in Elizabeth Field (now Davoren Park), and there's no way he would have got from Kilburn to Elizabeth Field in such a short time to take Steven wherever he wanted to go. My husband was at home with me all morning.' It's about a half-hour drive between the two locations.

Sylvia recollects that she was later told there was an incident that same day at the home of one of her sisters. 'I was told Steven had a handful of pills. He was threatening to kill himself. We all lived in the same area, it was just a short walk between all our houses.' However, none of the other sisters have ever heard this story, and they say the incident didn't happen at their homes. It's possible it was at Patricia's house, but unlikely, as she lived in Kilburn, and this was some distance from where her sisters lived at Elizabeth. Sylvia thought this happened at Brenda's house, but Brenda did not see Steven at all that day. It remains unknown where Steven was between the time he was picked up from Sylvia's in the morning until about 3 pm.

Steven turned up at Gloria's house at Elizabeth Field in the afternoon, and she says he was not upset or agitated in any way. She thinks he walked there. 'He asked my then-husband to take him to Broadmeadows railway station,' says Gloria. 'He said he wanted to go to Gawler. That was the last time we saw him. He seemed fine to me. Maybe he was going to Gawler, then somewhere else? I have no idea. I don't know if he knew anyone there. I thought he was just going to see somebody, or just go for a train ride.' Until I spoke with her, Gloria had never heard the story about Steven and the pills, and she didn't realise he had left all his belongings at Sylvia's or had been staying with her. The magazine article says Gloria rang Tammy and told her Steven had been staying at her house, and that Tammy had later been to Gloria and Bill's home, but she was too late to see Steven; he had already left.

Gloria's husband Bill, who has since passed away, dropped Steven at Broadmeadows train station at about 3 or 4 pm. This was the last time he was seen. According to Tammy, Bill bought Steven two bottles of beer on the way to the station from the Davoren Park pub around the corner. Tammy thinks Bill actually saw him get on the train. Sonia continues the story: 'My eldest sister Patricia – who isn't with us anymore – Steven rang her, and she said to him, "Keep in touch."' It was believed that phone call was made from Broadmeadows train station, but Tammy tells me that's impossible, as there were no phone boxes at Broadmeadows station. This suggests Steven made the call from Gawler.

'When my sister spoke to him on the phone, she could hear a train in the background,' says Sonia. The trip from Broadmeadows to Gawler is about 15 minutes by train. Brenda is able to continue the story, as she is certain Steven *did* catch the train to Gawler, and says he also rang her from the payphone there. She answered the phone to him and heard the STD pips. For those who didn't grow up in the pre-mobile phone era, there was a time when people made calls from payphones, and whenever the call was from a longer distance away than Telecom considered local, it was deemed a long-distance call, or what we'd refer to as an STD call (subscriber trunk dialling). 'I spoke to him, then he wanted to talk to John,' says Brenda. John was her husband at the time. 'He spoke to John, and he said he'd had enough, and he was taking off, he was moving on.' Brenda isn't sure what else Steven said to John, but knows he was the last person Steven spoke to. The phone call came late in the afternoon.

Steven Lockey has never been seen or heard from since this time.

'He left everything at my house,' says Sylvia. 'He left his motorbike, his clothes, everything. So, whether it was a spur of the moment decision to do it, I don't know. I never knew about the phone call from the train station. Whether he got on the train or not, who knows?'

Her former husband, Rick, has never been asked by police what happened that day or since. They were mates, and he thinks he knows why Steven just wanted to leave. 'I think he was just upset about … life,' says Rick. 'I don't think he was working at that point. Nothing was going right. He had troubles, and he was upset about how things were at home. I thought he was just going to piss off somewhere. He wasn't suicidal. I wouldn't have a clue where he might have gone. I didn't know he was really *missing*. Back in the day, he was sniffing a lot of glue, but he'd stopped that about when he had his kids. He started to get his head on straight, and he got a job. But then it all started to go wrong. I don't think he was depressed; he was more just pissed off at the way things had turned out. If he wanted to start a new life, then I'm not surprised he didn't contact any of us. It's understandable. But he got on with his kids really well, and I thought he might have contacted them over the years. Or one of his sisters, to let them know he was okay. But nothing.'

Gloria isn't surprised that Steven left without a word, as he was used to keeping things to himself and not telling anybody anything. 'I think he wouldn't even have told his mates, he would have just gone,' she says.

There must have been a great deal of pressure on Steven at this time. He had four children that were biologically his and his wife had an older son from a previous relationship. He had two failed relationships, had lost his job, money was very tight, his father had not been in his life growing up when Steven really needed him, his house had burned down and he was at one time suspected of being involved, and his workplace had also burned down, leaving him out of a job. It's easy to understand why Steven was at a very low point; why he might have felt like just leaving it all behind and trying to start again.

It was Brenda and her husband who reported Steven as a missing person to police, two days after he was last seen. Despite Steven telling them in his phone call he was intending to leave, something made them concerned enough to report him missing. Brenda says it was Steven's conversation with her husband that had them worried. It was about a week after Steven was reported missing that police visited Tammy.

'I didn't even know he was missing until the police came and questioned me,' she says. Gloria didn't realise Steven was a missing person for several weeks. 'When I heard, it went through my head that he was doing exactly the same as Dad did,' she says. 'Left his kids and off he went.' Sylvia started to become worried when he didn't return for his belongings or make any contact with her. 'I was concerned that something had happened to him, but Steven is Steven. He hardly ever talked about his problems, he just kept it to himself.' Sonia agrees Steven didn't open up about how he was feeling. She says: 'He tried making a good life for himself after he lost his job; in the end I think he just gave up. He lost a couple of jobs – the first one he lost because the business burnt to the ground. Steven had a lot on his shoulders.' Gloria thinks the glue-sniffing and heavy alcohol use contributed to Steven's problems. 'I think it was hard for him having a lot of kids,' says Gloria. 'I think he thought, that's it, I'm going to go. Just like Dad did.'

'We don't know why he left,' says Sonia. 'Whether or not he was still involved in criminal activity. We tried getting the police involved, but they said being a missing person is not a criminal offence. They eventually ended up taking the missing person report, but that was all they could do.' Brother-in-law Rick also recalls police did not seem to do very much to find Steven. 'I did hear a few years back that the police did do a search; they were checking Sydney and Melbourne. Apparently, someone had seen him over there? But I don't know much about that. I actually thought they'd found him and he didn't want any contact.'

Tammy was not surprised that Steven left his family, and she was very angry with him for doing it. 'I wasn't in the right frame of mind back then, because he'd left me,' she says. 'I thought it was a cop-out. I wasn't surprised that he'd just walked out. He said it in the note he left [at Sylvia's], "Life's a bitch, then you marry one." I didn't know anything about the note until I got called in by the police.' Incredibly, Tammy says that she was asked by police to check out all the possible reported sightings of Steven herself. 'My situation at the time was I was only 22, and I had four young kids, aged one, three, five and seven. Every time there was a so-called sighting of him, I had to separate all my kids and put them somewhere, and go and check out these sightings. And not once were they ever in South Australia. They would call me all the time. That was all off my own bat, no help from the police or anything. I had to go and see whether it was him or not, say yes or no, then come back.

'The only one I refused to do was a sighting in Tasmania somewhere; I told them I wasn't going overseas for anyone. So, after two years of doing that, I got sick of it, and I divorced him. I had to fight to get the divorce, because he's a missing person.'

I have never before heard of this happening, of the police asking a family to travel interstate to check possible sightings of their missing loved one. Tammy does not think police investigated Steven's disappearance very thoroughly. She has not heard from the police in over 25 years. 'We've heard nothing from the police at all,' says Sonia. Gloria also says she has never heard from the police, despite Steven having stayed with her. 'They never came around,' she says. 'I don't think the police ever investigated his disappearance properly. They should have absolutely done more than they did. It's very upsetting. I wish they had, as we might have had some closure, and find out what's happened.'

Jodie was about 12 when her father went missing. Like most of the others in his life who he was close to, Steven rang his daughter around this time. Curiously, he didn't tell her he was leaving, but instead said something different. 'I was seeing him every Saturday,' she says. 'I used to volunteer at the Riding for the Disabled, and in return I was allowed to join the pony club and ride their horses. Dad would pick me up from there, and I'd go back to their house. I'd usually stay the night. I remember one day he rang me, and said: "I won't be able to pick you up this weekend. Tammy and I had a fight, so I won't be there. But I'll ring you and I'll let you know what's going on." That was the last phone call I got, and I never heard from him again. For me as a child, how long is that period of time until you start to think, well, is he going to ring me? He almost just faded away. The phone call never came. On the odd occasion that I'd see my cousins they'd say, "Hey, Jodie, do you know your dad's missing?" So, I knew, but it was kind of hard to understand, at that age.'

A couple of years after Steven disappeared something strange happened. Sonia was living in Taperoo, a beachside suburb of Adelaide. 'My children were going to school one morning, and they came back to the house. They said, "Mum! There's a man outside that looks like Uncle Steven!" So, I went outside to have a look; this man was working on the road with a crew just out the front of my house. He was the spitting image of my brother. The same height and everything. I rang the police and they came and checked him out, and they said no, it wasn't him.' Sonia didn't approach the man. 'I had a good look at him, and he looked at me, but I should have said to him: "I want to see if you've got any tattoos." He sort of looked at me like he knew me. I was just curious, whether it was him.'

Sonia's son Damien was eight or nine when his uncle went missing. Damien has contacted me the most about Steven; for more than ten years he's been urging me to keep making appeals for his uncle. It was Damien who saw the man outside his house that day while he was going to school. Damien recalls that when he saw the man, he ran to get his cousins, who lived just a street away.

'Walking down the road we see this council worker, who we thought was Uncle Steven,' says Damien. 'We had some cousins who lived in the same suburb, and we all went to the same school together, so we got them and walked back to where this council worker was. All six of us there. We started talking (loudly) about Uncle Steven to see if it would cause a reaction from this man. None of us was positive if it was him or not, so we walked back home, and got my mother to walk back with us, as she would be able to confirm if it was or not.' At the time Sonia didn't think the man was Steven, but after speaking to a psychic, and thinking about him further, she changed her mind. 'I know for a fact it was him,' Sonia told me.

'I was eight years old when he disappeared,' says nephew Damien. 'I do believe he went off away from us, his family, of his own accord.'

Gloria also spoke to a clairvoyant about Steven. 'She said he's living in New South Wales, but he doesn't want any of the family to get in contact with him.' Steven had been to Melbourne, but never to New South Wales, so Gloria isn't sure where in NSW he would go.

There was another strange incident with a NSW connection. Gloria says: 'I was on Facebook one time and I could have sworn

I saw a photo of my brother with a woman. But when I tried to talk to the woman who posted the photo, she disappeared. She wouldn't answer my questions. This was over ten years ago. She lived in New South Wales. I was sure it was my brother. I messaged her asking, "Is that Steven Lockey?" and she didn't reply.'

Brenda also tells a puzzling story. 'My brother-in-law (on my first husband's side) messaged me one day. He was driving through Western Australia. He swears black and blue he saw Steven there.' Roger is the brother of David, Steven's close friend and brother-in-law, who was killed in the car accident.

I spoke to Roger myself and asked him about this encounter:

I knew Steven very well. He was my brother's brother-in-law, and I also worked with Steven for a couple of years, building pool tables. It was on my first trip up to Kununurra; I was a sales rep and this was about 1995 or 1996. I called in to the local pub, the Kununurra Hotel. I was in the bar and I saw this guy, and said to myself, straightaway, That's Steven Lockey. He was talking to this other man, and I moved so I was nearby, and could hear their conversation. I was staring at him, and I said, "Hey Steven!" The guy turned around, but didn't say anything, and just looked away. I went over and joined in with their conversation. I was there for about half an hour, and I was staring at him the whole time. This other man didn't know the guy (that I thought was Steven) and was asking him about himself. I was thinking the whole time, this is Steven. But I didn't want to say anything to him, as I wasn't 100 per cent positive. And I felt like he wanted to stay missing, so I didn't want to ask him if he was actually Steven. The other

man was asking him about Kununurra, where he'd come from
– and he didn't want to answer that. He just said, 'Around'.
That made me think okay, this is Steven, and I didn't want to
push him any further.

He said he was up there working in the mines. I didn't really
take much notice of the details, like his lazy eye, but that wasn't
very noticeable anyway, only if you were standing eye to eye with
him. Same with the tattoos on his fingers, I'm disappointed I
didn't take more notice. I reckon he recognised me. All the time
I was listening to him, I believed he was Steven. He looked
exactly the same as Steven Lockey, so either there's two of them,
or it was him. Even his voice sounded exactly the same. I just
let him go, I never really pushed him. When I got back to
Adelaide, I rang Crime Stoppers and reported what I saw. The
police went up there, and they found the guy, and had a talk to
him. Apparently he wouldn't have his fingerprints taken and
he wouldn't have a DNA test. The police said he did look very
much like Steven. To this day, I'm still 99.9 per cent sure it was
Steven Lockey in the pub in Kununurra. I was so sure that I
went back to the same hotel the next night, but he wasn't there.

Tammy thinks this sighting has the potential to be genuine.
'Steven and Rog were pretty close, and he's pretty on the ball, so
I think he probably did see him,' she says. 'He knew him very
well, and would have recognised him instantly.'

Like many of the families I have interviewed, the Lockey
sisters all asked psychics for help in finding their brother. They
got a variety of answers. Sonia contacted a psychic who told her
the man she had seen outside her house was her brother Steven.

'They said there's someone out there who knows who he is, and where he is. One of my sisters went to see another psychic, who came up with the words Coober Pedy. Another sister also went to a psychic, and my mum and dad and sister "came through". My sister asked the psychic, "Where's my brother?" and the psychic said that Mum and Dad don't want anyone to know where he is, but that he's "in the sticks". In the bush somewhere. She said he was still alive.'

Brenda, however, consulted a medium who told her that Steven had died. 'She told me he's on a dirt road somewhere, and no-one knows where it is.'

Steven's daughter Samantha has also been to a psychic. 'I heard what I needed to hear,' she says. 'I'm pretty sure he's dead. I haven't come to terms with that, but it was comforting to know he didn't just leave and forget about us. Being the father he was, I don't think he would do that. A lot of people have said, Well, he's just done the same thing as his dad, but I don't agree with that. He would work all day, then come home and do everything with us. He bathed and fed us. A person who does that wouldn't just leave their children. I don't believe he'd just walk. I do think Dad made some bad choices, and maybe got mixed up in the wrong crowd. Maybe he owed people money. I don't know. It's a feeling I have. He had a lot longer with Jodie, and he especially wouldn't have left her. He always made sure he saw her.'

Jodie is in total agreement. 'That's what's stuck with me through the years,' she says. 'That's what makes me think something happened. I knew Dad loved us kids. He wasn't the sort of dad who would up and leave. He tried for years for regular contact. He was so happy when we came back from New

Zealand, and we'd had almost a year of weekly visits.' At the time he went missing, Steven was seeing Jodie every weekend, so he finally had the wonderful relationship with her he'd always fought for. Why would he walk away from that?

Samantha didn't even know she had a half-sister until she was 12. 'It was actually through a detective, who was looking into the case, who was speaking to my sister, and Jodie said, "I actually have siblings, can you get me in contact with them?" Police went to see Jodie around the tenth anniversary of her father going missing. Jodie thought police went to re-interview her whole family at this time but was astonished to learn she was the only person they spoke to. 'After he went missing, contact dropped off with my siblings,' says Jodie. 'They were like my own living dolls when I went there. I used to dress them up and we'd go to the park, I'd give them bottles. But I didn't have contact with them again until I was 23. I was so nervous, but my heart was so full, getting to see them again.'

As well as living with the ambiguous loss of a vanished brother, the family also had to cope with the tragic death of their sister. Sylvia says:

My older sister, Patricia, committed suicide. It was many, many years ago. I later had the police come to me asking whether I thought Steven would have committed suicide, or whether I thought someone he knew might have had something to do with his disappearance. Earlier, I would have said no, he wouldn't have committed suicide, but because my sister did, I couldn't rule that out, that he did as well. I think it was the seven-year anniversary that the police came and asked me that. They wanted to pronounce him dead, but there wasn't enough evidence that he was. I told the police I couldn't say yes or no, whether he could have committed suicide. I don't know. If my sister could do it, what's to say my brother couldn't do it? Things change, and your whole idea on how things could happen can change. He used to go camping a lot, to a place with a lot of rocks, down on the Yorke Peninsula, so maybe he jumped off there.

Sylvia thinks the police did investigate at the start, but isn't sure they've done enough. 'Yes and no,' she says. 'They did come and ask me what my thoughts were.' There has never been an inquest into Steven's disappearance and suspected death, and Sylvia's other sisters have never been contacted by the police or a coroner about this. They have not given their DNA to police to be compared to unidentified remains.

After I interviewed Sylvia, she messaged me back to tell me something she'd forgotten – something that turns Steven's story in a whole new, sinister direction. 'My mother was approached by the police and told he may be one of the bodies in the barrels,' she says. 'I do remember the police going to my mum's, so there must have been some truth in it.' The 'bodies in the barrels' case is one of Australia's most notorious and horrifying serial killings. Also known as the Snowtown murders, they were committed by three men between August 1992 and May 1999. They killed 12 victims, ranging in age from 18 to 47, both men and women. The killers dismembered some of their victims and disposed of them in barrels, stored in a disused bank vault in the small town of Snowtown, and some in other locations.

Snowtown is more than 130 kilometres from the Salisbury area, where the Lockey family lived. Two victims were, however, found buried in the backyard of a house in Salisbury, close to where Steven was last seen. According to the timeline, the killers did not take any victims between 1992 and 1995, and this is unusual for serial killers. The first Snowtown victim was killed in 1992 but his body was not found until 16 August 1994. The final phone call from Steven was made to his sister on 11 August 1994. It's eerily close. The first victim was killed in Salisbury, but was found in a shallow grave in Lower Light. It's also chilling that the Waterloo Corner Road, Salisbury address is less than 3 kilometres from where Gail King disappeared, in Mortess Street, Brahma Lodge, in 1997. Police considered the possibility that Gail had been another victim, but it was quickly discounted (see Chapter 4 to read Gail's story).

Gloria had no idea her brother was at one time thought to have possibly been a victim of the Snowtown serial killers. Living in Elizabeth, she was well aware of the murders, but didn't make any connection with her brother's disappearance. 'The police didn't let us know,' she says. 'It was very hard to identify the bodies. He might have been one of the victims.'

Rick thinks it's possible that his brother-in-law did perhaps know the killers, simply because at that time everyone knew everyone else in the Salisbury and Elizabeth areas. However, Tammy disagrees and does not recall Elizabeth being a close-knit community. Samantha knew her father was at one time suspected of being one of the bodies in the barrels. She isn't surprised that her father may have been targeted by them. She recalls drug use in the family, and knows the Snowtown killers targeted drug users. 'There are definitely options, to what may have happened to him,' she says. She sees the phone calls to his three sisters and note left for the other as sinister. 'If you know something's going to happen to you, maybe it isn't unusual to call your family,' says Samantha.

Horrifyingly, Steven Lockey's story and that of the Snowtown serial killers are intertwined, because of a very big coincidence. 'I lived next door to the bodies in the barrels killers,' says Tammy Lockey. 'I was reported to the police when they got found out, because someone reckoned I put them up to it, to do Steven in. Someone rang up missing persons and told them I lived next door. I had to prove that I didn't have anything to do with putting the bodies in the barrels.'

Tammy says she did not know the Snowtown killers before Steven went missing:

> He was out of the picture before I met them. I wasn't with Steven then. I was just a single mother. If the killers would have put my name together with his, I think they would have said something to me, like, Are you anything to do with that missing person? I lived next door to Robert Wagner and Mark Haydon; they shared the house on Waterloo Corner Road. John Bunting lived down at Smithfield, but he used to come and visit at Waterloo Corner Road. Bunting would come around, and I daresay when they went out they were going to his house too. Whenever Bunting came around, there was just that look in his eye … I actually thought he was a paedophile. There was something that gave me the creeps about him, so I'd take my beer and go home.

Tammy says she regularly went next door and spent time with the men, who would all later be revealed as Australia's most sadistic serial killers. 'I didn't know Jamie (Vlassakis) well, I mainly knew Wagner and Haydon. I did know Elizabeth Haydon.' Elizabeth was the former wife of Mark Haydon, and was murdered by John Bunting in 1998. 'I have no sympathy for her,' says Tammy. 'She was allowing her son to be molested by her partner. That's why what happened to her, happened. I do know about that. One of the other people who ended up in the barrels was the perpetrator who was molesting her child. I also knew Vlassakis' mum and dad from the caravan park in Port Pirie, but that was way before they were killed. It wasn't until later that I put two and two together as to who they were.'

She says she had no idea what they had been doing until police started to dig up bodies in the backyard, under the water tank, next door. 'I thought, How can you do that and get away with it? They just had a normal life. You wouldn't have known. I had absolutely no idea what was going on.' Samantha remembers living at this house. 'There was a big tree in the backyard, and we always used to be sent outside to pick up glass. That's the last house I remember.'

Tammy says the Snowtown film, in the scenes that focused on the Waterloo Corner Road house, was not accurate in the way it suggested the killers were open about wanting to harm their victims. Tammy says they never spoke around her about wanting to kill people. Barry Lane also lived in the Waterloo Corner Road house, with Robert Wagner. Barry initially helped the killers dispose of at least one of their victims, before being murdered by them himself.

Steven's sister Brenda is well aware of the possible link with Steven to the Snowtown murders, and as well as the murders happening close to where she was living, Brenda actually knew Barry Lane, by sight, as he used to visit friends who lived a couple of doors down from her. She would see him walk down her street frequently. 'I do sometimes wonder if Steven was one of their victims too, as there are still bodies out there that they can't give names to, and haven't found,' she says. 'Those killers used to make their victims ring up their family or a friend, and tell them such and such, that they've had enough of their lives and they don't want to be in touch anymore.'

Tammy does think it's possible Steven knew the Snowtown killers before he went missing, as his sister lived in the same street Barry Lane visited, and Steven visited Brenda and her husband frequently. Tammy says there was never any suggestion or rumour that Steven was involved in anything that would have made him a target to the killers. 'He wasn't in the drug scene or anything like that. It was more the alcohol. He drank every day, but he wasn't paralytic. He wasn't a violent drunk. It was his go-to.'

A *Sydney Morning Herald* article on the murders from 2003 said, 'Police said … the killers did not hunt far from home.' Chillingly, the article also said: 'Each of the victims was known to at least one of the accused, sometimes because they lived nearby … Police said … it was difficult for them to know that some of the victims were gone because of the kinds of lives they led – these were not people who were necessarily missed.'

In 2006, author Debi Marshall released a book called *Killing for Pleasure*, about the Snowtown murders. I have had a copy for many years; I have helped Debi in the past with some of the research for her books, if they involved missing persons. I picked up the book today and the first page I opened to, in the middle of the book, left me cold. 'Where's Thomas?' Maxine asks when they return without him. 'He's gone to Gawler,' Bunting says, looking at Robert and laughing. The official court transcript from the trial also confirms the men said they'd taken victim Thomas Trevilyan to Gawler. That night, Trevilyan was driven from Wagner's house by Wagner and Bunting. Wagner came home alone. He told Mills that they had dropped Trevilyan off at Gawler. Trevilyan was murdered in 1997. His body was later located at Kersbrook, east of Salisbury, not Gawler. So, why did the killers mention Gawler? When we know that Steven made his last phone call from Gawler, this comment takes on a very dark hue. Did the killers laugh because they'd taken someone else to Gawler? Three years before?

Brenda was right when she said the Snowtown killers made recordings of their victims, and spliced them together into tapes that they played in phone calls to the victims' families, to make it appear they were still alive. The court transcripts from the killers' trial states:

> The tape recorder was produced and Bunting forced Brooks to repeat phrases. They were phrases couched in terms appropriate to be transcribed onto a telephone answering machine, and included abuse of his mother. Other personal details were extracted, such as PIN numbers, his bank accounts and other questions. At the trial, a tape containing what was said to be the voice of Brooks recorded while he was being tortured was played, and another voice, said to be that of Wagner, was also on the tape.

Vlassakis gave evidence of how the tape taken during the course of the torture was used to transfer messages onto Brooks' telephone message bank. During the course of police investigations following the discovery by them of the barrels, an audio tape was found in a plastic garbage bag in the ceiling of Bunting's house at Bundarra Court. It was the Crown case that the voice on the tape was that of Elizabeth Haydon and that the recording was made before she was murdered, so as to obtain evidence which could be used to conceal her death.

Associated with the evidence of the recording on the tape was evidence given by (a woman) of phone calls made about a week after Elizabeth Haydon's disappearance to Elizabeth Haydon's mobile telephone number. Her evidence was that on one occasion when she called the mobile number a voice which she recognised as that of Elizabeth Haydon said, 'Leave me alone, I'm all right.' When she rang back again, she heard the voice say, 'You're a slut, nothing but a dirty slut' and the phone then cut off. It was the Crown case that the evidence of Ms Ball as to the telephone calls confirmed the purpose for which the recording on the cassette tape was made. The statements 'Leave me alone' or 'I'm all right' appear on the tape recording ... the evidence of (the woman) was that at least on the second occasion when she got through to the mobile number, the voice sounded like a recording.

There was evidence that Bunting set up the computer so that Johnson's recorded voice was played over in telephone calls to Johnson's friend. Recordings of the phone call to (the friend) matched the voice on the computer hard drive. It is self-evident from the content of the recordings that they were made in contemplation of the killing of each of the deceased. The subsequent use of the recordings to create the impression that the victims were still alive by transferring the recordings to telephone answering equipment is a clear indication of one of the purposes.

There are a startling number of other missing persons and murders from the same area as Steven. Salisbury, Elizabeth and surrounds appear to be prone to acts of violence and mystery.

Carlene Ward was found beaten and stabbed to death in the bedroom of her home in Parafield Gardens, in 1992. Her killer has never been found.

Geoffrey McLean's partial remains were found in a wheelie bin in a vacant paddock in Salisbury South in August 2022.

Beverley Hanley was murdered in her home in Homington Road, Elizabeth North in 2010. The murders of Beverley Hanley, Phyllis Harrison and Stephen Newton have been the subject of review and further inquiries by Task Force Resolute. Phyllis was murdered in Harvey Rd, Elizabeth South in 1998. She had suffered multiple stab wounds. Stephen Newton was found in his home on Davison St, Mount Gambier in 2011. He died as a result of an assault. Police believe all three were killed by the same person.

Emily Wanganeen, aged 30 years, lived a transient lifestyle and had no fixed place of abode. She spent most of her time in the Salisbury and Elizabeth areas where she would stay with numerous friends. Ms Wanganeen was last was last seen on 27 February 2010 at a house in Elizabeth South. On 13 June 2010, two youths walking through a steep sided gully adjacent the Boral Quarry, Black Top Road, Hillbank, discovered the body of Ms Wanganeen who was naked with her clothing located nearby.

Peter Marshall, aged 35 years, was located lying on the bedroom floor of his home address in Northcote Street, Kilburn on 5 February 1992. Mr Marshall had suffered a gunshot wound to the head. He appeared to have been shot from outside of his apartment through an open rear window.

At about 8.00 a.m. on Saturday 19 May 1956 Kenneth Hearn, aged 21 years, was found in the front seat of a St Georges taxi on Golden Grove Road, Salisbury. He was a taxi driver. Mr Hearn had been shot once in the head at close range with what was believed to be a .22 bullet. His killer was never found.

Baby Darren Shannon was taken by his father from a home in Blackdown Street, Elizabeth West, in 1973. His father was involved in a fatal car accident in Roseworthy, north of Gawler, but baby Darren was not in the car.

Fifteen-year-old Michaela Godau was last seen at her Walpole Street, Elizabeth Field (now Davoren Park) on 19 December 1982.

Neville Richards left Salisbury North, South Australia, and was last heard of on 27 August 1997 at Dareton, New South Wales.

Russell Bradshaw was last seen by his wife leaving their Salisbury Heights home in January 1992. Russell Bradshaw, at age 35, and Damien Cauchi, then aged 21, went missing six years apart, but police have linked the two during an investigation into the cold cases. Their remains are believed to be somewhere in the region of Karoonda, Borrika or Perponda. Damien Cauchi was last seen in the St Agnes area in August 1998.

Jason Plews was last seen at a house in Para Hills, next to Salisbury East, where he was staying with friends on 24 November 2001. Jason lived in Salisbury North.

Craig Leonard was last seen his home at Douglas Road, Salisbury East on Monday, 11 January 2010.

Brian Cairney was last seen on 1 June 2010, when he left his mother's home at Salisbury after telling her he was catching a bus to meet some people he had met earlier that day. Detectives have established Mr Cairney visited his sister the day he vanished and borrowed some money before going to the Elizabeth City Centre. While there, he met a couple whom he had never seen before, and made arrangements to meet them later that night to go drinking at their house. The trio caught a bus and the pair got off at Elizabeth Vale.

Kenneth 'Kenny' Camplin was last seen alive at 12.25 am on the morning of Friday 27 December 2013 at a fast food restaurant drive-thru at Paralowie, near Salisbury. He lived in Elder Court.

***

Sylvia is keeping an open mind, but thinks she may be the only one of her sisters who thinks it's very possible Steven is no longer alive:

> *If he's out there, good on him, but if he's not, we'll never know. I don't know what his thoughts were. I don't think he's alive. If he is, and doesn't want to be found, well, good luck to him. But I've come to the conclusion that he's gone. I have to. I can't stress about if he's out in the cold, if he's not eating, I can't do that. I've got my own life, my kids, my grandkids to think about, as much as I miss him. Life's got to go on. It was his*

choice, not our choice. I can choose to make his disappearance impact my life, or I can't. I try not to let anything get to me, because if I did I'd be a mess. You've got to keep going, and you put that onto the side. Lots of people go through traumas, and you either let it get to you, or you learn to move on.

My kids know he's missing, but we never really talk about it, unless there's been something on TV about it, then they'll ring me to tell me. He's been on missing persons shows a few times over the years. I tell people sometimes that I have a missing brother, and they go Oh REALLY! And how are you? I tell them I'm fine. You've got to be fine. It's been almost 30 years. My son is 28, and never met him. I have lots of happy memories of him. Even though we used to punch on, he was my best mate. He was good friends with my ex-husband; we all used to go out into town a lot.

Sonia has no idea why her brother would have chosen to drop off the face of the earth. 'We don't know why he wouldn't contact any of us. He doesn't even know that our parents are now deceased. He doesn't know that our elder sister is now deceased, and he was close to her.' Steven's father passed away in 1997 and his mother in 2007, never knowing what happened to their son. Their mother did not talk about Steven after he disappeared. Sonia thinks it might have been too painful for her. She says she and her sisters don't share their theories about Steven. 'We don't really talk about it much anymore. We're all hoping that he's still out there. We do believe he's changed his name. I'd like to think that. I think he doesn't want to be found.'

Brother-in-law Roger thinks it's unlikely Steven has come to harm, as he would have fought hard against any attack. 'He wouldn't have let anyone stand over him,' he says. Roger also thinks Steven would have managed to start afresh without any belongings or access to his bank accounts. 'He was pretty switched on when it came to money,' he says. 'He wouldn't part with a dollar unless he had to.'

Brenda managed to check Steven's bank account, and found it had not been touched after he went missing, adding to the concerns that something sinister happened to him.

'I would have thought Steven would have kept in contact with his mates, because they were tight,' says Tammy. 'Some of them were like brothers. I know none of them had heard from him. I don't believe he's dead. I go to a psychic quite often and not once has she mentioned he's dead. A couple of times she's said he's out there somewhere. I believe he's changed his name.'

Steven's sisters also think he's using another name. 'He had a good mate whose dad didn't like Steven, for some reason,' says Brenda. 'So, Steven would sometimes use an alias.' That alias was the name Jeffrey. Tammy says his mate's dad thought Steven was a bad influence on his son, and blamed him for the boys getting into trouble, so when Steven would call the house he'd say it was Jeffrey calling and not Steven Lockey.

Brenda is keeping an open mind, not wanting to believe he's been murdered but also not sure he would have left and never returned. 'I thought he might come back one day,' she says. 'I've had dreams about him. They say when you dream about someone that means they've passed over. In the dream I was told he was in a hotel, and I went looking for him, but I couldn't find him.'

I asked Sonia if Steven's disappearance had an impact on her life and she is thoughtful:

At first, no, because I knew what sort of a brother he was. But people do change over the years, and I am hoping that he's still out there, alive. I would like to see him again, but I wouldn't know how to respond to him. It's been too long. I think it would be a strained relationship. I would just be happy to know what happened to him. I think about him. Every now and then I'll look on the internet for missing people, and I come across his name. I think of him on his birthday, Christmas. The birthdays of his children; I wonder whether he thinks of them. I'd like him to be found. I'd like to hope he's still out there. If he doesn't ever want to come back, then a phone call or a letter would do.

Gloria says she was very affected when Steven first went missing, but after almost 30 years she's had to accept it. 'I think, oh well, he's gone. If he's going to come back, he'll come back. Just like Dad did. Maybe one day.' I asked Gloria if believing Steven is still alive has made it easier for her to cope with his disappearance, and she thinks this is the case. She doesn't believe he's been murdered or took his own life. 'Just like Dad, he'll come back when he's ready. It might take a few years. It's been a long time, though.'

'I've always had a sick feeling about it,' says Jodie. 'I didn't like how everyone moved on very quickly afterwards.' Like Samantha, Jodie didn't know about the letter her father left, and had never seen it until I sent her a copy. It was nice to be able to tell the girls that the last action of their dad before he left was to write about how much he loved them. Jodie says:

> *It's hard for me to say something bad happened, without any concrete justification, but it just seems so out of character for him to just choose to walk away. When you're young, you don't really know what kind of drug and alcohol situations are happening in people's lives, but it's become pretty clear that there was alcohol abuse and probably some drugs. Maybe that played a part.*
>
> *I remember hearing from someone in the family that there was concern that one of the bodies in the barrels was Dad, that maybe they would find his body there. Maybe he didn't want to tell me the truth about him actually going away; I know he wouldn't have wanted to upset me.*

Amazingly, Samantha has never been contacted by police, either in relation to her missing father, or because she was living next door to serial killers. She was raised by her aunt and is close to her grandmother. Samantha has relied on stories from her family to fill in the blanks about her father:

> *They always told me that he'd gone off and had another family. I never really liked that. But I can understand why they said it; they wanted to believe that. But it wasn't good enough for me; it doesn't sit well with me, and I don't believe it. I probably should have met with my aunts a long time ago to talk about him. There are a lot of cousins too.*

Niece Fiona, who is Brenda's daughter, also messaged me, asking me to write Steven's story. She remembers her uncle with great fondness. 'He was a shit-stirrer. They tell me there was a way he could make me smile just by sticking up his pinky finger. It's important to me to find out what happened and where he is, not just for me, but for his children and grandchildren. We'd welcome him back with open arms.'

'There are times when I do think, *Steven, where are you?*, says Sonia. 'It's been a long time. He's got grandchildren he doesn't know about.'

Gloria would absolutely love her brother to come back, although she says she'd probably 'hit him in the mouth' after hugging him: 'For doing this to us,' she says with a chuckle. If Steven is out there, the message Gloria would like to send is: 'His sister Gloria loves him very much, and she wants him to come home.'

Brenda is more wary. 'If he was to walk past my house, or walk past me, I wouldn't recognise him,' she says. 'And I wouldn't know what to do, if he said, "I'm your brother." I wouldn't know whether to hug him or beat him up. I agree with Sonia, I'd be angry about what he's done, in leaving us not knowing, but then again if he was to stand in front of me, I probably would hug him. My message to him would be – where are ya? How have you been? Long time, no hear! Where he is, no-one knows but himself.'

Sylvia would welcome her brother back with open arms. 'Of course, I would,' she says. 'For a lot of years, I was angry with my sister who committed suicide. She left a six-month-old baby behind. You either let the anger eat you up or get over it. I had to let it go. There was a reason she did it, she obviously just couldn't cope. I think other people need to let go of their anger that Steven went missing. It doesn't matter what people have done, they're still family.'

It's been almost 30 years, but Tammy says she thinks about Steven all the time. 'I get angry when I think about it, because of what he did to the kids. He could have left me, that's not a problem, but why did he have to walk out on his five kids? And his family? I don't know why. He was so close with the kids.' She wishes for her children to have some answers about what happened to their father. 'We can't even get a plaque put up in a cemetery, as we don't have a death certificate. The kids have no place to mourn him. For their sake, I would like answers, and deep down in the back of my mind, I would want it too.'

Steven's son Michael was very young when his dad went missing, and as a result he feels the disappearance hasn't affected him very much. He didn't really think about his dad, growing up, he just knew he wasn't there. 'I've become accustomed to it, I guess,' he says. He doesn't feel his life would change if his father came back, and doesn't know if Steven would be a part of his life.

I asked Samantha how she'd feel if her dad walked back into her life, and she struggles to answer. After a while she says: 'It would take a while. And I'd have to hear the full story. But I think I'd just be happy to have answers and closure. The hardest thing is not knowing anything. I have three children now of my own, and they know I don't have a father figure. They know of Steven, they know he's my real dad, and it's hard to answer their questions. I'd like to know medical stuff. I've told my kids a little bit, just that we don't know where he is.'

Strangely, during my phone call with Samantha, the phone line dropped out three times, for no reason, as neither of us was moving around. It was always when I had asked her a crucial question. Almost as if someone were trying to tell us something. 'Someone's toying with me,' says Samantha wryly. 'I hope it's Dad. I want all the secrets to come out. I listen to a lot of true crime podcasts, and I hate them, because they're not solved. I think I prefer to think he's passed, because that means he was still a good person. I mean, if he left, that doesn't mean he isn't a good person, but our lives haven't been easy, and he would have known he was leaving us to a difficult life. That would be hard to accept. But if you're out there, Dad, just come back. I don't care about the reasons. I'd be sad, I'd be mad, but I'd get over it. I just want to know that he's okay. And that he didn't forget about us. Even though I only had three short years with him, I know that I was loved by him a lot, and it has left a lasting impression. He has always had, and always will have, a place in my heart. He will always be my dad.'

Jodie says having a missing dad absolutely impacted her life. 'I encourage my daughter to have a relationship with her father, and not having my dad around definitely made me do that. I have never had a consistent father role model, and haven't had healthy relationship modelling, so Dad going missing has affected lots of aspects of my life. Trying to navigate your own healthy relationships when you haven't had that modelled for you, and you haven't had that support in your life, it's hard. My childhood was very unsettled. It was better when Dad was in my life, when he was around. That was always my happy place, when we moved back to Adelaide and I got to see my dad.'

People ask me all the time if missing persons often just leave everything and everyone they know and start a new life, and the short answer is no. Sometimes, of course, it does happen, but it's rare. Most of the time, something has happened to the missing person. But in Steven Lockey's case, I think there's a chance he might read this. A chance he might just go home.

In mid-2023, Sylvia put in a request under the *Freedom of Information Act* to see if she was able to access 'all relevant information regarding the disappearance of Steven Lockey'. Access was refused. South Australia Police gave the following as their reason:

> *As of the date of this determination letter, this matter is still under investigation. The premature release of the document may hinder current enquiries and adversely affect the investigation or any future prosecution by disclosing information provided to police and particularly given the matter is under active investigation. In consideration of public interest factors I am of the opinion that releasing this document could inhibit any further investigations by making details of the investigation to date public knowledge. On balance, it is contrary to the public interest to release any documents the subject of this investigation to any party at this time.*

It is heartening to see in writing that police consider this an active investigation, but given the lack of contact between police and every single witness and family member in the case, for decades, it is difficult to understand what they mean by 'active' and 'current enquiries'. If they are actually still actively investigating Steven's case, as this letter says, then by all means keep the details confidential. However, we need to hold police to this promise, and we expect them to actually undertake the investigation that this letter states they are conducting.

On 13 July 2023, I put out a call on my Facebook page. I wrote:

STEVEN LOCKEY – are you out there? I'm working on the follow-up book to Vanished *and I'm currently writing Steven's story. He was last seen in Broadmeadows/Gawler Adelaide in August 1994. This is very unusual, but I want to say to Steven, if you're out there, NOW is the time to make contact, if you don't want me to write your story. I have been digging deep and uncovered so many stories, and there's enough evidence to make me think you really did just walk away and are probably reading this now. All you have to do is walk into any police station and say, 'I'm Steven Lockey and I'm a missing person in South Australia.' They can take you off the missing person list and everyone can stop looking for you. By law, police (or me) cannot tell your family where you are without your permission. No-one can make you go back, and if you have chosen to stay away that is your right, it isn't a crime to go missing. But if you don't want me to tell your story, you need to tell me that. It's your decision.*

However, there're also many things about Steven's story that make me concerned harm has come to him. It was widely shared, but Steven Lockey didn't walk into a police station or message me. I also joined the Kununurra Community Facebook pages and shared Steve's photos, asking long time locals if they remembered him as a regular in the pub – as Steven was a drinker – or working in the mine 28 years ago. Again, no-one remembered him, including the staff who had worked in the pub. Roger Coulter and I did an ABC radio interview and also online news article, talking about Steven, hoping someone would remember him from Kununurra, but no response.

Is he still out there? There are so many possibilities. He wrote a goodbye note to his sister and brother-in-law, asking them to tell his kids he loved them. He phoned his other sisters and said he was leaving. He told his sister and brother-in-law he was leaving on the train. But he called his eldest daughter, saying he couldn't see her that week and he'd call her soon and tell her what was happening. Why did he break that promise? Why did he leave everything he owned behind? Why did he go to Gawler on the train? Were the sightings actually Steven? If so, why doesn't anyone remember him? And if he's still alive, why hasn't he contacted his children, who he was devoted to? Or told police he's not missing? If he's been a victim of foul play, was it the Snowtown killers? Or someone else?

Steven Lockey, even though he is 60 now (2024), would still be recognisable from his unique features – he has a 'lazy eye', from birth, several tattoos on both arms and hands, a Pegasus tattoo on his chest and an eagle on his back. He is 175 centimetres tall with hazel eyes.

It's not a crime to go missing, so you won't be in any trouble, Steven, and police won't tell anyone where you are without your permission. But you have a beautiful family who love and miss you. You have grandchildren. They want to meet you. Please give them a call.

If you know anything about what happened to Steven Lockey – or Steven, if you're out there – call Crime Stoppers on 1800 333 000. You can remain anonymous.

CHAPTER TWO
Joanne Butterfield

Joanne Butterfield, aged 37, was last seen on 25 June 1998, around 7pm when she set off on the Captain Cook Highway, at Mowbray Queensland, telling friends she intended to hitch hike to Sydney. Her clothing and belongings were found three days later scattered on a railway line near Mossman.

Joanne Butterfield was a free spirit, a woman who didn't live a conventional lifestyle, but loved her children and her family fiercely, and whose disappearance is a true mystery. After speaking with her family and writing her story, I am left thinking that Joanne might actually be reading these words now. It's very possible she's still out there, alive and well.

The Butterfield family lived in beautiful Mittagong and Bowral in the NSW southern highlands. Joanne was born in Camden. There were five children in the Butterfield family – Marc and Joanne were born first, then their father formed a new relationship and Belinda, Barry and Shane were born. Marc and Joanne's mother also had two children from a previous relationsihp - Norell and Garry. Norell is still devastated by Joanne's disappearance, and remembers going on the train to Mittagong to visit Jo and Marc after they went to live with their father. Joanne and Marc were aged bout four and five years old when they came to live with their father and his second partner. Remarkably, the other children had no idea Marc and Joanne were their half-siblings until Barry was 17, and his parents called the family together for a talk, his father telling them he and their mother were going to get married.

Barry had no idea his parents were not married, and had no idea his brother and sister had a different mother. 'We lived as a pretty tight little family,' says Barry. 'They called us all together and told us they had some news. Marc and Joanne were pretty close; they must have known they were full brother and sister, but they never told the rest of us. They have lots of other siblings too, from their mum. I remember times when Mum and Joanne would have a go at one another, and the same with Marc, but they always had that love for her too. I think they had a lot of respect for her. Joanne always called her Mum. Our lives growing up were mostly good, but there were times where it was terrible as well.'

His sister Belinda recounts her childhood memories: 'Dad was a concreter and bricklayer, and Mum was a nurse and a taxi driver,' she says. 'She did a bit of everything. They worked really hard. Dad was always working; we didn't see him from early morning to late at night, he just worked for us kids. We were poor growing up; we had hand-me-downs, but we were grateful, we loved everything we got. At Christmas you never got much at all, you might have got one or two presents, but that's all they could afford.'

I asked Belinda if it was a happy house. She isn't so sure:

It was a bit abusive, our family, growing up. Mum was very, very hard. She was so strict, and I think that really did some damage to both of us, me and Joanne. I think she put all her fears onto us, like fear of sexual abuse, that sort of thing. She wouldn't let us go out. We would sneak out so we could have some fun. I can never remember being cuddled by my mother. That was pretty sad. She'd always be yelling and screaming ... and I mean really screaming. We used to get beaten too. She'd sleep most days. I think she had terrible depression.

It was a hard life growing up with Mum. But now that I'm older I realise that it must have been harder for them in those years, they weren't so lucky. They must have loved us. I know Dad did. Mum loved us, but in her own way – she never showed it.

I don't think Mum could really cope with five children. The boys seemed to have an easy life, but us girls were the ones who had to scrub the floor, do the washing up, all the chores while boys were out playing. If you didn't eat your tea she'd make you sit there until you were heaving and spewing; you'd still have to come back and eat what was on your plate. I had a terrible eating disorder because of it.

The boys are all good, but it affected our lives; me and Joanne ended up with problems. I ran away when I was about 14 and lived on the streets of Kings Cross. It was pretty hard, but I don't regret any of it, because it taught me a lot and I've still got good morals. It helped me raise my children into good human beings.

Her mother's strictness seemed to push Joanne in the opposite direction to her intentions, and Jo turned into a bit of a wild child. 'Joanne had lots of boyfriends,' says Belinda. 'That was the exact thing Mum was trying to stop happening to us by being so strict, but it happened anyway. Jo would always be off with the boys, from a very early age. Her and Mum were fighting all the time; Mum was so hard on her. I think Mum was harder on her than me, but we both copped it. We'd have to pick a stick and skin it and whip it and if it made the *crack* sound then it was right, and we'd just have to stand there. I never remember the boys getting belted like that.'

Barry remembers it differently, however. 'In my recollection of my childhood, we were all treated the same, but my mum was very tough. If she called us to come in, we *had* to come in. I think the girls rebelled a bit; they were both buggers in the end.

My brothers had their own issues. Dad and I talked a lot, and he was always worried about Joanne, but we also talked about my brothers. My family were very much loved by both my mum and dad, and I believe we were all treated equally. I think my baby brother was always looked after just that little bit better,' he adds with a chuckle. 'He was a spoilt bugger. Our parents were tough, but I think that's made me the person I am today; we had a tough upbringing. We always got a kick in the backside or hit with the feather duster or the belt.'

Barry's wife Rachel adds: 'Everyone's perspective will be dependent on their own experiences. We've been married for many years, but I only knew Barry's mother for a short time. She died when Barry was 21. I think that Belinda's perspective will be different.'

Joanne's difficult home life meant she struggled through school, and she left early. According to Belinda, the harshness of their upbringing caused both daughters to leave home in their teens. 'Joanne ran away from home too; earlier than me – she was about 15,' says Belinda. 'She met a butcher. He was in his late twenties. They lived in Bowral and Maroubra. Her and Mum seemed to get on better when she wasn't living at home. Joanne and the butcher moved to West End in Queensland, where she had a baby, Melissa, who was born with her stomach outside her body. She only lived for 35 days. I think that's what really destroyed Joanne. She was pretty mixed up, poor honey. They moved back to Mittagong, and she had two more children, Jason and then Skye. When Skye was about 18 months old my sister decided to leave the butcher. She moved in with a friend in Mittagong, then she met a truck driver. He was such a beautiful man, he treated her good, and they got married.'

Barry has very happy memories of his sister at this time. 'Joanne and I were very close,' he says. 'I loved my other sister, Belinda, just as much, but when Joanne moved out of home I used to go to her house on weekends and visit her. Most of my childhood memories of Joanne are visiting her at her little house on the Hume Highway at Mittagong. I'd go there when I finished school and say g'day and hang out with her kids. When I started work, I'd go to her house and have a coffee with her.'

Rachel says: 'I got to meet Joanne twice before she left the Southern Highlands. Once, when Barry and I were dating, he pulled up at her house at Moss Vale to borrow a bottle opener for a picnic we were going on. She reminded me a bit of my mum; she was just a normal mum with her kids, doing life. I met her again maybe six months later at the RSL club. There was a band playing; she was on a night out and her hair and makeup were done. She didn't even look like the same person. She saw Barry, and was dancing with him, and I didn't recognise her; she'd changed so much that I asked him who the hell he'd been dancing with! That's how much she changed from day to day.'

Barry believes Joanne kept much of the darker side of her life a secret from her little brother. He says:

I know she was busy with truck drivers, but I was younger then and it really didn't cross my mind. I realised what she was doing when I got older. We grew up pretty tight, but there was lots of stuff I didn't know about Joanne. I'm sad I didn't. You know when you think you really know somebody, but you really don't? She kept things from me. I was at her house all the time, and I didn't know she was into drugs. She didn't sleep a lot. But in all the times I went to her house she never offered me drugs, never told me she used drugs. I was under the impression she was a drug addict, but I never saw her use it. Whether that was showing a bit of respect to me as her younger brother, I don't know.

One night I went to her house, and I asked her what she was going to do the next day. She said, 'Oh nothing, we're just going to hang out with the kids and stuff.' I said, 'All right, cool, I'll see you tomorrow afternoon when I finish work.'

So, the next afternoon I went to her house, knocked on the door – no answer. I thought, well, that's weird. Then I peered through the window, and the house was empty. Everything was gone. That was the last day I ever had any contact with Joanne. She just disappeared off the face of the earth. I was devastated. I didn't know where she went to. It was probably a lot my fault too, because I never tried to contact her. I just thought, Oh well, if that's what you want to do, that's what you do.

She was pretty good at doing that. She'd be in one location, pack up and then she'd be somewhere else. As her brother, I'd cop that on the chin, but I was upset that she'd never said anything to me. I don't hold that against her, though, I never have. I don't hold grudges, I just think well, you wanted something different in your life, you wanted to get away from here.

Belinda was also aware of her sister's erratic lifestyle, but is sympathetic to her reasons for going down that path. 'I think

Joanne was too affected by her past,' says Belinda. 'She and her husband moved to Melbourne as he had a house there, and he raised her children as his own; he was a damn good person. While he was away driving trucks and supporting her and the children, she stripped her husband's house of everything one day and moved. So, her marriage was over.'

Belinda sadly described how her sister's life was spiralling downwards. 'She moved back to Queensland, and I can remember her ringing my mum and telling her she had a job in a massage parlour. Mum nearly fell over. I remember conversations Mum and Dad had about that phone call. From then, Jo was out of control. She moved around places a lot, then she came back down to Campbelltown in Sydney. By this time Jason was about six and Skye was three or four. Jo was given a Housing Commission house.' Belinda says she was always there for her sister, and frequently took in Joanne's children when it was clear she needed help.

Belinda says: 'There were times over the years when Jo wasn't coping, and by this stage I was old enough and had my own place, and I'd take the children for weeks on end until she was able to cope with having them back. She started to show signs of a mental illness, like she started yelling and screaming and doing things that were not normal. She suffered so much trauma in her life that I don't think she knew who she was anymore. She was lost in amongst all that trauma. After losing Melissa, that was it, she just became different, she didn't want to be close to people, she was pretty mixed up. Because she was my sister, I loved her no matter what she was doing. She was a tough cookie, though. I remember one time we caught the train from Mittagong to Campbelltown, and the train broke down. My sister had a broken leg and was on crutches. She didn't want to wait on the train until it was fixed, she said: "We're going!" So, here we are, jumping off the red rattler, with her on crutches, and off we went!'

Joanne's need to be loved led her to alternative religious groups. 'While she was living in Sydney she got involved with this church group in Campbelltown,' says Belinda. 'Jason said to me years later: "Aunty Belinda, Mum was okay up until we moved to Campbelltown and she got involved with that church. She changed horribly." She started doing bizarre things, like she was found walking along beside the highway without any clothes on.'

Barry is also aware of Joanne being involved in the organisation. 'She got involved in something that was not very nice, but I'm unsure what it was,' he says. 'There was something weird about it. But Joanne attracted weird people. She led a pretty wild life and she sure attracted the dickheads.'

Joanne was living in a Housing Commission house at Claymore, and got a job at a factory that made doorknobs. Belinda continues her sister's story:

While she was there she met this man. Jo really loved him, and she fell pregnant to him and this beautiful little baby, Thorne, was born. He was so tiny, only 4 pounds. He spent a lot of time in hospital because he was premature.

However, Joanne was not coping with her baby, and when he was only a few weeks old she asked her sister to take him. 'I jumped straight in the car and went to Campbelltown,' says Belinda.

'I went over to his cot and he was just lying there; he was the most beautiful little baby. I was pregnant myself with our second child. I took Thorne home. I'd ring her and say: "Jo, come and see him," and she'd say: "He's not my baby, he's your baby now." I told her he was *her* baby and she needed to have some kind of connection with him. I was getting quite attached to him; he was my nephew, but I was also raising him.'

Belinda tried her best for the next few years to get Joanne to have a relationship with baby Thorne, to no avail.

I remember driving with my family and Thorne down to Wombeyan Caves. I saw my sister coming towards us in her car! I called out and made her stop. I pulled up right beside her and said: 'Jo, come and look at Thorne!' But no way would she get out of that car. That tore me apart; I tried so hard to get them together.

We continued to raise this little baby, then one night out of the blue, about 11.30 pm or midnight – Thorne was in bed in his cot, sound asleep, we were all asleep – there was a knock on the door. It was my sister, and she said: 'I've come for Thorne!' I said: 'What? I don't have a problem with you having Thorne, but you're not taking him out in the middle of the night like this!' She said: 'No, I want my son now!' I told her she couldn't do that.

I asked her where she was living and what she was doing. None of us knew what she was doing at that time. She said: 'I want him! That's my child!' I said, 'I know he's your child! I've been trying for years to get you to have something to do with him! And now, out of the blue, in the middle of the night, you think you're going to just walk in here and take him out to God knows where? That is not happening!'

I was seven or eight months pregnant at the time and we ended up having a fist fight as she tried to push past me to get into Thorne's bedroom! I told her she wasn't taking him out. She said she had a place in a caravan park in Cairns. I asked her what kind of life did she have to offer this boy. I told her we'd talk about it in the morning, and I'd check out her accommodation, and how stable she was, and work out a plan. I told her she could have her baby, but she wasn't waking him up that night.

The next morning Joanne got up and she was different, she was nice and quiet again, her normal self, so we sat and talked. I rang the caravan park in Cairns to confirm her story, and they told me they'd given her a cot and set it all up for Thorne. To this day, it was the hardest thing I have ever done, to hand over that baby, not knowing what was going to happen to him. He screamed for me when she left. I don't think I've ever cried so much in my life. I was so attached to him. He got his first teeth with me, he crawled, he was just like my baby. I went downhill after that.

Joanne took her three children and moved to Cairns. It was a fresh start for the little family, but Joanne's untreated mental illness continued to worsen.

One person who remembers Joanne's life in Cairns is her friend Lucy. In 1992, Lucy moved to Port Douglas and became Joanne's neighbour. The two women struck up a firm friendship when they moved into the same block of units. Thorne was about three and Lucy remembers him being still in nappies. 'I didn't know Joanne for that long, but we went out a few times, and we'd go over to each other's places. Her eldest son, Jason, was a nice boy and my son was friends with him,' she says.

When I ask Lucy what sort of person Joanne was, she hesitates. She is concerned that her answers might tarnish Joanne's children's recollections of their mother, but I reassure Lucy that it's important to have an accurate picture of Joanne's lifestyle and behaviour in order to have the best chance of working out what happened to her.

She was a really nice person, but she really didn't seem 100 per cent with-it most of the time. She was off with the fairies. She wasn't crazy or anything, but she was just a little bit different. Once we went for a walk down the beach and there was this guy sunbaking naked, and Joanne said: 'Oh, well, let's join him!' I just went home and when I saw her the next day she told me they'd walked home naked. She did crazy things like that.

If we went out, she'd see someone she'd like to hook up with; a couple of times, if I was with her, I'd take her home, but it was the times I wasn't with her ... she'd tell me about it the next day and I'd think, oh no, you're going to get yourself into strife one day.

One night she must have brought some fella home, and in the morning we were going to Cairns. I asked her where the kids were and she told me at home. Then I said, 'Where's this fella?' and she said, 'At home.' I said, 'With your children?' and she said: 'Oh, they'll be all right,' and I thought,

Oh God. I wanted to go back but she said no. So, she was a little bit airy fairy about looking after the children, but she did love them. She just never really thought of the consequences of things. But she had a good heart. She was a nice person, but she had this side to her that is really probably what got her into trouble.

I include this story not at all to shame Joanne, but because of what was to happen later, on the day Joanne disappeared.

While Joanne was living in Cairns, she worked at a resort in Port Douglas as a cleaner. It was around this time that she had another child. Belinda is unsure who the father of the child is, and the baby was later given into foster care. Belinda says: 'She rang me and told me about this dream she'd had about a mother on a white horse, and I knew she'd gone off the rails again. It happened quite a lot.' Joanne and Belinda kept in touch regularly by phone and Belinda had increasing concerns about her sister's mental health. 'She started going downhill and I could tell,' says Belinda. 'I picked up on it quicker than I ever did in the past. I realised my sister had a mental illness. I said, "Jo, I think you need to go and see a doctor. I love you but your behaviour is becoming bizarre again. Maybe you have manic depression." So, she did go off to the doctor, and he said she could be schizophrenic, and I thought that could explain a lot. She rang me a week later and said she was sending Thorne to Sydney to live with his father.'

Joanne only had a phone number, no address for where her son was living, although she knew where he was going to school. After a while, she decided she wanted Thorne back. Belinda says she found Thorne and told Joanne, who said she would travel to

Sydney to get him. 'She said: "All right, I've got to get a bit of money together and I'll start heading down next week." She said she was going to walk into the school and just take him. That was the last time I ever spoke to her.'

The events of the following days are unclear, with no-one sure of when, or if, Joanne left Cairns. She was last reportedly seen on 24 June at home and on 25 June 1998, in Mowbray. She was 37. Belinda is certain Joanne was headed to Sydney to find Thorne. After Joanne told Belinda she was coming to Sydney, Skye moved out and stayed with friends. A couple of weeks later she hadn't heard from her mother, so Skye went back to her old home and found her mother was gone.

'That was the two weeks where none of us knew what day it was that Joanne was last seen,' says Belinda. Skye rang Belinda and told her aunt that her mother was missing. Belinda says: 'She said, "I can't find Mum, nobody's seen her for two weeks." I thought she'd probably just driven off somewhere, stayed at someone's house; she'll come home. But as time went on and she didn't come home, I told Skye to call the police and report her missing. It was unusual for Jo not to ring me.'

The police spoke to Skye and obtained photos of Joanne and compiled a missing person report, but Belinda doesn't feel much else was done. 'Because of Joanne's past, they thought they'd give Kings Cross a go, and check all the homeless places there to see if anyone had seen her. No-one had.'

Police said Joanne was living in Mossman, and was last seen in the small town of Mowbray, south of Cairns. Mowbray is about 20 minutes' drive from Mossman. She was visiting a friend named Kevin, who has since passed away. Kevin told police Joanne said she was going to hitchhike south. Joanne's belongings were later located 'scattered' on a cane train railway line near Innisfail, south of Cairns. They were found near a lookout, on Henderson Drive, Pin Gin Hill, near Currajah. This is 245 kilometres from Mowbray, where Jo was last seen. They were found on 28 June 1998, three days after she was last seen. Included with the items found were the dress Jo was last wearing and the embroidered handbag she took everywhere with her.

It's very open and mostly flat countryside, with a train line running through it. From Mowbray you'd expect Jo to have hitchhiked down the Bruce Highway. To get to where her belongings were found direct from Mowbray meant likely going back to Mossman, where she lived, yet she didn't go home. That route is inland, through Mareeba, with less traffic than the Bruce Highway, which would have provided many more lifts for her if she was heading south.

Belinda says: 'I think it was a farmer who found my sister's belongings – her passport and ID and clothing on an unused train track. That is when it got serious, and a detective was assigned to the case.'

Daughter Skye adds another part of the puzzle – around the time she went missing Joanne sent an envelope to Skye's school. Skye said to me, 'I still have the envelope with her handwriting on it that she sent to me care of my high school with no letter … just some of her personal ID, ATM card and her rent book with a postal stamp from Cairns in the days following her disappearance. It was school holidays and by the time I received it the police had already contacted my pop after finding her belongings and remaining ID scattered on a railway line near

Innisfail.' More than anything else, this suggests Joanne chose to disappear from her Cairns life.

The biggest mystery of Joanne's disappearance is these items found on the rail tracks at Innisfail. Normally, finding a person's clothing would be cause for great alarm, but Joanne was known for removing her clothing, so that may account for her clothes being discarded. The passport is the strangest item found; Joanne had never left Australia, and had neither plans nor any funds for an overseas trip. Belinda is equally baffled. 'Why did she have a passport? She'd never been on a plane. Surely she knew she didn't need a passport to fly in Australia? She'd said she was 'going to work her way down' to Sydney. I thought drive. But maybe she was going to catch a plane. She wasn't educated, so maybe she thought she needed a passport. She'd never travelled out of the country. I don't know why she had a passport at all.'

Barry disagrees with Belinda's theory about domestic travel and says: 'No, Joanne wasn't stupid, I can tell you that. We all went through school to year 10. I said to Dad, "Since when did she have a passport?" I don't know what she was doing with a passport. The thing I struggle with is if somebody did take her and dispose of her, why did all her cards get sent in an envelope to the kids' school? Who else but Joanne knew where the kids went to school? My dad and her were very tight. If you said to my dad, "I've got a million dollars and I'm going to bury it in your backyard, tell nobody about it," then that would be the last you'd hear about it. I reckon Joanne cut a deal with him. I think she said: "Dad, I'm okay, but I've been a terrible mum and I'm out. I've done this, I've done that and I don't ever want to be found. I don't want my kids to know where I am." If I know Joanne as well as I think I do, that's my take on it.'

After about eight years of Joanne being missing, her case was featured on the television show Missing Persons Unit. The opening line in Joanne's case described her as a 'Missing mum of four and party girl'. The program filmed NSW Police following up a lead in Kings Cross, and Queensland Police Detective Sergeant Trevor Perham travelling to NSW to investigate. The show's narrator reports that police had a tip-off that Joanne was living on the streets in Kings Cross. Police visited homeless shelters in the city and showed Joanne's photo around, then went to the Wayside Chapel in Kings Cross. Detective Sergeant Trevor Perham said on the show: 'Her activities perhaps brought her into disrepute, and she didn't want to have that reputation hanging over her children's heads.'

In 1998, Joanne promised her friends she was 'going to change her ways'. Detective Sergeant Perham said: 'She made comments to a number of people that her children would be better off without her, and she was going to disappear for their benefit.' The detective said Joanne went missing after visiting her friend in Mossman:

> She visited Kevin just after she was seen hitchhiking on the highway and she hasn't been seen since. Her dress that she was wearing and her carry bag and her passport turned up on a railway line two hours south. What's it doing there? How did it get there? We don't know. There's a number of possibilities with this case ... that she's met with foul play or that she's simply cut all ties with her family and has relocated somewhere else and is living somewhere else as she said she intended to do.

He said there was a greater chance of finding Joanne in Sydney than anywhere else. The show followed Detective Sergeant Perham and Sydney police as they interview Belinda and her father. Belinda related the conversation she had with Jo just before she went missing, about going to Sydney. Police said they believe Joanne was heading to see Belinda. The show detailed how Belinda took in Thorne and she told the audience: 'Basically, she'd be very depressed and feeling like she couldn't go on with the children. It wasn't until a couple of months before she disappeared, she was so down that she had gone to the doctor and they said she was schizophrenic. She'd told a number of people that she intended to disappear for the sake of her kids, because she thought she was a bad mother.'

Belinda said Jo often felt that way. As mentioned, she had Thorne living with her for almost two years at one stage, from when he was only six weeks old, and the other children for months on end throughout the year depending on how well Jo was. 'But she'd never leave it this long,' Belinda says on the show. 'Something's gone wrong and I just don't know what. Young Thorne had been flown over to Sydney to live with his father, and Joanne was concerned because every time she rang the school they said they no longer had a boy there by that name. She was really trying hard to find what school he was in. She said to me: "Look, I'm coming down, I've got to find him, just to make sure he's okay," and that was the last conversation that we had.'

Detective Sergeant Perham told the show that he had witness statements from Joanne's friends. He said that the witnesses had told him: 'Joanne fled to Sydney to change her identity eight years earlier. But her sister Belinda says Joanne was actually looking for Thorne, who was then living somewhere in Sydney with his father.' At the time Thorne believed his mother would turn up one day. On the show, Joanne's father, Barry, said: 'It was a hell of a shock when they said she'd gone. She was a roamer, but never ever thought that she'd … I think that eventually they'll find her bones. But I don't know.'

Belinda made an appeal to the camera, saying: 'Sis, if you're watching this right now we'd love you to contact us please. Dad's not well and your kids miss you so much, and so do I. So, please, if you are watching, please call us.'

Thorne said: 'Mum, if you're watching this, I want you to know that I miss you, I didn't really know you when I was young but I just want to get in contact with you.'

Belinda continued: 'Please come home. Or if there's anybody out there that knows anything please call Crime Stoppers.' Belinda comforts a clearly emotional Thorne.

Belinda and her father were also interviewed for another TV show, *Australia's Most Wanted*, not long after Joanne went missing. The television appeal came as a surprise to at least one member of their family. Barry says:

I was living in Moss Vale, and we had a couple of kids of our own. I was lying on the lounge and the Roger Climpson show came on, Australia's Most Wanted, missing persons and stuff. They said: 'The next missing person we have is Joanne Butterfield, alias Brown.' I didn't know what to say or do. I sat bolt upright. It gives me goosebumps just talking about it. It blew me out of the water. I had no idea Joanne was missing. They'd been and interviewed my dad and my sister, but at no stage did anyone tell me my sister was missing. On the show they put up a photo of Joanne exactly how I remembered her — red hair, freckly face, a big smile. That's the last image I have of my sister.

I was in two minds whether to ring my dad straightaway or wait until the show was over, but I watched the rest of it, and there they are interviewing my dad on the doorstep of my sister's house! At first, I felt hollow, and I didn't know what to think. Why did they keep me out of it? Why had they said nothing? I could see the look on my dad's face, and I thought there's something not right here about that on its own. So, the entirety of it was that I think I know my dad pretty well, and he was the type of guy who, if you said to him: 'Do not ever repeat this, lock it away forever,' he would, he was that type of guy.

I rang him after the show and asked him what was going on. He said: 'What do you mean?' Just like that. I said: 'What do you mean, what do I mean! You've been interviewed, my sister's missing, what is going on!' He said: 'Oh mate, you know, I didn't want to bother anybody.' I told him I was really disappointed I'd been left out of the loop.

After that I started to do my own research, and I found out the cards had been handed in to the school, and they found her clothes strewn along the railway line in the sugarcane fields. Dad told me she had a passport, and he never knew that, and neither did I. I was extremely upset that my sister had gone missing, but what do I do? What's my next move? So, I rang Skye. She told me she'd been looking after her brothers ever since they were little, because her mother was never home. She'd done it all herself, raised those kids. Skye has grown into this incredible adult and person. So, as time went by, I spoke to Belinda, and I sat back and listened to what was going on. I got on the internet and looked to see if there was anything about Joanne being found. There was nothing.

Despite the family's heartfelt appeals, the original show only generated one phone call, which was followed up and mentioned on the second show. With no leads and no sign of Joanne, the case soon went cold.

Belinda still looks for Joanne in crowds. 'I haven't told the detective this, but I have an aunt who lived in West Gosford and years ago she said to me: 'I'm sure I saw your sister. I was getting some bread and saw this woman in a car. I stared at her and she kept staring back at me. I swear it was Joanne.' My aunt and my sister never got along. If they had got along, my aunt would have gone up to the car. I sort of fobbed it off and didn't think it was very credible, though. But I don't know. There is not a day in my life, when I am at the shops, that I am not looking in the faces of people. At one point my sister fell off a horse, so she had a metal plate put into her foot, so I watch how people walk and I'm looking for that little limp she had.'

Barry has an even more eerie story:

In about 2015 my wife and I had been to Wollongong, and we stopped to get fuel at a little place called Yallah, down the coast. I walked into the shop, and at the same time this female and I crossed paths. I thought, 'Far out, that's my sister.' I stopped, she stopped. I basically froze. I recall in the middle of Joanne's back was a tattoo of a dreamcatcher, and this woman had a blue singlet on and I could just see the top of this tattoo. Her hair was cut really, really short and it was jet black. She had the same little bubble nose. It was just incredible. This woman got in her car, and I was still frozen in the shop. She crunched her gears like there was no tomorrow, didn't even put her seatbelt on, and she sped out of the service station.

I got back into my car and all I had in the car was my work hat, and I wrote down the licence plate on the hat. It's still written in my hat today. I've never given it to the police. Whether I should is a different matter … I don't know. I've never told Skye about that. If it was Joanne that day, crossing paths in that service station, she could have said something to me if she'd wanted to.

We were both shocked; we were so close we almost bumped into each other. We looked at one another, and there was no reason for this woman to get into the vehicle like she did and really crunch the gears. I wish I'd had my phone on me to get a photo. I just have in my mind, 100 per cent, that was my sister. I don't care what anybody says. And for her to stop like she did … I've changed a lot, I'm older now and I've probably put on twenty-odd kilos, and she's probably done a second-take as well, thinking: 'Wow, that looks like him … is it?' and we both stopped. So, I hope that day, that if it was her, she's thought: 'Well, maybe that was my brother.'

If that was my sister, then it was confirmed for me that she doesn't want it known that she's still alive. I sometimes wonder if it was fate, that that day we literally bumped into one another. It was so weird. I've got goosebumps again telling this story.

Barry is also convinced that his father knew exactly what had happened to Joanne. 'My dad had become very sick. I took him to Bowral hospital, and I knew he was going to die. There was one question I had that I needed answered. I asked him if Joanne was still alive. He looked me square in the eye, I can still see his face right now – and this is years ago – and he said to me, "Mate, everything's okay. Don't worry about nothing." To me, that was "Joanne's still alive". That's my opinion and I'm going to stay with that forever.'

Belinda has never given up trying to find out what happened to her sister, despite mixed reactions from the rest of her family. 'A few years ago I met up with a clairvoyant,' she says. 'She gave me a big map of where she reckoned my sister was buried. I knew it was probably nothing, but I thought I better tell the detective. I rang him and he said it was probably just mumbo jumbo, but I said, well, she's said an exact location, was it worth looking into? He said, "Okay, send it to me." I sent him everything. I asked him if we should discuss it with Skye and he said, "No, Skye's been through enough." He felt so sorry for Skye, and you would, because she's been through so much. He did look for my sister, but I don't think the police tried hard enough. The detective was lovely, but it's been years since I talked to him. I would like an inquest. I see other people have one and I say, why can't they have one for my sister so we can try and understand what happened?'

The strange thing is, there *was* an inquest for Joanne – in 2014. I spoke with Belinda in 2019. It's alarming that the family are unaware that this inquest took place and seemed to have taken no part in it, nor were they advised of any findings by the coroner's office. The coroner ruled that 'Joanne is likely to be deceased and is likely to have met her demise at the hands of others', in the words of Detective Acting Inspector Kevin Goan.

Barry has actually never had any contact with police regarding his sister's disappearance. 'The police have never spoken to me about my sister,' he says. 'Belinda suggested they could speak to me, but I never heard a word. I quite often go onto the internet and just see if there's any further news, but there's nothing.'

'Joanne's disappearance has affected her entire family,' says Belinda. 'I don't really get together with my brothers to have dinner or coffee or anything, but we get along. They don't really talk about Jo.'

Barry says, 'I've asked our brother Marc a few times if he's ever heard from Joanne, or if he thinks about her. He said, "Well, she's my sister," so, he thinks of her, but he's never heard from her. I asked him once what he thought had happened to Joanne, and he didn't give me an answer. We just moved on. We've got a very mixed-up family, though. I often think I would love to get all my family together, but then I think, there's going to be that missing piece. Should I not do it because of that missing piece? It's horrible. I lost my mum when she was only 44 and I was extremely young, and my dad died at 71. I feel I'm missing something in my life but I just don't think that I should be selfish about that. I've got a beautiful family and a beautiful life, but I keep Joanne in my background, most definitely. There's always going to be something missing. The relationship that I had with her ... I used to call her Red, because she was a ranga. She'd put her fist up to me and say: "Stop it! Don't call me that!" and she'd laugh at the same time,' Barry recalls with a chuckle. 'She had a beautiful smile. She was fun to be around. We were very close. I enjoyed her company and I think she enjoyed mine.'

In recent years Thorne has become determined to find out what happened to his mother, but has had all his efforts thwarted. He posts about Joanne on Facebook and on one of his posts his sister Skye has replied: 'She wasn't a hippy, Thorne, she just needed someone to love her and look after her. I hope she's found that. Behind that smile and crazy is a beautiful soul and I'm proud to say that she's my mum.'

A friend wrote to Thorne: 'She would be so proud of the person you have become Thorne.' Thorne spoke to journalist James Taylor of the *Southern Courier*, who wrote:

Thorne Nyker vividly remembers the moment he found out his mum had vanished. At the age of six, he was sitting in his father's living room when the words that would torment him for life flashed up on the screen: 'Missing: Joanne Butterfield'. The words he didn't fully understand, but he knew the smiling face. 'I was confused and thinking, Is that my mum? I didn't really know what to think ... then my dad sat me down and told me what was happening,' he said.

'I will not stop until I find her,' Thorne said. Thorne said his daughter was a catalyst to begin the search again. 'As you can imagine, I wanted my daughter to meet her; she asked me once and I didn't really know how to explain where Nan is now. I don't really think (she is alive), most of the family doesn't think so either, but you never know – she might have changed her name and everything to get away from it.'

Joanne's family continue to miss her every day, and Belinda says she often struggles to cope with having a missing sister:

I have really bad days because I miss her so much. It's horrible. You cry all the time. You could be anywhere and it will come across your mind and you just cry because … where are you? I don't know where you are. I want to know where you are. I miss you, so much. I love my sister, I want to find her, I want her not to be forgotten. I love my kids, my grandkids and animals. But I just feel empty all the time. You feel this big hole. I see other women with their sisters, wishing their sisters happy birthday. My loss, it feels like I've lost an arm or a leg. Part of you dies. You don't want to live with the loneliness. Life was chaotic, but she's just not there anymore.

I used to think she was alive, then maybe she is, and then maybe she's not, but the more time's gone on the more I think no. She always called me, no matter what. If she was in a psychotic mood, I'd be the one she'd ring. She knew she could depend on me. I know if she was alive, she would have contacted me. She always did in the past when she wasn't well. She'd never ring our brothers and say how she was feeling, that she wasn't coping, no way would she ask them for help. She always put her tough persona on.

When she went missing they thought: 'Knowing Joanne she'll be just moving around,' but I said no, something's wrong.

Barry is happy to talk about Jo when people ask. 'Someone at work came across it and asked me if I had a missing sister and I said, yeah. They'd Googled "Butterfield". So, they talked it about it and asked me how I felt about it.'

Everyone I have spoken to has a different idea about what they think happened to Joanne Butterfield. I asked Belinda if there was any chance Joanne took her own life, and her answer was an emphatic no. 'No way in the world,' she says. 'I can say that 110 per cent. I feel someone else may have taken her life, or I've often thought, is she stuck in a mental institution somewhere? And she didn't beat around the bush, if she didn't like something she'd tell you straight out. But I believe she's met with foul play.'

Joanne's friend Lucy also thinks someone may have harmed her. 'When I first read about her being missing, and they said her clothes had been left somewhere, I thought, well, maybe she's just wandered off and she'll wander back, because I knew she liked to take her clothes off. So, I thought maybe she'd just come back, and I didn't hear any more about her. Then I saw an article about Thorne, and from that it looks like something has happened to her. Maybe she picked up the wrong fellow. I wasn't surprised that something had happened, but I'm so sad about it. I didn't know her for very long, just a few months, but I did like her. She did care about the children. I just don't think she knew any better. She was off in her own little world. Either that, or she wandered off and went to live somewhere else. I can't imagine it happening in one way because I know she really loved her children. But in another way, I could see it happening, because she might just sort of forget, and just wander off. She might have forgotten, if she was on something. I just don't know.'

I asked Lucy if Joanne ever seemed worried or scared during her time in Cairns and she thinks back. 'I do vaguely remember her talking about when she left New South Wales, but I can't remember why she did. I don't think she was in touch with any of her family at the time. I told her she'd be better off if she did speak to her family, but we didn't talk very much about that sort of thing. But she had a sad life. I can't see her just leaving the children, unless she had some sort of episode. If she got into a state of mind she might have decided to just disappear, because up there it's very easy. I just hope we do find out, eventually, what happened.'

Barry, however, firmly believes his sister is still alive. He believes Joanne may have even gone into witness protection and changed her identity:

That's also why I think she's still alive. She's thought, 'It's never too late to change my life; if I can get away from this stuff up here (in Cairns) and run away from everything. They're better off without me.' And if she's in witness protection, the police aren't going to tell you that. If she is alive, she obviously has some very bad issues to deal with, and I don't think she was a very good mum to her kids. Whether or not that's playing on her mind, and she's thought: 'You know what, I'll make it look like something terrible has happened to me,' I don't know. Joanne is extremely good at what she does. After what my dad said before he died, I have no reason to believe that Joanne is not still alive somewhere close by. Maybe she keeps an eye on her kids through social media.

For me, my sister was a beautiful person. She was very protective of me, and we did get on extremely well. I often think about her, and I miss her. I looked at her as my full sister, not half. I still do today. I wish and hope one day she might reappear, but I think in my own mind, she's alive somewhere. Unless something's happened to her in those years since I asked my dad. Dad's quote remains in the back of my head forever, that she's okay. I'm confident that Joanne is alive. As time rolls by you don't ever forget about her, she's always on your mind.

Tragically, in April 2020, Joanne's sister Belinda passed away. Family told me one of the biggest regrets Belinda had was dying without any answers about what happened to her sister. I hope Belinda's memory is honoured in the telling of her story.

Thorne was devastated to lose Belinda, who was very much a mother to him from the time he was born. He wrote:

Yesterday we lost our queen …
The closest thing I've ever had to a mum
The strongest lady I've ever met.
She loved everyone and gave everyone a chance. Her door was
open to anyone
You fought well!
Will miss your big smile …
thank you for everything you did for me
To all the family, I love you all and please know I'm here
anytime for anyone!
I love you

For her birthday in September 2020, Thorne wrote that Belinda was the best thing that ever happened to his life. Belinda's words in this chapter speak so strongly of her love for her nephew.

In July 2021, Queensland Police announced a fresh enquiry into Joanne's case.

Far North District detectives are renewing a public appeal for information relating to the suspicious disappearance of Mossman woman Joanne Butterfield who went missing in North Queensland over two decades ago.

Joanne, aged 37 at the time of her disappearance, was last seen around 8pm on Thursday, June 25, 1998, leaving a house in Mowbray near the Captain Cook Highway. She told friends she was planning on hitchhiking south.

Three days later, on June 28, 1998 personal property belonging to Joanne was found near Innisfail between a public lookout and bank of a cane train track at Henderson Drive, Pin Gin Hill (near Currajah). This included an embroidered bag that Joanne took everywhere with her.

On July 8, 1998 an envelope containing Joanne's Medicare card, bank cards and personal documents was delivered to her Mossman home.

Joanne was last seen wearing a short black dress with shoulder straps, black flat shoes, and carrying her floral embroidered bag. She is described as Caucasian, approximately 160cm tall, with long auburn hair and blue eyes.

Detectives are confident more information could lead to a breakthrough in the case.

Specifically, detectives are wanting to speak with anyone who may have seen a woman hitchhiking between Port Douglas and the South Johnstone area between Thursday, June 25 and Sunday, June 28, 1998.

Anyone who travelled along Henderson Drive, Pin Gin Hill and saw any other vehicles, or any people, near the lookout on that road between those dates, are also urged to come forward.

Something to note here is Skye told me the envelope with her mother's documents and cards was actually mailed to Skye's school, addressed to Skye – not delivered to her Mossman home as this statement indicates.

The ABC interviewed Acting Detective Inspector Kevin Goan, who said police had reopened the cold case following several new tip-offs that had been made to Crime Stoppers over the past 18 months concerning her disappearance. He told the media:

An inquest in September 2014, found that Ms Butterfield had died shortly after last being sighted on the 25th of June in 1988, that it was unlikely that she had taken her own life and more probably that she was killed by a person or persons unknown. We suspect that she might have been collected in a vehicle and that her personal belongings were discarded in that area.

Acting Detective Inspector Goan said they had begun re-interviewing people in the Mossman area about Ms Butterfield's disappearance. He said they were particularly interested in speaking to those with information about two men. 'We have an interest in the two men who might have had recent dealings with Joanne at that time in the Mossman area. We would like to speak to any person who may have information in relation to the men and their connection to Joanne. We have been in continued contact with Joanne's family and the ideal scenario is that we can, with the public's assistance, recover Joanne's remains and give some closure to the family by prosecuting those persons we suspect are responsible for her disappearance,' he said.

After this appeal, in August 2021, journalist Grace Mason wrote in the *Cairns Post*:

> *Far North Det Acting Insp Kevin Goan said they had received multiple calls and anonymous reports through Crime Stoppers which had generated 145 'investigative tasks' which would be looked at by detectives. He also confirmed two men considered persons of interest, who had links to Ms Butterfield and both still resided in the Far North, had been identified. 'They have been spoken to and obviously there are lines of inquiry that need to be followed up on,' he said. 'We're very happy with our response from the public, particularly those who had the presence of mind to make contact with police directly.' Det Acting Insp Goan said police felt certain there remained people in the community worried about coming forward due to fears of retribution and moved to reassure them they would be protected. 'There is nothing to fear and we will work with them with regard to safety issues,' he said. Ms Butterfield's DNA profile has also been added to their records which could be potentially matched against any remains found. 'While we don't know what occurred, it would be good to be able to recover Joanne's deceased remains for the family's closure and the opportunity for them to pay their respects,' he said.*

Police clearly think Joanne was murdered. But was she? What about the woman Barry saw? What did her dad know? And what about the belongings Joanne herself sent back to her daughter, as if in a deliberate attempt to disappear?

The inquest findings for Joanne are not available on the Queensland Coroners Court website. Joanne is also not on the National Missing Persons Co-ordination Centre website run by the Australian Federal Police.

In June 2023 Thorne wrote a tribute to his mum on the 25th anniversary of her disappearance, on Facebook:

> *Today is 25 years of our mum going missing.*
> *This is my favourite photo of her and sadly one of*
> *the only I have xxx*
> *It's hard to think that someone out there knows*
> *something but we may never know.*
> *If you have a mother, make sure you treat her like your*
> *queen and appreciate every little moment.*
> *My heart and soul would rest with just one of her hugs xx*
> *We will find you one day I promise.*

The photo he mentions is the one I have added to the beginning of this chapter.

I held this chapter back from the first volume of *Vanished* because some of Joanne's children had concerns about it. It is very important to them that Joanne is remembered with the respect she deserves, as their mum. They miss her every day, and still need her in their lives. They didn't want their mum portrayed in a bad light, or that it would be suggested she was a bad mother. On the contrary, I think Jo was the best mother, because she recognised when things were getting hard, and when that happened she asked others for help, like handing over Thorne to her sister. She clearly loved her children deeply. Her last acts before going missing were to plan to go to

Sydney to find Thorne, and to send her belongings back to Skye.

Joanne absolutely led an unusual and bohemian lifestyle, but it's important to remember she had suffered a great deal of trauma in her life, and was coping with an undiagnosed and untreated mental illness. She did the very best she could, and her children are rightly proud of her strength and resilience, and love and miss her deeply. I knew I had to tell Joanne's story, especially now, to honour her sister Belinda, who never stopped looking.

Joanne, if you're reading this today, it's not too late to make contact with your family. They've never forgotten you – indeed, they miss you every day, and your loss is a giant hole in their lives that only you can fill. If you want to let them know you're okay but want to keep your details private, you can contact any police station, or look up Australian Missing Persons Register on Facebook and send me a message, so I can let them know you're alive, and the police can stop looking.

It's never too late.

CHAPTER THREE
Rigby Fielding

Rigby Fielding was last seen on 15 August 2015. He had been visiting friends in East Perth, Western Australia and was intending to catch a train home to Rockingham. His belongings were later found in bushland near Kwinana.

You might have read that Rigby Fielding is missing, but chances are you don't know much about him. I know I didn't before I started writing his story. And Australia needs to know about Rigby. In all the media reports I've read about Rig's disappearance the case is regarded as a homicide, but with no reasons why being given by police. I was very interested to find out the true story. What I learned has made me agree completely with his sister: that something terrible has happened to Rigby Fielding.

I spoke with Rig's sister Stephenie, who is one of an astonishing eight siblings. Rigby is the second eldest and Stephenie is fifth in line. The family lives in Rockingham, Western Australia, a suburb of Perth, about 47 kilometres south-west of the city centre. It's a beautiful coastal town, with sandy beaches and abundant marine life in Shoalwater Islands Marine Park, where visitors can swim with wild dolphins. The family emigrated from the UK to Australia in 1969, when Rigby was about seven.

'We are a very close family,' says Stephenie. 'Dad was a schoolteacher, and Mum was a mum. I'm still living in the same house we grew up in. We had a really good childhood, and our parents were really involved in our community. We did a lot of sports. Dad was very invested in kids, and ran the local army cadet unit. Mum's time was mainly spent driving all us kids to our various sports clubs and dancing lessons. Dad even bought her personalised plates that read KIMSWAN, as our local taxi service is called Swan Taxis. She was always down at the school helping with the reading. Our younger sister Tina has Down Syndrome, and Mum was often at the school with her; they didn't want her going to a special needs school, so they helped her through mainstream.'

Her brother Rigby always stood out and was not one to blend in with the crowd. 'He was quite creative at school. He was pretty different!' Steph laughs. 'The Aussie boys were the surfers, but the English boys were punks and mods. He was well known for wearing punk clothes, and he had a mohawk. He'd get around the shopping centre in these striped pyjamas with safety pins all through them. I remember my friend's parents saying to me once: "Your brother Rig was the politest punk we ever met." He was really into anarchy, but on a very peaceful level. He liked music and went out to see live bands. He liked a lot of English stuff from the 70s and 80s.'

When he was 18 Rigby went back to the UK and lived there for a while, then returned to Australia. He went to technical college and studied cooking, and from there became a successful chef. He opened his own restaurants with his partner in Melbourne and New Zealand and did very well. 'He was always the cook at family gatherings, feeding everyone, nurturing everyone,' says Steph. 'He came to see me all the time, and I often popped in to their place; we all did, all my brothers. It was a house where there were lots of visitors, lots of kids.'

Rigby was married to a woman before he came out as gay. 'He got all us kids to be there when he was ready to tell our parents,' says Steph. 'I think he was more worried about it than they were. Until then Mum thought his partner was just his travelling partner. They hadn't bought the restaurants together at that stage. When he actually came out, we all just said, "Okay. Who wants a cup of tea?" After that, Dad would always introduce Rig's partner as his other son. He was very included in the family.' The couple were together for about 15 years before separating.

When his father became unwell, in about 2011, Rigby sold his restaurant in New Zealand and moved home to Perth to help out. Rigby and his new partner lived in Perth city. Tragically, Rigby's partner was diagnosed with Huntington's disease with chorea and, unable to cope with the inevitable bleak future this incurable illness offered, he took his own life. He didn't want Rigby to become his carer. It was a terrible shock to Rig. The couple had just travelled around the world together.

Soon after, Rig's father passed away, and his mother was diagnosed with cancer. Stephenie had moved back into the family home to help care for her parents and sister, but after the death of their father Rig told her he would move back in and take over their care, allowing Steph to move back into her own home. 'He was really invested in Mum's care,' says Stephenie. 'He rarely left home, and when he did he'd tell one of us where he'd be. He'd say, "I'm staying in the city for the night, can someone check in on Mum?". But he'd only do that maybe once a month or less. Mum had cancer in her stomach and bowel, and had a really major surgery. She refused to have cancer treatment.' After the death of his partner, Steph thinks Rig dated casually, but didn't bring anyone home to meet his family. 'We spoke about him using Grindr, and other dating apps. We told each other most things.'

Grindr is the world's largest dating app serving the LGBTQ community. Rigby cared deeply about justice and the rights of the LGBTQ community. He supported marriage equality, and the safety of LGBTQ asylum seekers. He was very politically active in his local community and spoke out in support of protection for gay people in Russia and Africa. Rig volunteered at pride parades and was a vocal activist for climate change, human rights and the Green party. One of his Facebook posts reads:

I am totally over the level of racism we are seeing in this country now, if your vote yesterday was based around keeping asylum seekers from access to their rights please de-friend me now.

On Friday 14 August 2015, Rigby went to Perth by train, intending to see his friends and stay the night. He told his mother he'd be home the following day. On Saturday 15 August 2015, Rigby called his mother at 4 pm and told her he was on his way back to Rockingham. His mother was expecting him home for dinner. The trip from Perth Station to Rockingham takes around 40 minutes. At about 7 pm Rigby's mother called daughter Stephenie, and told her Rig had not come home, and asked if Steph had seen him. 'I just kept saying to her, he'll be home,' says Stephenie. 'He's probably had a beer with someone and is still on his way. But I knew that night, when his phone was off, it just didn't feel right.'

Stephenie had been trying to call him, but it just went to voicemail. 'I went down to the police station quite early on, because we just *knew* straightaway, on that first day when he didn't return home. I was calling his friends and the hospitals, I thought maybe he'd had an accident and maybe didn't have ID on him, I just kept thinking things like that.'

Reporting Rigby as a missing person to police turned out to be much more difficult than Stephenie anticipated:

I had to report him missing three times, at our local police station, before they actually took the report. They just dismissed what I was saying. They had the same response each time: oh, he's 53, he can go missing. I explained our situation, that he was living at home with Mum, who had been diagnosed with cancer, and our younger sister, who has Down Syndrome. Mum wasn't travelling too well with the cancer, which is why he was living at home and keeping an eye on her. I was telling the police all that; he's not someone who would just go missing. He just wouldn't leave them like that. He'd make arrangements with one of us. And if he stayed over in the city, he'd always call and ask us to go and check on them. It was really out of character.

I gave the police a lot of good information, which the lady behind the window was writing down, so I was thinking, that's her making a report. Then I left it for a week or so and called back, but that lady was on leave. They told me they had no record of me going in the first time. So, I went back and did it all over again, with the next person. I gave them a couple of weeks to do a bit of groundwork on it and went back in — that person was now on leave. I just got so frustrated. I asked police, when I was going in to the station to try to report him missing, when the last transaction on his card was. They said, Yeah, we'll get onto that. Then two weeks later when I went back in, I told them again, you need to get on to the bank, was he still taking money out of his account? That's how I was going to find him.

Each time I went in to the police station I was there for quite a while, giving them the whole rundown. I told them what I'd found and where I knew he'd been, because by then I'd spoken to his friend and I knew he'd been at that place and then that place. And then again, weeks later they still hadn't even put in the report. The last time I went I really lost it with them. I told them they needed to get a sergeant or someone in charge to talk to me because I was not bloody happy. Then that guy went on leave. I just thought they were playing games! How can that many people go on leave?

I'd never even given them a statement. All the times I'd been in there, and I thought they were writing it all down, all the things I was saying, they were never logged, I never signed anything. I've never had to sign a statement or make a missing person report before, so I just went along thinking they were doing what they were supposed to do. All the information I gave them was going nowhere. That's when we went to the media. All along, the police kept saying, don't go to the media, don't talk to them or we'd hinder the case, because people would ring in with false information. They were just so negative. They just really didn't want to help.

Despite repeated instructions from local police to not speak to the media, Stephenie and her brothers felt it was the only way of getting something done about Rigby's disappearance. Their decision paid off, and the case was finally escalated. 'It wasn't until we went to the media that Major Crime in Rockingham became involved,' she says. 'They were brilliant. Within a day they'd run the bank checks and checked his phone activity. The first guy we spoke to did so much leg work; he found out where he'd been and all of that. He was able to tell us his bank accounts hadn't been touched, things like that. He was so apologetic about all we'd been through to that point, and said, "We'll deal with Rig's thing first, but down the track, if you want to put in a complaint I'll help you through that process." I said, I don't want to complain, I just want you guys to help me! I don't have time to put in a complaint! Just somebody help us! I didn't think we were asking for much.

'The major crime guy was great; what he found out in a few days, even in just a few hours, was brilliant. It was also disappointing, because we knew the next day that his bank account hadn't been touched, so because of that, we thought, he's dead. I just knew.'

Stephenie struggles to tell me what that realisation was like, as she is overcome with grief. Her distress also brings me to tears. 'It was devastating,' she eventually manages to get out through her tears. 'It still is. I still just think – why? We all let him down. He was let down by the police. And I should have jumped up and down that first day. I just think the outcome might have been different if they'd worked on it sooner, and been looking in the right place sooner. Tracked his phone sooner. All those things.'

There's that survivor guilt that I have heard countless times over my years working with the families of missing persons. Stephenie is not to blame even slightly; she did not let Rig down. By the time she went to police, whatever terrible event that took Rig's life had already happened. I remind her what an amazing sister she is, as she's been fighting for Rigby, she's been his voice since the day he didn't come home. Despite all the negative responses and difficulties she's faced from police, she has never given up.

The case was handed over from Major Crime, in Rockingham, to police in Perth. Things had been progressing well to this point, but Steph says this is where her relationship with police began to sour. 'I got the feeling early on that these guys just couldn't be bothered,' she says. 'We felt like we were inconveniencing them, and they were quite homophobic. I would say that my brother was gay, and they'd make offensive comments. I feel like because they weren't interested in looking, that's why they haven't found any more.'

The family found out, from speaking with Rigby's Perth friends, that on the Friday he had been to see a friend who lived in East Perth. Rigby then went to Galleria shopping centre. There is a taxi record showing Rigby was picked up from the shopping centre, in Morley, north-east of the city centre. The taxi took Rigby back to East Perth at about 2 pm. The official police report states Rigby was last seen in Goderich Street, East Perth. His phone last 'pinged' on the corner of Broome and Beaufort streets in the Mt Lawley, Highgate area, which is about a seven-minute car trip from Goderich St.

'We went to the street, there's lots of cafes in that area,' says Steph. 'That was one of the first things we did with the media.' The family handed out missing person flyers near Elmar's Smallgoods, a deli in Beaufort Street, Highgate. The information about this being Rigby's last location was given to them by his friend, who could see the location on the Grindr app, meaning Rigby must have had it open at the time he last made contact with anyone. The family felt this was of vital importance. 'His friend was really helpful and showed us on his phone where he could see that last location,' says Steph. 'But the police didn't even bother to speak to him. The people giving us information were people we trusted, people Rig went to school with. It wasn't like they were not known to him. I was asking his friends what his frame of mind was like on that day, as it was all so out of character.'

A 2022 article from the ABC by Tobias Jurss-Lewis details the alarming number of users of dating apps who have been subjected to sexual violence. The article quotes a man who uses Grindr, who said that each time he meets someone he would

> ... turn on his location, send his friend a photo of the person he was with, their phone numbers, as well as a link to their social media platforms. He's had too many bad experiences to roll the dice. That's how bad it can be, that people are messaging each other to say, 'just in case I get murdered or attacked, this is who I was with.' ... Eighty per cent of us have experienced sexual violence in person from someone we've met online.

Is this what Rigby did on that last day? We know he sent his location to his friend. Was this because he was meeting a stranger?

Frustrated by the lack of police action, the family hired a private investigator to look into the case. 'We hired the private investigator fairly early on, because we didn't feel the police were doing a lot,' says Steph. 'The police didn't want to work with her. The private investigator gathered information, from talking to people, but police didn't want to see it. She was really helpful to us; she had lots of information.' Rigby's family and the private investigator spoke to 9 News Perth three months after his disappearance. The private investigator said she hoped she wouldn't have to hand a file to police, telling them they were looking at a murder. Rig's brother Matt said, 'As time goes on, it looks like that's what's happened, and we don't know whether to grieve.'

The media publicity resulted in people coming forward with information, both to police and to the family directly. Steph had a disturbing encounter with one of these people. 'We had a guy come forward, who ended up being an absolute nutter. He said he'd seen Rig weeks after, in the city. The police went to talk to him – many weeks after – and he changed his story. He was really quite strange. I don't know what Rig's connection with him was. He contacted me through Facebook, then sent me a nude photo of himself.'

It's horrific what the families of the missing have to endure, aside from their own fear and grief over their missing person. Stephenie is able to laugh about it, thankfully. 'If I catch up with Rig, I'll be telling him what I've been through, because of him!' she says in jest. The police were not so amused. Stephenie says she asked them to go and interview this man, and afterwards they complained to her because the man had acted strangely towards them. They told Steph the man had answered the door wearing a woman's dressing gown.

The family's strained relationship with police continued to get worse. 'We'd arranged to meet the police at my other brother's house, as we didn't want the police talking in front of Mum and my younger sister,' says Steph. 'We'd always do it there, or meet with police at the station; we didn't want Mum to have to deal with that.' Steph says police told her they didn't want to look into the Grindr app, and feels the police were homophobic towards Rigby.

They said to me: Was your brother a bit camp too? That's when my other brother told them to get out of his house. I was so angry. The police kept saying, 'The more you talk to the media, the less we can help you.' I said that sounds like a thinly veiled threat to me. They said, 'We're just telling you, you just have to stop talking to them.' I said, 'Mate, they're the only ones doing anything, they're the only ones getting the story out there.' After I said that to them, they finally did a media briefing in East Perth.

Even then, things still did not go right.

They got things wrong, like the date. They said the last time Rig spoke to anyone was the 14th I kept saying to them no, it was the 15th. The police said, 'Fourteenth, fifteenth … whatever.' That's the kind of attitude they had. The media release said he had brown eyes, but he clearly had blue; I said they needed to change the release, and they said: yeah, we'll get someone on that. And it was never changed. I know they're small things in the scheme of it, when I look at it now, maybe not a big deal, but it was a big deal to me.

In a missing person case, the little things are the big things. If you're asking someone to remember what they saw on a particular date, then that date is vitally important. If you're asking someone to remember a person they might have noticed, and they discount the sighting because the person had blue eyes when the media release says brown … big things.

There was a breakthrough in December 2015 when Rigby's belongings were found in bushland. The location has been described as Wellard but it's actually an area called The Spectacles, closer to Kwinana. Almost the entire suburb is a wetland reserve. Police tracked Rigby's phone, and traced it to a man who lived in Kwinana, only about 10 minutes from Rockingham. The man also had Rigby's bag. He told police he had found the phone and bag in the bush, and he took police to the location. It is unclear why the man had been in the bush. Police told the family the man was not a suspect. Steph asked the police if they could tell her who this witness was, and if she could please talk to him herself, but this was refused. Steph at least wanted to know his name, as she would have been able to tell police if he was a friend or acquaintance of her brother. The police response was to tell Stephenie she watches too much *CSI*. 'I told the detective that what I was suggesting wasn't that outrageous. I wanted to check if maybe this guy was Facebook friends with Rig or something. I also wanted to know if maybe this was the guy he'd been chatting with on Grindr. It wasn't weird that I was suggesting these things.'

After the bag was found, police organised a search of surrounding bushland. It only lasted one day. Nothing further was located. There are two large, shallow lakes in The Spectacles but at the time Rigby went missing they were mostly dried up. Stephenie sent me a photo of herself walking through thick mud as she searched for her brother. 'They did a couple of hours of searching in the bush with police horses and SES volunteers,' says Steph:

It was very frustrating, feeling that nothing thorough had been done. My friends and I went out there, and I asked the police if they could give me a round-about spot where the belongings had been found, as the bushland was huge. They refused to tell me. They knew exactly where in the bush this guy had found it. They never told us the exact spot. We were out there for weeks, and we made our own little grids that we'd search. Then we realised we were looking for a needle in a haystack.

And he may not even be there. He could be anywhere, and someone's just dropped his bag there, as a distraction or decoy.

The private investigator organised to take cadaver dogs through the bush. They were brilliant, K9 Trackers Perth. But taking dogs through there so long after he went missing felt really futile. They were amazing, they volunteered their time. It was when they didn't come up with anything that we started to think we could well be looking in the wrong spot.

K9 Trackers is an amazing organisation. They provide their services free of charge to the families of missing persons, to help locate the remains of their loved ones.

I also want to give a shout-out to Por Drone Solutions who have donated their time and skills to fly drones looking for the missing. In 2023, a drone company located the remains of missing man Corey O'Connell, whose case was quite similar to Rigby's. Corey's car was found out of petrol in bushland at Nannup, Western Australia in June 2022, and a bag of his belongings was later found concealed in the bush. Despite a police search of the bush, Corey was not found until the drone was used in May 2023.

In September 2023 I spoke with Daniel Wood from Working Drones Australia, who tells me his company is more than happy to provide this free service to the families of missing persons. They are truly unsung heroes. Daniel is currently developing software that will make it even easier to locate items of interest in thick bushland.

The location where Rigby's bag was found has been suggested to be a known hook-up area, or gay 'beat'. After a little research (that was not for the faint hearted), I discovered that The Spectacles is listed (with a 5-star rating) on at least two gay cruising websites. One of them includes the information:

The Spectacles is a popular gay cruising spot. Car park is nearby, cruising takes place in the bush/shrubs near the trail. Park up and see who wanders into the bush and follow.

It's worth noting that The Spectacles is directly opposite Kwinana train station. As we don't know exactly where the bag was found, it's hard to pinpoint where a person may have entered. There's no direct access when coming out from the station, but if they hopped the barrier beside the highway they are in The Spectacles, and it's only a few steps to a series of connecting tracks leading all through the wetlands. However, to walk from the train station (southern end of The Spectacles) to the carpark mentioned above, which is on the western side of The Spectacles, is at least a 45-minute walk.

Warnbro Beach at Rockingham is also listed as a gay beat. A 'beat' is a place where men can anonymously pick up other men for sex, or head to for sex after meeting elsewhere. They are all over the country. Google reviews mention repeatedly that the sand dunes at the beach, which is a designated nudist beach, are often occupied by older men performing sexual acts. Travelgay. com also recommends these sand dunes as a place for hook-ups. Wells Park at Kwinana also has ratings, and on one site I found a recommendation for a spot near Kwinana train station, down a path to the bird tower. This spot, at the roundabout intersection of Sicklemore and Sulphur Roads, is extremely isolated, in bushland, not a house or building in sight, and just a couple of minutes walk from Kwinana train station. This is just eight minutes by train from Rockingham station.

Police now had Rigby's bag and, crucially, his phone. However, the phone had been wiped of all data. It is unclear whether DNA testing was done on the bag and phone. Stephenie has never been told what was in Rigby's bag when it was found, apart from his phone. 'Police had his bag, so they knew exactly what it looked like. They sent me all these photos of bags for me to identify. They sent me photos of women's handbags.'

The family felt this was another subtly homophobic jibe towards Rigby, and say they felt 'tormented' by the attitude of police. Steph says police never sent her a photo of Rigby's actual bag, and she's bewildered why they sent her photos at all if they had the bag in their possession all along. She has also not been told if his phone was already wiped when they seized it. 'They took a lot of Rigby's stuff from home,' says Stephenie. 'His laptop and things like that. Many months later the police said I could go and pick them up. They gave me his phone, but they didn't give me his bag. So, they've still got it; they said they need it for evidence. But I thought, why don't they need his phone for evidence? Why did they give me everything else back, but not the bag? I would have thought the phone would be a key piece of evidence.'

One strange aspect of the case is the train fine. An infringement notice was posted to Rigby's home address, dated 15 August, the day he was last seen. The fine was issued for riding the train without a ticket. 'Rig was not someone who would deliberately not buy a ticket,' says Steph. 'He had a lot of money, and he probably also had one of those transport cards that you swipe.

That was strange, it was so weird for that to happen.' The chilling thought that comes to mind in this scenario is that it was not Rigby who presented his ID to transit police, but someone who maybe had his wallet and ID. Frustratingly, police were unable to view the CCTV footage from that day, as it had been wiped by the time they requested it.

Adding weight to this theory is that the train the person was on was coming from Mandurah; it was heading in to Perth, not out of it. Mandurah is south of Rockingham. So, if Rigby caught the train home, as he intended to do, and something happened to him either on the way, or after he alighted at Rockingham, it is certainly possible that whoever harmed him and took his wallet caught this train back to Perth, where they had come from. Rigby's bag and phone were found near Wellard. This is on the same train line that would have come from Mandurah, through Rockingham and back to Perth. Everything points to Rigby getting the train back to Rockingham, as he told his mum he would. Did he have someone with him on that return journey? Was he followed? Or did he meet someone when he got back?

Rigby would normally catch a taxi or Uber home from Rockingham train station. There's also a bus that runs directly past his house. All of these methods should have been checkable, and some would have had CCTV, so why were these not all investigated by police? Steph thinks Rig would have likely called a taxi, because we know he took a taxi in Perth. Months after that ride the taxi company was able to provide police with a recording of Rigby making the booking. It gave Steph hope that records were kept for longer and there might have been something to point them in the right direction, but it doesn't appear the taxis in Rockingham were checked at all, in case Rig called for one at that end of his journey. To walk home would have taken about 40 minutes, 5 or 6 kilometres. Stephenie lived a 10-minute walk from the station, so if Rigby had started to walk, he would have likely gone to her house to say hello and ask for a lift home.

'If he'd missed the bus, or didn't have his wallet, if he'd been robbed or lost it, or lost his phone, he could have walked to my place.' She is very frustrated that there is absolutely no CCTV footage anywhere of Rigby's journey, despite it being all on public transport. 'How can all the footage from the train stations be gone, from every train and every train station? Why weren't they scouring all that? They tried to tell me it all gets wiped. But what about the Cloud? Nothing really disappears if you're good at looking for it.'

Stephenie feels the key to the puzzle may lie in the Grindr app, which we know Rigby was using on the afternoon he disappeared. The app has a messaging feature, and Rigby was using this to speak to his friend that day. He could have just used text messages, so for him to be using the Grindr message system he would have needed to open the app. This suggests he may have been looking to meet someone that afternoon. 'His friends were very helpful; I'd known many of them for years, we'd gone to concerts together and stuff like that,' says Steph:

They were all out looking for him too. I contacted everyone. He wasn't with any of his mates that day, so it had to be someone he'd just met. He had long time friends who were on the Grindr app on the same day, so they knew the exact location of where he was, that's how we knew he was in East Perth. It pings when you're talking to someone you know, and they can actually see where you are. He was talking to one of his friends through the app, and that friend got in contact with me.

I asked him if Rig seemed not like himself, was he drunk or anything, and he said no, he seemed fine. I asked if he thought Rig might have been on the app that day hooking up with someone, and he said quite possibly. I was trying to get through to the police that they needed to look into this app. We contacted the Grindr company in the USA, and they said if we could get a Federal Police clearance to look into it, then they'd release the information. So, we did all that; I spoke to some Federal coppers and they said yeah, we can do this. They went back to the head of the investigation, who said he didn't think it was necessary. It felt like we were bashing our heads against the wall. There were lots of little things like that that seemed big to me.

This is unbelievably frustrating. I record the interviews I do to make sure I can quote people perfectly, so I can also hear my own responses. During my interview with Steph I gasp indignantly many, many times at what she tells me. It's unbelievable to me that something that seems like a crucial step in solving this mystery has not been pursued.

I never set out to portray police in a negative way, and I love hearing stories about great police who do a fantastic job, like the Major Crimes officer Steph dealt with. However, it's been difficult to find areas in which to praise police in this story. I was reading up about Julie Cutler's case – she was a young woman who went missing in Perth very mysteriously in June

1988. Her car was located floating in the ocean just off the beach at Cottesloe two days later. Eight years later, in 1996, a purse, 1988 diary and pen were found half buried in a sand dune about a kilometre from where her car was found. They were thought to belong to Julie. The man who found them handed them to police after seeing a missing person appeal for Julie. What did police do with these potentially important pieces of evidence? They destroyed them. I had hoped we'd moved on from the mistakes of past decades, but there we were in 2015, with little to commend.

Police and family considered the possibility that Rigby took his own life, but the idea was quickly dismissed by family, who knew him best. Rig had experienced first-hand the terrible shock and grief a suicide impacts on the people who loved them, and Steph knows he would never have put his own family through that. 'I just know he had no intention of taking his life,' says Steph. 'Although he was grieving, he wasn't that type of person. And he would have told me; we were really close. He was really angry with his partner for doing that, and never telling him.'

In December 2015, Major Crime Squad Detective Senior Constable Bruce Wishart told the media the case was being treated as a suspected homicide due to the length of time since Rigby had been in touch with his family. All of Rigby's siblings believe the same thing – that he was murdered. They believe he met someone at some point in his return journey to Rockingham and something sinister has occurred. Stephenie has no idea who could have done such a thing to her kind and gentle brother.

'We can't think of anyone that he was with or anyone he knew that would want to hurt him. He was too well liked. He was very generous. Very passive. Maybe he didn't meet the person on Grindr; it could have been anywhere. A lot of men do go missing from Rockingham. Maybe there's a crazy serial killer out there that's picking off gay guys.'

In 2020, three teenage boys used Grindr to lure 56-year-old Peter Keeley to Broulee, in southern NSW. He thought he was meeting an 18-year-old boy. Peter was found dead, bound at the wrists, head and ankles in Broulee bushland on 2 February 2020. The boys were only convicted of aggravated kidnapping. They claimed they had used the app to contact Peter, mistakenly believing him to be a paedophile. How many other men has this happened to? As an aside, Justice Michael Walton denied an application by prosecutors to allow Mr Keeley's family to read their victim impact statements in court. It feels like the victims are being revictimised by the system that is meant to help them.

Rigby was a wealthy man. He had sold his very successful restaurants for a lot of money, and also had an inheritance from his partner who had died. He was living rent free with his family. He did not owe anyone a cent, so a debt is not one of the theories in this case. Rigby had a painful arthritic condition that had led to his early retirement from the restaurant business, and he self-medicated for this. 'It wasn't like he was taking drugs to go out partying,' says Steph. 'But the police asked me if I think my brother was a junkie. I just said, "You guys have no tact." I told them he had health conditions that stopped him cooking, his hands were quite painful. He was going to doctor appointments for other stuff too. He wasn't someone who was giving up on life, he was attending all these appointments and taking care of himself. He'd been through a lot. We didn't talk about any of that with Mum as we thought it would have just upset her, but I remember during an interview she actually talked about it. We were trying to protect her from what she really didn't need to know, but she already knew. Rig was really honest, and he would have just told her himself. He was highly functional; he did Mum's cleaning and kept the house nice, he was always fixing things, took Mum places, cooked for her.'

It's important to include this, in case Rigby's disappearance is in some way linked to his self-medicating. Maybe he had arranged to buy illegal medication near the train station in Rockingham, and a simple regular transaction perhaps went very wrong. Perhaps people realised Rigby had a lot of money, and they demanded more than he was spending. Perhaps they tried to force him to go an ATM. Which again, would have had CCTV if checked. Steph says that if someone had demanded more money from Rigby he would not have fought back, he would have just given it to them. He was a gentle and peaceful man.

Rigby's mother passed away in 2019, without answers. 'Mum kept his room the same, and would not let anyone go in there,' says Steph. 'I think she knew he wasn't coming back, but she didn't have the heart to move anything. Neither could, I for years. Even now, there's a lot of stuff still in boxes. I can't bring myself to throw it out. It's his life there. I've been going through all his paperwork for the last seven years. And I can't let anyone else do it. I don't trust anyone else, and no-one else would do it as thoroughly as I would. We'll need it if there's a coronial inquest, but I can't even get the ball rolling on that. I don't want them to do one, because I want them to find him.'

Like many families, the thought of an inquest makes Stephenie fearful, because she sees that as the end of the police investigation. 'That's the other side of the coin. Yeah, I want to wrap it all up at some point in my life and have some resolve, have a funeral, sort out his affairs, and I can move on from it. But to do that, that's it, isn't it? That leaves someone out there who did it, and we also need to find him. I do think someone's got away with murdering him.'

Younger sister Tina knows everything that's happened, and Steph describes her as very switched on. It must be particularly hard for her, as Rig was her carer as well as her brother. Initially the family tried to protect their mum and Tina from what had happened. Steph says this was also because the police attitudes towards Rig would have upset their mother terribly, and being so unwell they were determined to not make her condition worse. Now, they are very open with Tina.

Stephenie became obsessed with finding her brother, and the constant vigilance began to take a toll. 'It consumed me,' she says. 'I had to take a step back from it all.' She continues:

For the first five years, it was all I ever talked to anyone about. My other brothers got to a point where they were like, can you talk about something else! They just dealt with it better than I did. It wasn't that they weren't feeling the same feelings of loss and grief like I was — they certainly were. But they were trying to tell me, get on with life. It still affects my work, my relationships. I'd love to not think about it all the time. It's all consuming. It's something I can't switch off from. Sometimes I'll go a few months without thinking about it too much, and I start to feel a little bit guilty. But I want to be in that spot where I can let it go. I can't actually do anything. I've come to that realisation there's not a lot I can physically do without a lot of money to spend on other people searching. I can't take any more time off work to be doing this.

Now that Mum's passed, I also now look after my younger sister, I'm her full-time carer. I've really got to put the time and energy that I do have into making sure she's all right rather than staying all wrapped up in my brother. It feels hopeless. Until somebody else comes forward ... I really believe he was with someone. Someone knows something. Until they find more evidence, or his body, or someone comes forward there's really not a lot I can do It's too big a space out there to look for him.

I know that there aren't enough police to work on every single case 24/7 for a year, and they have to take the next case that's more important, I do get that Rig's is right down the bottom of the pile now. Occasionally I'll get a call from Missing Persons Unit to say his file is still open, have we heard anything, and I always say, has anyone looked into Grindr yet? They say, we'll get back to you. It was February the last time I spoke to them.

Stephenie misses her brother profoundly. 'I was just thinking of a funny story about Rig, when he and I went to Bunnings to buy some plant pots. We were in the outdoor garden section, and Rig had reached up to pull a fairly large pot down. It was full of water and it absolutely drenched him. I still laugh at the way he yelped and was dancing around. I was literally on my knees crying with laughter. It still cracks me up.'

The final words are from Rigby himself. In 2011, Rig prophetically wrote on Facebook, in reply to birthday wishes:

Thank you everybody for your kind regards. All I can say is life is so short, make sure you stand by those who are close to you. Time is a precious thing. Bless you all.

If you have any information about the disappearance of Rigby Fielding please contact Crimestoppers on 1800 333 000

CHAPTER FOUR
Gail King

Gail King, aged 28, was last seen when she left the family holiday home at Minlaton, on South Australia's Yorke Peninsula on 7 July 1997. Her car was found at the family home in Brahma Lodge, Adelaide, but it's unclear what happened to Gail.

I hope that Gail King had some happy moments in her life. I hope she rejoiced in the smiles of her children, and I hope she knew she was loved by her family. But as hard as I tried to find the happy side of Gail, I could not see it. All I can do is tell her story and hope that brings her peace, and brings her home.

Gail was one of three children born in the suburbs of Adelaide, South Australia, to Wilfred and Joyce King. The couple, after being unable to have children for many years, adopted a daughter, Julie. Two years later, a miracle happened, and Gail was born. Six years later, little brother Peter came along. The family lived in Pooraka, and dad Wilf was a hard worker, holding down three jobs to feed his family; he was a storeman by day, and at night he would help out the undertaker down the road. On weekends he drove taxis.

'They were both happy-go-lucky people,' says Peter. 'They drank a bit, smoked a bit. Mum was very hard working too; she worked with Dad for a bit, then at another place. She worked up until she had us, then she stayed at home. We weren't rich, but we weren't poor.' The three children didn't have an idyllic childhood. Peter remembers lots of arguments in the family as they were growing up. 'It wasn't an overly happy childhood,' he says. 'Gail and Julie used to fight all the time, and I don't think Dad understood me. He always wanted a boy, to keep the family name going, but he was a very angry person. Maybe it's just that he was tired all the time, from working so much. I tended to get a few smacks.'

Peter says dad Wilf was very close to Gail. 'He'd tell her off, but he didn't like doing it,' says Peter. He has some fond memories of his sisters as children, going away on holidays in a caravan, but struggles to recall truly happy times in their childhood. He tries to give his own children the opposite childhood to the one he remembers. 'I don't look back on my childhood and think, what a wonderful time we had. I don't really remember many fun times. It's sad.'

Gail was an average student at school and was not the sort of girl to attract attention to herself. Gail was not happy at high school, and Peter and his wife Cathy have only discovered in the last couple of years that Gail was bullied quite badly during her time there. Peter hesitates when trying to explain why Gail may have been a target for bullies, as he clearly loves his sister very much. 'She wasn't the most attractive person,' Peter says, reluctant to criticise Gail. 'She didn't really look after herself. She had a few issues. She didn't have much self-esteem. She wasn't very happy at home, either.'

Cathy has spoken to some of Gail's friends from high school and says: 'Gail was bullied by many students as she was "different", and didn't fit in. Her friend from school said she and Gail were both bullied, so they stuck together. Gail had acne, and she was partly deaf. She also made a "tick" noise, so that could also be why.'

Gail left school in year 11 without any real goals for her life. 'Dad thought that if you could get a job, you should leave school, so that's what Gail did,' says Peter. While in high school Gail had a part time job picking fruit and vegetables at a market garden, a job she enjoyed every much, and continued after leaving school. She made some true friends there, who stayed with her through into her adult years.

Gail later became a carer for the intellectually disabled, and was still working in the care industry when she went missing. Leanne Salmon, who worked with Gail at a nursing home in about 1987, remembers Gail as 'a very nice, friendly girl who would help anyone out if needed'. Gail had a couple of close friends, but not many. One of her friends, Alison, remained her closest friend through school and until she went missing. With her work friends, Gail would go to the pub for drinks on a Friday night, and sometimes ten-pin bowling, but she remained a quiet girl.

After leaving school Gail moved out of the family home to the small seaside suburb of St Kilda in Adelaide. Gail and Peter still kept in touch, but Peter said he didn't know much about what was going on in her life. 'She was a very secretive person, we're finding out now,' he says. 'We had our suspicions (about what sort of life she was living) before she went missing, but we're finding out more.'

Gail had a couple of boyfriends in her teens, but her life changed when she met Marvyn. Gail and Marvyn met over drinks at the Brahma Lodge Squash Centre, and soon afterwards Gail brought him home to meet the family at their weekly dinner. These dinners continued as the children eventually all brought home partners, and everyone came together each Wednesday night. Peter can't recall his initial impressions of Marvyn, but believes he thought he was okay. Gail was not experienced at being in a relationship, and Peter feels that when Marvyn showed an interest in her, she responded simply because he was paying her some attention. 'She was never the pretty girl who wore makeup,' says Peter. 'She was a bit of a tomboy. So, anyone who paid attention to her, she would have leaned towards.'

A year later Gail and Marvyn moved in together, and soon afterwards their first child was born.

'They always said they were going to get married, but they didn't have an engagement party or anything,' says Peter:

I later spent a bit of time with Marvyn, so I saw a different side of him to what Mum and Dad did. Gail changed a fair bit when she moved in with him. He owned the house they lived in. I remember Gail came to our place a lot to eat. She came down for lunch once, and at the local shop you could get a serve of chips for $2. I told her to grab some chips on her way down and I'd fix her up when she got here. She said she didn't have any money. I said, 'You don't have $2? In your car, somewhere, you don't have $2?' She said no. She just got to the point where she would not spend any money unless she absolutely had to. She was earning fairly good money at the time, and she had a fair bit of money in the bank, so she must have been doing okay, but she didn't ever spend any money.

I tried to talk to her about it a couple of times, but I was the younger brother, and she'd say, 'Shut up, it's got nothing to do with you.' She got very angry and defensive. It almost felt like I was the only person who could see what was happening, no-one else could see it. I'm not sure if Mum and Dad didn't want to see it, or just couldn't.

Peter was becoming increasingly worried that his sister was changing, and being manipulated:

She wasn't the sharpest tool in the shed. And if you've been bullied all your life, you probably just don't think much of it. I think she had that low self-esteem her whole life. Gail was (outwardly) a happy sort of person, but I don't think she was happy with herself. Towards the end, after she had the kids, I think she felt like she was maybe stuck (in the relationship), and trapped. Once they had the kids, she would have felt obligated to stay with him. She was not a happy person at that stage of her life.

Peter isn't sure why Gail didn't leave Marvyn if she was unhappy. 'I don't think leaving was an option, but it should have been. She had a bit of money tucked away, so whether she was doing that, putting money aside so she could leave him, I don't know.'

If Gail had decided to leave Marvyn, her old room was still as she left it in her parents' house, and older sister Julie had already moved out, so Gail's children could have had their own room too. Peter said the friends she had from the vegie-picking days would also have done anything for her, and helped her without question if she'd asked.

'I talked to her about leaving him,' says Peter. 'I asked her was it worth being with him, and she said yes. I tried to talk to her a few times but she'd either change the subject, or not really answer me. Or she'd say she was happy with him. But I could tell she wasn't. It was like she was trying to convince herself. Towards the end, we had more arguments than anything else. I remember one time, I tore the ligaments in my ankle, and I phoned her to ask if she could drive me to the hospital, as I couldn't really drive. Gail said Marvyn told her I should be fine, and should be able to drive myself. I was thinking, "You're my sister, I didn't ask anyone else, I asked you." I drove myself, in the end.'

Peter recalls Gail as a caring mother, but her nonchalance towards her own hygiene extended to her children. Peter remembers one day watching in disbelief as the family dog licked food from Gail's children's faces in the car for several minutes, while Gail seemed unconcerned. Peter believes his own views on parenting were quite different from his sister's, but says: 'She was happy that she was a mum, and she did what she thought was best for the kids.'

Marvyn's parents lived at Yorketown, about 200 kilometres from where the couple were living in Adelaide. Gail didn't get on with his family, and declared she would not visit them if she had to stay at their place. Detective Brevet Sergeant Tanya Mason later said to the media: 'She wasn't happy at the prospect of being there all the time. We know she wasn't happy being around Marvyn's family and they were not all that keen on her either.'

It was decided Marvyn and Gail would buy another house in the same area so they would have somewhere to stay on their own when they visited on weekends. They bought a farm at Minlaton, about 25 minutes from Marvyn's parents' place. It's a pretty little farming community of about 800 people on the Yorke Peninsula, and is known colloquially as 'the barley capital of the world'. However, police have said the couple argued about the property, and Gail didn't want to move there permanently, away from her job and friends in Adelaide, and close to a family she didn't get on with. Despite this, the family spent most weekends at the Minlaton farm.

On Friday 5 July 1997, Maryvn took the kids to stay at the farm. Gail stayed back in Adelaide on the Friday night, worked on Saturday, and drove to Minlaton after work. According to Marvyn, Gail said she had a workplace health and safety meeting scheduled for the Monday morning, so was planning to drive back to Adelaide early. Police said they found it very strange she would have gone all the way to Minlaton just for one night, and indeed Gail spent just 24 hours there. However, police enquiries at the aged care facility at Gilles Plains where Gail worked showed there was never any meeting.

According to Marvyn's statement to police, Gail left to make the two-hour drive back to Brahma Lodge at about 7 pm on Sunday night on 7 July, and stated that is the last he saw of her. Gail left her children, aged six and four years, with Marvyn. On the Monday morning Marvyn and the children visited several locations on the Yorke Peninsula, including Troubridge Point and Pondalowie Bay, before going back to the Minlaton house at 5.30 pm on Monday evening.

The following day Marvyn and the children drove back to Adelaide, arriving at Brahma Lodge at about 6 pm on Tuesday 9 July. He told police that when he arrived home he found Gail's car, a white Toyota hatchback, parked in the driveway. The overnight bag she'd taken to Minlaton was inside the house. Her house and car keys were missing, as well as her black vinyl handbag and purse. A single light was on in the lounge room. Nothing was disturbed. Marvyn later told police there were photo albums taken from the home. When Gail left Minlaton she was wearing a green tracksuit. This was found inside the house and had been washed, but the other clothing Gail had taken away with her remained unwashed in the overnight bag. Marvyn told police he washed the tracksuit when he'd returned from Minlaton, with some of his own clothing. He also told police there was a half-eaten chicken takeaway in the fridge, which the two children later ate.

Peter learned his sister was missing when Marvyn called him and his parents on the Tuesday evening to ask if Gail was there. Peter was still living at home with his parents at the time. Marvyn told them Gail's car was at the family home, but she wasn't there. 'I thought that was a bit strange,' says Peter. 'If I came home and saw Cathy's car was here but she wasn't, I would think she'd just gone for a walk. I wouldn't be ringing her mother. I would think she must be around somewhere, she can't be too far away. Apparently, as soon as Marvyn got home, he rang us.'

Peter's initial thought was to guess that a work colleague had perhaps picked Gail up. 'You just don't really think much of it, I guess. You just don't think something like that will happen to you. You don't assume the worst.' Peter recalls having to wait for a while before they could report Gail as a missing person, and in the meantime his parents started ringing Gail's friends to see if anyone had heard from her. They were concerned, but not too worried at this point.

South Australia Police told me that Marvyn was the first to contact police. He made a missing person report on 9 July 1997, two days after Gail was last seen. Police interviewed Peter and his parents, and Marvyn. 'At the time, Marvyn seemed very concerned, he was getting very emotional,' says Peter. 'I never thought that he'd hurt her. But he said that she was having an affair, and she'd run off with someone. I thought, well, that doesn't make sense, as she'd be using her bank account, and keep in contact with Mum and Dad – especially Dad, as they were very close. And if she'd run off, she would not leave her kids.'

Peter does not believe that his sister was having an affair. Cathy also does not believe this, and says it wasn't in Gail's nature to cheat, that she was committed to her family. Police have spoken to a man Gail was rumoured to be having an affair with, and he has cooperated with them. He is not regarded as a person of interest. To everyone's surprise, it was revealed later in the police investigation that Gail was three months pregnant when she went missing. Dad Wilf was the only person who knew Gail was pregnant. Peter isn't sure whether Gail would have been happy about this situation. 'She might have been happy that she was having another baby, but not happy (about the father),' says Peter. 'Looking back on it, although they were still living together, he went his own way and did his own thing, and so did she. I think they were only together for the children. That's how it seems to me. Whether she wanted to get away from Marvyn or not, I'm not sure,' he says.

Gail's disappearance was featured in newspapers and on television, and the more the case was discussed, the more Peter wondered what could have happened to his sister. Peter's parents didn't suspect any harm had come to Gail at all, but had no idea what could have happened. Police asked them did they think someone close to Gail could have hurt her and they said no, definitely not. When the police asked Peter, his reply was yes, he thought certain people were capable of murdering her. The police asked Peter what he thought of Marvyn and his reply was: 'You don't want to know what I think of him.'

At the time, Peter didn't think the police were doing a good job investigating the disappearance, but in hindsight he realises they simply didn't tell the family the details of the case, as is standard with most investigations. The whole thing was very strange, early on. 'I understand they don't tell us everything, but it just seemed not good enough.' Peter felt very excluded from the investigation. 'From my point of view, it was like I wasn't there. I would tell the police to talk to certain people that Gail and Marvyn knew, and they'd get back to me six weeks later about it. It was like nothing I said was taken seriously. If they had suspicions about a certain person from early on, I would have thought they'd have listened to me a bit more, as I knew the most about it. I'd spent a lot of time with them both.'

Police went through the Brahma Lodge home meticulously, seizing several items for testing. They found no evidence that anything untoward happened in the house. The case went cold. After Gail went missing, Marvyn sold the Brahma Lodge house and moved permanently to the Minlaton holiday home he and Gail owned. When he visited Adelaide he would allow Gail's parents to see their grandchildren. Peter says his parents were never left alone with the children; Marvyn's new girlfriend or his mother would come along and stay with them. Eventually Gail's parents were prevented from seeing their grandchildren at all, a situation that was very upsetting for them. Peter sadly tells me he also has no contact with his niece and nephew, despite being very close to them before Gail disappeared. 'Mum and Dad basically brought Gail's son up, until she went missing. Gail and Marvyn both worked a lot, and Mum and Dad would have the kids all day, and I saw them a lot too.'

The trauma of his sister's disappearance was compounded when Peter discovered a stranger attempting to profit from the family's misfortune. Peter and Cathy were at a market one weekend and came across a stall selling a book. 'It was a "choose your own adventure" type book, as in choose how you die,' Peter says grimly. 'I was reading the back of the book, and I realised it was about Gail. I just walked away. Cathy went back to talk to the woman on the stall, who'd written the book, and she said it was based on a woman from around the area. She told Cathy she'd spoken to Marvyn about it, and actually sent him a copy of the book, and he was fine with it. I'm thinking, *we* weren't told about it. We went to the police about it and they said there's nothing in it that she wasn't allowed to put in. They agreed it wasn't right that she'd done it, but couldn't do anything about it. I went back to her and said: "This is about my sister", and she still made me pay the full price for the copy of it. I just wanted to see what she'd written about Gail.'

Like most of the siblings in this book, Peter has consulted a psychic about his missing sister:

We spoke with a psychic who does the Sensing Murder show in New Zealand, and she came out to appear on the Today Tonight *show here in South Australia. I believe in that sort of thing anyway, but I'm looking for any way to help, any way to close it, by any means possible. It might be one little thing that helps the police solve it.*

The psychic medium is Sue Nicholson, and during the Seven Network *Today Tonight* show she walked through Gail and Marvyn's former Brahma Lodge home. A mother and daughter now live in the house, and believe they can feel Gail's presence still there. The mother says she's heard wardrobe doors banging on their own, screaming noises on their phone line that the phone company can't explain, and front doors slamming in the faces of males as if to keep them out. She and her daughter have both heard a female voice in the house, in between the hallway and bathroom. Sue feels Gail was murdered in the house, her body taken to the shed, then dumped at sea. She has told Peter they will never find Gail's body.

'This case is really, really complicated,' said Sue in the TV program. 'It wasn't just a murder, then dump the body … there were other people involved. There was a lot of goings-on, affairs, things like that. I feel like there's two people involved. One did it, the other one knows about it, but the other one got rid of the body.' Sue held a photo of Gail, and a coffee cup that had belonged to her. She sensed Gail was 'in a dark place'. 'There's something not right about the head,' says Sue. 'I'm feeling like something's happened around her head. My head really, really hurts, like I've been hit with something, or hit on the head, or knocked and hit my head. And she keeps showing me water.'

Sue feels Gail's clothing is significant. 'She had it on, but it was taken off,' she says. 'But I'm not seeing a sexual attack, or anything like that. I can't even see a stranger. She knows him.'

Peter and Cathy have passed on Sue's information to police, and are grateful for Sue's input. 'She picked up a lot of things that she couldn't have known, like the affair, and the baby,' says Peter. 'A lot of what she said made sense. She said that Gail didn't actually come home for a work meeting, she came home to meet a man. Sue has said to us a few times "American" and on Kangaroo Island there's a place called American River. If Gail went missing from Brahma Lodge, it would be more logical to take her to that sort of area.'

Speaking with psychics is often a source of comfort for the families of missing persons, perhaps making them feel like they are doing *something* to try to find out what happened; however, it's important to note that psychics who become involved in criminal investigations often create headaches for police.

Detective Brevet Sergeant Tanya Mason from the Major Investigation Branch of South Australia Police, who has worked on Gail's case, responded to my questions with great detail and candidness, and for that I am most grateful. She was very firm when speaking about the difficulties created when police are given information from psychics:

Police cannot use any information provided by psychics. Whether you believe in them or not, the information they provide is not evidence based – some of it is from what is already out in the media. Police can't act on this information. Police have many people claiming to have psychic abilities contact us. None of which have ever proven to be accurate or ever resulted in anything helpful in the past. Many psychics give families false hope. This is actually quite cruel when you think about it.

Families tend to believe a psychic person more than the police because they're actually telling families stuff they want to hear. Dealing with psychic information wastes police time and resources when we could be focusing on evidence based information. In the past, I've wasted a number of days dealing with information provided as a result of psychics, water diviners, pendulum swingers, as the families have been convinced the info is accurate.

I have to agree with Tanya. I have included in every chapter of both my books the details about families of the missing consulting psychics, because it is not my place to judge what they choose to do in their painful journeys. Whether or not any of these psychics are accurate or helpful is not for me to say, but I do agree with Tanya that they can often cause greater pain and grief for families already dealing with tremendous pressure and fear. In many high profile missing person cases I am contacted by people with 'visions'. I remember one person contacted the mother of a missing young woman, and told her she'd had a vision of her daughter, and the daughter had been raped and murdered and was to be found naked, bound and gagged and in an abandoned shed near water. The girl was found safe and well the next day. Can you imagine how that mother felt, until she got the news her daughter was fine? Tanya is absolutely correct that such contact from people is very cruel.

I would never tell a family of a missing person not to consult a psychic, as this is their journey and not mine, but I will not hesitate to prevent the 'pendulum swingers', as Tanya puts it, from contacting vulnerable families. In almost 19 years of missing person work, I am yet to see a psychic locate a missing person. That's my usual response to them – if you 'see' in your visions that a missing person is buried in a shallow grave in a forest, by all means you go out there with a shovel and start digging, and if you find them, I will be the first person to shake your hand. It hasn't happened yet.

Having a missing sister has taken its toll on Peter. 'I used to be a happy-go-lucky sort of person before, but I'm not now,' he says. 'According to Cathy I'm grumpy … but I want justice. I can't deal with not-justice.'

Cathy has been a tower of strength to Peter. 'She's been really good,' he says. 'I'm a quiet sort of person, but she's very vocal. She promised Dad she would do the best she could to find Gail, and she will ask the questions, she will push things, she's really good.'

Despite having never met her husband's sister (Cathy and Peter started dating about a year after Gail went missing), Cathy is determined to find the answers for her family. It is Cathy who runs the Facebook page, making appeals for Gail. 'I really want to find closure for Peter, and be able to get justice and closure for Gail,' she says. 'She isn't just a memory, she was real and deserves to be remembered, and we won't stop until we get this. Peter only has her, and for him, not knowing is affecting him greatly. He needs to know that she is okay, or if he can lay her to rest.'

Cathy sat down with Peter's dad before he died and asked him what she could do to help him. 'He said to me, "Just find my girl, find my baby girl," and I said, "Don't worry, it doesn't matter what happens, we will do anything possible to find her." I made him a promise.' Cathy saw Gail's father crying – and this was a man who was adamant that men don't cry – and felt compelled to help.

Peter has struggled with the frustration of knowing his sister was unhappy before she went missing, but being unable to do anything about it. 'I always felt guilty, I felt like I should have done something and said something, but I couldn't and didn't. I've also had to see what Mum and Dad went through, and then losing them. The kids now don't have grandparents, they were robbed of that.' Mum Joyce passed away in 2006, and Wilfred in 2008. Peter is sure the immense stress and grief they experienced when Gail went missing contributed greatly to their decline in health, and eventual deaths.

'It did kill them inside. They went downhill pretty quickly after she went missing. Mum was going through breast cancer at the time, right when Gail went missing, and she was so sick from that. Dad was only 67; my grandparents were in their eighties when they died, so Dad was robbed of at least 15 years of life. After Mum died, he started drinking a lot more, and he had ulcers that were bleeding. It destroyed them both.' No doubt these serious health problems were a result of the immense stress Wilf was under, with a missing, presumed murdered, daughter.

Peter says his family had to navigate their way through the murky waters of grief and ambiguous loss without any help. 'We were never offered any counselling; it was only when Cathy looked into it recently that we got some support. Until now, we've been offered nothing. I'm on my second counsellor; hopefully she can help me a bit.' Peter is happy that progress seems to be being made on Gail's case, but admits the constant pressure does take a toll. 'It's easier if it's not in your face every day, even though it's always in the back of your mind. Now, it's harder, it's in your face more often, but it's good because you're hopefully getting closer to some sort of closure. It's helpful to meet and talk to the families of other missing persons who are in the same situation.'

South Australia police have told me they regularly reassign investigations to different detectives so that everything can be looked at with fresh eyes. They ask the new crop of detectives to check all the details of Gail's case to try to pick up something that may have been missed. South Australia have new DNA analysis equipment and the family, at time of writing, were waiting on the results from testing evidence from the case. Peter has been approached by potential witnesses, whose names and details he passed on to police. Police assured him the witnesses had been interviewed. 'The police did say to us the other day they can assure us that things are happening behind the scenes. If they can arrest somebody, then we'll get closure that way. It won't make me happy, but at least if someone says, Yes, I did it," then you get some closure. At least we'd know why and how.'

In August 2017, police told the media they had been in contact with someone who provided 'a different taint' to the investigation. Detective Inspector Greg Hutchins said: 'While I can't comment too much on what we have, I can confirm that we have information that is credible and needs to be explored. It is another avenue we need to look at.'

In 2018, police launched another enquiry into Gail's disappearance. Major Crime officer in charge Detective Superintendent Des Bray said detectives wanted to speak with anyone who knew how Gail's Toyota Corolla came to be at the Brahma Lodge house. He said: 'Either it was brought back to Adelaide by someone assisting the offender or she drove it herself. Confirming either of these possibilities could change the direction of the investigation.'

Detective Sergeant Tanya Mason from South Australia Police said: 'We don't have any proof that she left the Yorke Peninsula and made it back to Adelaide. We have had a person of interest who we've tried to incriminate or eliminate and at this stage we haven't been able to do either. It is difficult, there are certainly some odd things about it that came up in the early days that caused us to look at one individual.'

Marvyn has always co-operated with police, and has always denied any involvement in Gail's disappearance or death. He, himself, acknowledges that he would naturally be considered a person of interest by police, and told the media police made it clear to him that he was a suspect. In 2019 he told Channel 9's Ben Avery: 'I was probably one of the last persons to see her. But there's somebody else out there too who actually knows what's happening too.'

Crime Stoppers SA have this on their official appeal: 'While investigators continue to keep an open mind in the investigation, they believe there are two likely possibilities. Firstly, she was killed by a close associate in the Minlaton area, with someone then returning the vehicle to Adelaide to stage the scene, or secondly, she was killed by another person, who is most likely known to her, after returning to Adelaide.'

Peter has no qualms about giving his opinion about who may be responsible for harming his sister, being certain that person was close to Gail. He makes no secret of his feelings.

If I can rattle a few cages, I'm happy with that.' Peter doesn't think he will ever find Gail's body. 'If she is in the ocean, as I've always thought and the psychic thinks, then we'll never get closure that way. But if we can get an arrest, at least, that will be some sort of closure. I know who did it, I know who killed her. But I just can't prove it. I need more to prove it.

He feels they are closer than ever to finding answers, as it seems like recently people have taken much more of an interest in Gail's case.

> *Over the years we've had bits and pieces. If she'd been on Crime Stoppers or whatever, but this year's been unbelievable, there's been so many leads come in.*

There is a $200,000 reward available for anyone who can provide information that leads to a conviction in this case, or the recovery of Gail King's remains.

If you can help, please contact Crime Stoppers on 1800 333 000 or report online at sa.crimestoppers. com.au

CHAPTER FIVE
Anthony Jones

Tony Jones, aged 20, was last seen on 3 November 1982, as he left Townsville, Queensland, intending to hitchhike to Mount Isa. It's believed he may have met with foul play in Hughenden.

You may not know this, but National Missing Persons Week, which is held every year in Australia at the end of July, was started because of Anthony Jones.

Twenty-year-old Tony has been missing since 1982. It's such a long time, but his family are just as keen today to find their answers as they were more than 40 years ago. Tony comes from a big family: 'You'd think with there being so many of us, we wouldn't miss one!' jokes brother Mark. It's a joke he's made many times, and unless you know him, you might be taken aback by such a quip, but it's typical of the straightforward, matter-of-fact way this family has dealt with this terrible event in their lives. They are not the sort of people to go to pieces. They know that won't help them find out what happened to their brother and son in Queensland all those years ago. They need to find him, and they won't stop until they do.

The Jones kids were typical Aussie larrikins, who loved being active and living their lives to the full. They grew up in suburban Perth and rode their bikes everywhere, exploring the neighbourhood. 'We'd find a hill and set up a ramp, and fly off the side of the hill on our bikes,' recalls Mark. 'All eight of us were at school at the same time, so it was a fair bit to keep track of.' Mum Beres had an unenviable task with so many children to look after who all wanted their own adventures.

Her brood were Deborah, Paul, Leanne, Brian, Tim, Mark, Tony and their indigenous foster sister, Bobbi. Dad, Kevin, was working two or three jobs much of the time to make sure his children could all attend good schools and have the things they needed. They were a big, happy family. Brian Jones wrote in his book *Searching for Tony*:

> *Though luxuries were few and far between, Dad had provided us with a Catholic school education and all the essentials of life. My mother, Beres, was a gifted and cheerful housewife who coped graciously with the turmoil of a large family.*

Brian also wrote about the family get-togethers:

> *Every Sunday afternoon we gathered at the family home in Dianella to be together, or to play squash, or indoor cricket, or charades, or Trivial Pursuit.*

The Jones family were clearly very close, and devoted to one another. At the time he wrote the book about his brother's disappearance Brian was training to be a Catholic priest. He has a wonderful turn of phrase, a trait shared by his brother Mark, who I spoke to extensively over several years for this chapter.

'A good insight into what we were like as kids is the fridge story,' says Mark. 'The Fridge Story' actually made the local news. Tony was seven years old when he went missing the first time. 'Three of us were in the shed, which was an out of bounds area,' recalls Mark:

> *We made some sort of secret club. We were making up all these different hand signals that we were going to use and all of a sudden, we had to actually USE one of them, as we heard Mum coming. We used the signal for 'hide' and Tim and I jumped out the window and went off and kicked a football around, and completely forgot about Tony. We actually didn't know what he'd done, but Tony had jumped in the old fridge.*

Just before, he said to come back and get him, but we didn't hear that bit!

When their mother could not find Tony, police were called and a search was organised through the local streets. As they were about to start searching a new area, their mother told them to wait while she checked the shed for the third time. She could hear a muffled sound and opened the fridge. There was Tony, unconscious and severely dehydrated. He was rushed to hospital but, incredibly, recovered very quickly from his brush with death. He'd been in the fridge for five hours. You'd think this experience would have taught Tony a lesson about being safe, but Mark goes on to tell me a second story about Tony's adventurous spirit:

A week later we were down at the local Police & Citizen's Club; they had a big, long hall and at the back is an old fireplace with some tunnels, so we went and bought some torches to explore. I went about 10 metres down, but there were too many spider webs for my liking. Tony went in there and disappeared. Fifteen minutes later we were there, shouting out to him but no word from him. We sprinted home and got Mum and Dad. They came back with us and, eventually, Tony came out, looked around at us all in surprise and said, 'What are you doing here?' He'd been right through the entire tunnel system underneath this hall. So, any worries about him having claustrophobia, or after-effects from the fridge, were soon dispelled!

Tony had a close group of mates as he grew into a teenager. 'They all idolised him,' says Mark. 'We did too, really. If we were a bit intense, Tony just found that all one big laugh. He didn't get people who took themselves too seriously. He was very laid back. He used to laugh at me doing the crossword, but I remember I left it one day and I got back and found he'd almost finished it. But he'd never let anyone know he had the brains to do something like that. He was all about being a knockabout bloke.'

Mark thinks part of this was the family dynamic, which ensured no-one got away with anything. 'We used to have some pretty intense games of Scrabble between the lot of us and Tony never got involved in that, he could never understand why we were all so competitive.' Being the youngest, Tony, Mark and Tim were known as 'the boys'. They were all close and did just about everything together. They'd go to the pub, see a live band. Tony liked to go away for weekend rabbit shooting trips and would spend the next six months telling stories about his adventures. He was a great storyteller, having written an 18-page account of his fridge ordeal at the age of seven, and Mark says he feels 'ripped off' that on top of the horrific events surrounding losing his brother, he also lost the chance to hear the wonderful stories Tony would have told about the epic trip he took across Australia before he went missing.

'If he could have written the script of his own life, he probably would have made up something along those lines,' Mark says with a sad smile. 'It would have been a murder-adventure, or something like that. If someone had said to him "write a story about your death" he would have made it a young death, and an interesting one, full of mystery and intrigue.'

Tony was working as a technician with X-Ray Laboratories,

but in May 1982 he decided to take a six-month trip around Australia. Brian writes:

Tony was a fine-looking lad; he was tall and lean with brown, shoulder-length hair and a dark-gingery beard which framed a winsome smile. Good natured, affable, and easygoing, he was regarded as a 'great bloke' amongst his friends, and endeared as the 'kid brother' of the family. Sky-diving, gold prospecting and roo shooting had failed to satisfy his thirst for adventure, so just before his twentieth birthday he announced his intention to embark upon a working holiday.

Tony had a girlfriend in Perth – Natalie – so it would have been a difficult decision to leave her for six months, but his wandering spirit prevailed, and he vowed to keep in regular contact with her by phone. Tony set off with a few mates from school. Older sister Leanne had decided to move to Sydney, so Tony saw this as a great opportunity to start his journey by driving her car across the Nullarbor Plain. He went to Adelaide, Melbourne, Canberra and Sydney, and the Snowy Mountains. It was here that Tony had a car accident and sustained a minor head injury. They were able to continue on to Sydney and spent a few weeks there, helping Leanne settle and also catching up with their brother Tim, who was living there at the time.

Tony looked for a job in Sydney but didn't find anything suitable, so jumped on a train to Brisbane. He stayed in Brisbane for several months, working at the Ekka (Brisbane show) and as a labourer in a canning factory. He made friends and was enjoying himself. Tim made a surprise visit to see Tony in Brisbane and they started to make plans to travel back to

Perth via north Queensland, at the same time, but separately, with Tim intending to cycle and Tony intending to hitchhike. The brothers spent three weeks travelling to Mackay, Airlie Beach and Townsville, meeting up with each other along the way and phoning home to Perth, and also to Leanne in Sydney, to relay messages to each other.

Tim and Tony met up at Airlie Beach and stayed with a couple of mates they'd made along the way, Steve and Eric. They continued on to Townsville and the four of them spent a week together in a caravan, at the Sun City Caravan Park in the suburb of Rosslea. In late October Tim set off on the Flinders Highway to cycle 900 kilometres to Mount Isa, and Tony travelled to Cairns. The brothers planned to meet up in Mount Isa. Brian writes: 'Thinking that Tim would need at least a ten-day head start, Tony hitchhiked further north to Cairns for a few days before starting the westward leg of his journey.'

Tony returned to Townsville from his Cairns trip on 3 November. It was their sister Bobbi's 15th birthday and her brothers wanted to wish her a happy birthday, with both of them phoning that night. Tim called home before Tony. Tim said he was at Mary Kathleen, a town about 60 kilometres from Mount Isa. He told his family that somewhere along his cycle journey he'd lost his wallet and bankbook, and he was struggling. Later that night, Tony phoned home from Townsville. Beres told him that Tim had already arrived in Mount Isa, which surprised Tony. He must have realised that he needed to get a move on in order to meet his brother, as Tim was waiting for him in Mount Isa so they could travel the last leg of their journey home together. He was concerned when Beres told him about Tim desperately needing money for food.

Brian writes that Tony said to his mother: 'Tell Tim I hope to be in Mount Isa tomorrow or certainly by Friday.' Beres told Tony she'd put $150 into his bank account, money that was to be shared with Tim. Tony told his mum his bank account was down to $3.99, so news of her deposit must have been very welcome. Tony spoke to Mark and told his brother he'd been sleeping on the beach in Cairns, and that it had been tough to find lifts up the coast. After he spoke to Mark, Tony called Natalie. Mark, Beres and Natalie recounted what was said in these phone calls as accurately as they could recall, in Brian's book:

'Hello, Mum. Tony here.'

'How are you, love?'

'Fine. Is Bobbi there? I'd like to wish her a happy birthday.'

'No, she's playing basketball tonight. She'll be sorry she missed you. I'll tell her you rang.'

'How's Dad and everyone at home?'

'We're all well. Dad's much better now and is in Melbourne for the Cup. He had a good day yesterday; even backed the winner of the Cup. Listen, Tony, Dad met a young chap from Mount Isa who said there was plenty of work up there. Why don't you get a job for a while before you come home?'

'Trouble is, Mum, you have to stay there for a minimum of three months in the mines, and I want to get home soon.'

'How are you going for money?'

'I'm all right thanks, Mum, I've got a dole cheque due on Friday.'

'Listen, Tony, Tim phoned earlier. He arrived at Mary Kathleen today and expects to be in Mount Isa by tomorrow. But Tim has had some bad luck. He had run out of money, and also lost his wallet and his bankbook. I was unable to send him any money, so instead I put $150 into your bank account. If you need any of the money help yourself, but give a fair share to Tim because he is rather desperate.'

'Okay.'

'Tim will be phoning back later. Is there anything you want me to tell him?'

'Tell him I hope to be in Mount Isa tomorrow or certainly by Friday. I'll phone again when I get there to find out where he is staying.'

'Take care and God bless.'

Beres then handed the phone to Mark.

'Hi, Tony. How are you?'

'Pretty good thanks, Mark.'

'What have you been up to?'

'Not much. I've been up to Cairns; beautiful country up there.'

'I suppose you are nearly broke are you, Tony?'

'Yeah. I've had to spend a couple of nights on the beach. Can't afford a caravan anymore.'

'When do you think you will be home?'

'Well, Nat's having a party a week before Christmas, so I hope to be home before then.'

'Have you been able to get lifts all right?'

'It was easy going up to Cairns, but it has been a bit harder coming back.'

'Listen, Tony, I'm just off to see the Dave Warner band at the pub.'

'That should be a rage. What else have you been doing?'

'I'll tell you when you get home.'

'Great. And by the way, Mark, I hope you've got my old bed set up for me.'

'Not yet. But don't worry, mate, I'll have it set up before you come home. Anyway, I'd better go now. See ya, mate.'

'Thanks, Mark, I'll catch you later.'

After this call, Tony phoned girlfriend Natalie.

'Hello, Nat.'

'Hi, Tony. Where are you?'

'I'm in Townsville.'

'What are you doing there again?'

'Well, it's the only way I can get out to Mount Isa.'

'So, how's it going?'

'Great, Nat, but I'm surprised at Tim. I can't believe he got out to Mount Isa so quickly. Anyway, I hope to catch up with him tomorrow or the next day.'

'Tony, have you shaved your beard off yet?'

'Yeah, on Friday; but it looks terrible so I think I'll grow it back again. And how's work going, Nat?'

'Good, but I had a day off today. I've been a bit depressed with you being away, so I went to see a doctor.'

'Are you sure you're all right?'

'Yeah. I'll be fine as soon as you get home.'

'Hmm. Well I won't be long now, Nat, I can't wait to see you again. I'm really looking forward to getting home.'

'Listen, Tony, I've been saving some money up in the bank. Maybe ... '

'That's good! I might get you to send me some so I can get home quicker. And by the way, Nat, could you do me a favour? I sent all my luggage home recently; would you mind picking it up from the railway depot?'

'Sure.'

'Oops! The red light is flashing; I'd better go now. But listen, Nat, I'll ring you again on Monday. I hope to be in Alice Springs by then. Bye now.'

This was the last time anyone was to hear from Tony Jones.

When Tony failed to arrive in Mount Isa by Friday as planned, Tim contacted his family to ask if Tony had called home to say his plans had changed. He hadn't. This is when the Jones family began to realise that no-one had heard from Tony since the Wednesday 3 November phone call, but at this stage there was no real concern for him. They initially assumed that it had taken Tony longer than anticipated to travel the 900 kilometres from Townsville to Mount Isa. Tim continued to wait for his brother. After four or five days, by the following Wednesday, the family started to become concerned, and talked with each other about how strange it was for Tony not to phone home.

Brian was at the movies, eerily watching a movie called *Missing*, about an American journalist missing in Santiago.

When he returned home that night from the cinema there was a message from mum Beres, asking him to call home, which he intended to do the next day. Brian writes: 'The next morning I was awoken about seven by a telephone call. It was Mother telling me that my brother Tony had disappeared.'

The family spoke to Tony's girlfriend, Natalie, who said that Tony had promised to call her on the Monday, but had not. It was the first time he'd ever failed to phone her as promised. The family tried to piece together his timeline and tried to logically work out his movements. They knew he'd said he'd be in Mount Isa in two days. 'Had he got a lift with a truckie down a back road and was just laid over for a while?' wonders Mark. 'We just speculated about anything and everything without really knowing realistically what the possibilities were. We became increasingly more worried as time went on. The theories became more and more unlikely and bizarre, but we just tried to think of every conceivable thing that could have happened to him.'

The family felt strongly, even at this early stage, that Tony would not have simply forgotten to call, or become distracted. After his experience in the fridge as a child, Tony always made sure his family knew where he was. He called home regularly, and exactly when he said he would, for the entire six months of his journey. Tim had suggested that they surprise the family by turning up back in Perth unannounced, and Brian writes that this idea made Tony angry, with him saying: 'You just can't do that, the folks will be out of their minds if they don't hear from us.'

Mark says their mother Beres wasn't a hysterical type of

woman, and remained stoic during the search for Tony, but she was certainly terribly worried. Mark shares a deeply sad story; the pain this brings in recalling it is evident in his voice. 'The 11th of November, Remembrance Day, was also the anniversary of the day Tony was locked in the fridge. We didn't know, but Mum and Tony had a pact that on that day, every year, he would always let her know where he was.' Beres was already worried that he was missing, but when 11 November passed with no contact from Tony, she just *knew*. Brian writes that Beres said: 'If Tony doesn't ring soon then something must be wrong. He wouldn't let me go through that again. Even if he had to crawl to get to a phone, I know he would ring me today.'

After 11 November, the family knew something was terribly wrong. They told Tim to go to Mount Isa police and make a missing person report. Unfortunately, the police did not take Tim's report seriously. Beres later had to phone them to confirm Tim's account, and the officer asked Tim to come back in so they could actually get the information from him. Brian writes: 'For the second time in thirteen years Tony had been reported to the police as a missing person on Remembrance Day.' The following morning Brian went to see his parents to discuss what needed to be done next. At this stage, Tim was staying at the St Vincent De Paul centre in Mount Isa, as he still had no money, and was waiting by the phone for contact from his family.

The physical distance between Perth and Mount Isa made it very difficult for the family to search for Tony themselves, and they really had no idea what sort of terrain Tony had been travelling in. But Tim had made the trip safely on a bike –

why hadn't Tony made it in vehicles? The Flinders Highway is a vast and often lonely road, stretching 754 kilometres through western Queensland. It's flat as far as the eye can see, with the distinctive red dirt that you know means the Aussie outback. It does pass through some townships along the way, but they are few and far between. The area was once gold and copper mining country, and the area is still popular with gem fossickers, with beautiful garnets being found near the Fullarton River. Today, it's mainly used for cattle grazing. The highway doesn't go all the way to Mount Isa, it terminates at Cloncurry and becomes the Barkly Highway, heading to Mount Isa and beyond. The Barkly, too, is a highway I have become familiar with due to several unusual cases of people going missing along its stretch where it joins the Stuart Highway, near Tennant Creek.

When Brian walked into his parents' home on 12 November they told him that there had been a sighting of Tony, by a police officer, near Julia Creek, 250 kilometres east of Mount Isa. The family had no idea where that was. They waited for more information about the Julia Creek sighting. In the meantime, Beres contacted Tony's bank to see if there had been any new transactions that could indicate where he was. The bank gave them the details of his last transactions and the information came as a devastating blow when they realised that Tony had not touched the $150 his mother had deposited, and had not lodged the form to receive his dole cheque since the middle of October.

After she read the details of Tony's bank transactions Beres dissolved into tears. On 1 November he withdrew $15 in Cairns.

On 2 November he withdrew $7 in Tully. On 3 November he withdrew $7 in Ingham, the same day that he phoned his mother and Natalie. This was his final transaction, and his balance was just $3.99. 'Before the phone call from the bank we were all concerned, says Mark. 'But we were all just thinking there would probably be some logical explanation. Concerned at the same time, but once the call from the bank came through we all pretty knew much straightaway that we weren't going to find him alive. It was a telling bit of evidence.'

It's not an immediate conclusion to make when someone goes missing – that they have been murdered. As Mark says, it was an evolution of thinking that finally led the family to the horrific theory about what they believed had happened to Tony. Kevin Jones had recently returned from a work trip to Melbourne and had become quite ill, so in these early days of the investigation it was left to Beres and their family to try to make sense of what was going on. Mark says:

In those first few days, when we knew something was wrong, there were round table meetings every day. But there wasn't really much to do, as only a few things came up. There was not really a lot of emotion in it, at that point. I didn't get emotional about anything much in those days, and I think all the men in the family were trying to work with the logic of it. There was a lot of worry, but I don't think I was really that concerned. I guess just confused, and because none of us had been there we didn't really know what it was like, if there were back roads, or if he'd been bitten by a snake, would someone have seen his body … it's hard to really remember all the different things we thought of.

We were trying to find out a bit more about the place, look at maps, talk to people. Get a feel for it. Did he go off and get some work somewhere? Or whatever ... just about everything we came up with seemed unlikely because we kept coming back to 'Well, why hasn't he bloody called?' So, we had to think of something that gave an answer to that – that he didn't have money, or he couldn't get to a phone.

Until we got the call about his bank details, we were mainly concentrating on things that would mean he was still alive. We didn't see any point in speculating that he was dead, because we didn't see anything productive about that, and not wanting to think that anyway. We were all pretty pragmatic about things at that stage, and I guess pretty disconnected (from the emotional side), but we really just concentrated on the logic and what was the best way to proceed with it, and what were the likely outcomes.

Brian's book acknowledges that his whole family contributed to the writing of *Searching for Tony.*

The family felt helpless. They were pinning their hopes on the Julia Creek sighting, but with no further news being given to them about that they didn't know what to do next. Brian phoned the Catholic parish priest in Mount Isa, who was very helpful and said he was planning to drive to Julia Creek the next day, and would look along the road for Tony. But there was no contact from police. The family realised they needed to be in Townsville in person to find out what police were doing to find Tony. A police officer friend in Perth told them: 'Get over there as soon as you can! If you want the police to take any notice you have to be there.' Sister Deborah was furious at the lack of police communication. Brian writes that she said: 'They don't understand! They haven't done anything! Why doesn't anyone believe us?'

Mark decided he was catching the next plane to Townsville. The trip would cost over a thousand dollars, but there was no question that the family needed to go. Dad Kevin was unwell, so Beres decided to join Mark on the trip, and Brian also decided he needed to go along. As the family prepared to leave for the airport, Kevin said to Brian, quietly, 'I really think it's too late, Brian; I just hope he didn't have to suffer.' Brian wrote: 'He was echoing my deepest fear, yet, I preferred to imagine that Tony was somehow waiting for us to rescue him.'

When the family arrived in Townsville they were approached by a young man who went out of his way to help them, offering his personal vehicle for them to use to get around Townsville. He had been asked to help by Father Branagan, a priest Brian had contacted. The family were forever grateful to him, and others who offered to help them so far from home, in the direst of circumstances. Mark, Brian and Beres made their way to Police Headquarters and met with Inspector Grant. Brian writes that the inspector said to them: 'Mrs Jones, I must tell you, we get hundreds of reports like this each year. They are mostly runaway teenagers and they nearly always turn up after a few days. If it is only eleven or twelve days since you last heard from Tony then, to be honest, that doesn't really give us much cause for alarm. If he were a girl it would be a different story, but boys will be boys...'

The inspector spent about half an hour with the family and made several phone calls to check locations such as the hospital and morgue. The family asked him about the Julia Creek sighting that Mount Isa Police had advised them about, but Inspector Grant had no idea what they were talking about. He phoned Mount Isa police but could not speak with the officer in charge. He promised to send out the missing person alert for Tony to all police stations between Townsville and Mount Isa. He told the family that the media would only run a missing person story if the case was 'very urgent', which again angered and frustrated the family. Beres replied: 'But, Inspector, why do you think we came all this way? Don't you believe this is an urgent case?' Her plea prompted police to act and the local TV station put out the missing person alert that evening. Inspector Grant told the family that when missing person appeals went to air, the missing person always turned up within 12 hours. Although still believing strongly that Tony was already dead, the family clung to that number. They felt their expensive trip of more than 5000 kilometres was finally seeing some results. Brian wrote: 'Our being there had certainly got things moving.' TV and radio started broadcasting appeals for Tony.

The family stayed in the Sun City caravan park in Rosslea, Townsville. At the time they booked in they were not aware that this was the exact park Tim and Tony had stayed in a few weeks before. In the meantime, Tim arrived back in Townsville from Mount Isa, where he'd still been waiting for his brother or any news. Mark picked him up from the railway station. It was an emotional reunion with his family, who he had not seen for more than a year, and Brian writes that Tim looked very weather-beaten after his long travels in the outback, on the bike.

Brian writes that Tim relayed a story about the time he spent in Townsville with Tony:

One night we went for a drink down at the pub with a couple of mates, and while we were sitting around the table we got into an argument. At least I did; Tony was innocently standing at the bar at that stage. A big, burly bouncer came along and ordered us to leave. As we were going he turned towards Tony and told him to rack off. So, Tony slowly finished his beer, threw his stubby in the air, and said: 'Hey, mate, catch this!' Then he ran for his life, with the bouncer in hot pursuit.

Tony escaped, but the bouncer must have followed the rest of us to the car. When Tony reappeared a short time later, still laughing, the bouncer caught him by surprise; he punched Tony in the face and nearly knocked him out. And then, just when we got in the car ready to take off, Tony wound his window down and yelled out: 'Do you want me to tell you who my old man is now, or when we get to court?' We went to the Central Police Station and reported it, but they said there was nothing they could do. We then took Tony to the hospital to get a few stitches.

The incident happened at the International Hotel, not long before Tim set off on his ride to Mount Isa. The family wondered if it was possible that the bouncer spotted Tony on his own a few days later? What would the bouncer have done if he'd found him?

Father Branagan continued to help the family generously, even cooking for them. The Jones found so many people in Townsville willing to help them, and the local paper, the *Townsville Bulletin*, was more than happy to run the story. Today, the same paper is still publishing stories about Anthony Jones. However, when trying to trace Tony's calls, they found Telecom to be uncooperative, according to Brian. As Tony had phoned home reverse charges, the family wanted to know where he made that call from. Telecom said it would take at least three weeks; that's if they could find out at all. Brian writes that Beres said to this: 'I can't wait three weeks. That could make all the difference between finding him dead or alive.'

The family again went to see Inspector Grant at Townsville police station and asked him to try to get the information from Telecom. Beres told him that Tim had arrived in Townsville and Brian writes the inspector replied: 'I've heard some unhappy reports about him. Apparently, he said some unpleasant things to the boys down there, and he is lucky he wasn't thrown in the lock-up.' It seems astounding that police could threaten the family of a missing person. They seemed to view the family as an annoyance, and that they were overreacting. I wish the passage of time had corrected that view, but even today the family are still being accused of causing trouble. Beres was firm in her response to Inspector Grant, says Brian: 'Well, no doubt he had a reason to be upset. The Mount Isa police have done little to help. And by the way, Inspector, have you heard any more about the Julia Creek sighting?'

Once again police were giving them vague, unsupported sighting information, then not bothering to update them for days about the results of their enquiries. Brian reminded the inspector he'd told them missing person cases that appeared on TV always turned up within 12 hours, but that was not the case with his brother. While they were at the station, Telecom called the inspector to tell him they'd traced Tony's last phone call, made at 8.50 pm, to a phone box in Bowen Road, Rosslea, not far from the Sun City caravan park, the same park where the family was now staying, and the same telephone box the family themselves had used during their stay in Townsville.

Inspector Grant told the Jones he was handing over the case to Sergeant Des Burke, who was at Mundingburra, a suburb of Townsville. The family found they got on well with him, and he was helpful. Brian wrote that he had a 'genuine and caring manner' and went out of his way to help, even on his day off, and gave them his home phone number. While they were in Mundingburra a report came in about another apparent sighting of Tony. This was passed on to the family by police, but also turned out to be a false lead, like the Julia Creek sighting. The next day the family found a campsite under a bridge near the caravan park in Townsville, but Beres knew it wasn't Tony's when she found a tin of baked beans amongst the debris – a food Tony hated.

Around this time the family started to wonder about Tony's hat. It was his favourite: a reddish-brown leather cowboy hat. Tony had recently sent his luggage home to Perth, so Beres called Kevin to ask if the hat was amongst his belongings. Kevin confirmed the cowboy hat was not in the luggage, meaning Tony must have still had it with him. Tim recalls that it was probably in the backpack and not being worn each day.

Also significant is that Tony sent home his rifle case, but it was empty. Did he still have the dismantled rifle with him in the backpack?

Not willing to give up just yet, the family decided to search the road from Townsville to Charters Towers, but found no trace of Tony. They made themselves known to the local police when they arrived there, but despite Inspector Grant assuring them he had sent every police station between Townsville and Mount Isa the missing person alert, Charters Towers police had never heard of Anthony Jones. It must have been incredibly frustrating for the family. They were glad they'd made the trip out there in person, so they could talk to police face to face instead of relying on them to read a bulletin. Finding nothing, they returned to Townsville and decided to check out an all-night service station in Bowen Road. They felt Tony may have gone in there at some stage. They spoke to every truck driver who entered, but no-one recalled Tony.

Interestingly, a little way up the road Mark noticed a young male hitchhiker trying to catch a lift. He approached several cars and trucks, but all declined his request. The family later spoke to him, but he had not heard of Tony. As they left him, Beres asked him to call his mother. I'm sure it gave her comfort to think she at least could watch out over someone else's son, if she could not see her own that night. Watching the hitchhiker made the family realise it might not have been easy for Tony to find a lift, and maybe he accepted a ride with someone he would normally have been wary about. We know he was anxious to reach Tim in Mount Isa and he may have had to accept whatever lift was offered.

On the other side of the coin, the family watched a couple of young female hitchhikers get a lift on their first try.

In 2016 I received a chilling message through my Australian Missing Persons Register Facebook page. It was from a woman who had a frightening story to tell:

Back in 1983 we were hitchhiking from Townsville to Darwin, there was a guy in a dark blue XW or XY ute at every place we stopped, we ended up at 3 Ways roadhouse, couldn't get a lift, ended up getting a lift with him, plied us with pot and vodka, in the middle of nowhere he stopped at the side of the road, car idling, my mate in the middle, I looked in the mirror and saw the butt of a gun, split second decision, told my mate if he shoots me just drive, I jumped out and screamed 'what the fuck are you doing?' He let off 2 shots into the bush, put the gun back in the ute and got back in the car, not a word was said, I nearly shit myself, my theory was if he killed me, my mate would get away and he'd be caught! He said his name was Paul, about 25, 6ft tall, sandy hair, large nose! Don't know whatever happened to him!

My first question to the woman was, did you tell police? She said as soon as they got to Darwin she reported the incident to police, but they were 'not interested'. At my urging, she said she was going to call them again that day.

The Threeways Roadhouse is at the intersection of the Barkly and Stuart highways, near Tennant Creek. North Queensland was certainly a dangerous place for hitchhikers, and missing girl Anita Cunningham is still on the Missing Persons Register. Anita and her friend Robin Hoinville-Bartram were hitchhiking in 1972, heading for Bowen, Queensland, when they disappeared. Robin's body was found at Sensible Creek under a bridge on the Flinders Highway, approximately 80 kilometres west of Charters Towers. She had been sexually assaulted and shot in the head with a .22 calibre rifle. No trace of Anita Cunningham has ever been found. Robin and Anita were two of seven female hitchhikers who were killed in Queensland between 1972 and 1976. Police have not ruled out that the women may have been the victims of a serial killer. Information indicated the pair, who began their journey from NSW's Hume Highway, had gone to Darwin before travelling to Mount Isa. The other women were Gabriele Jahnke and Michelle Riley in 1973, Lorraine Wilson and Wendy Evans in 1974, and Margaret Rosewarne in 1976.

When you have unexplained missing persons in a particular area that are possible homicides it's easy to think they may be linked. There is, of course, always the possibility that a serial killer has stalked victims and is responsible for several disappearances, but the reality usually turns out to be that the cases are all attributed to separate offenders, or the missing persons have died by other means such as suicide or exposure to the elements. Google 'Flinders Highway Murders' and you get all sorts of gruesome headlines like 'Highway of Death!' and 'Thrill killer has struck twelve times!', and plenty of comparisons with the horror movie *Wolf Creek*. Mark Jones regards these claims with scepticism, and so do I.

There is one case in the area, though, that does bear similarities to Tony's case: an older couple also from Western Australia named Ovens, in 1977, were shot after picking up hitchhikers on the Flinders Highway near Richmond. Richmond is a little over an hour's drive from Hughenden. In Tony's brother Brian's book, *Searching for Tony*, he mentions that the Ovens' killers were two young hitchhikers who shot the couple 'for the thrill of it'.

A triple murder also has caught Mark's attention. In November 2015, Mark spoke to the media about his belief that the Spear Creek killer might also be Tony's killer. In October 1978 the bodies of three young people – Karen Edwards, Gordon Twaddle and Timothy Thomson – were found at Spear Creek, 12 kilometres west of Mount Isa. All three victims died from a gunshot wound to the head fired from a .22 calibre rifle. The killer has never been found. Mark said to journalist Andrew Koubaridis, about the killer:

> *I believe that he can still be found [and] it's my mission to do exactly that – or to at least put a name to him. I think it was a man travelling extensively through northern parts of the country and killing opportunistically. He wasn't just your run-of-the-mill bloke, he's very distinctive. I just wonder how many people saw him.*

In 2019, a man – in fact, a retired senior prison officer – was finally charged with the Spear Creek murders. However, in July 2023 all charges against this man were dropped. The court was told one of the reasons was because a number of key witnesses had either died or were not in good health to give evidence before a trial. Justice Peter Callaghan said there had been 'terrible' communication between the police and the Director of Public Prosecutions office about the issues surrounding the witness list.

Sounds familiar, doesn't it? It's very worrying to think that by the time charges are finally laid in Tony's case, they may have a similar outcome.

Beres was still upset after their queries at the service station produced nothing, and she decided she wanted to go to Townsville hospital, despite it being 11 pm. There they found the doctor who had stitched up Tony's head after the pub fight on 27 October. The doctor reported that Tony was in 'perfectly good health', according to his medical notes. Her desperation is painful to imagine. The family were so anxious for the tiniest piece of information.

The next day the family decided to follow up on the phone box information. Police had refused to doorknock the area, so the four Jones' decided they had to do it. Brian wrote: 'Mother and Mark canvassed one side of Bowen Road while Tim and I did the other.' Mark still can't believe the family had to doorknock the street themselves. He says:

We traced the phone box where he called from and we asked the cops to doorknock that area, in Bowen Road, Rosslea. They refused, but they said we could do it. That's when we came across this man who said, 'Yeah, I saw a guy sitting on his backpack out by the junction of two highways.'

I actually think some of our old-fashioned police work is more effective in missing persons cases; modern police are so used to bringing in the forensic teams and working from there, but with missing persons cases, you usually don't have anything for the forensic team to get involved in. You've got no crime scene, no body. In the old days they were used to getting out and asking questions, looking around, and they didn't even do that, they didn't even doorknock the area around the phone box. They didn't even have to find the phone box – we did all that for them.

Brian and Tim knocked on the door of the man who was to tell them he saw Tony at the phone box that night. Brian writes that Keith Kemp said: 'He was sitting on his backpack by the side of the road about two weeks ago waiting for a lift in the direction of Mount Isa. I was dropping my friend home after a game of cards. It must have been a Wednesday night about two weeks ago; third of November, I think. And it was about nine or ten o'clock at night.'

Brian asked the man to show him where he had seen the man and Keith took Brian and Tim down Bowen Road. The man said: 'It's about a mile down the road. It's opposite the Walkabout Service Station.' I am unsure if the Puma Rosslea was once the Walkabout, but if so, it is at 79 Bowen Road. Across the road, now, is the Banjo Paterson Motor Inn. I haven't been able to find out if it was there in 1982, but with just $3.99 in his account, Tony would not have been able to stay there. Certainly, opposite the Puma would be the spot to try to get a lift to Mount Isa. The Sun City caravan park is no longer there, neither is the phone box. The family spoke to everyone they could find in the area, but no-one remembered seeing Tony.

Mark is angry that the police didn't actually interview their witness, for years. 'It took them that long to interview the only person that we came across who saw Tony hitchhiking on that night. The last person to see him alive. It took them 29 years to interview that person. And by then the guy couldn't remember anything about it, he was just too old.' As all contact with Tony Jones abruptly ceased immediately after those two calls from the phone box, it was arguably the only eyewitness evidence they had. And police did not even interview the witness who saw him there. At least the family now had someone who had actually seen him. Brian believes after he called the family and Natalie, Tony walked about 2 kilometres down Bowen Road to the crossroads and tried to catch a lift in the direction of Mount Isa. And that's where the trail ended.

After this, police said there was nothing more they could do except wait. Tony had been missing for two weeks. The family could not know they'd gather in Townsville again when he'd been missing for 35 years. Defeated and exhausted, they flew back to Perth on Friday 19 November. Kevin, still unwell, was having a hard time on his own back in Perth without his wife and family, and was becoming irritated with people telling him not to worry. Beres wrote in her diary about how she was feeling at this time, and as she is no longer here for me to speak to, her words are precious:

It seemed a long flight home; the tiredness, disappointment and emotional strain were hanging heavy; I was very unsure of how I would react on seeing Kev, Deb, and the rest of the family. Home! It was great to have Kev meet us and to feel the comfort of his arms around me. He looked much better than I expected to find him and his spirit helped lift my tiredness and anxiety. Deb came in after work; the strain of the past two weeks showed, but as always she was a tower of strength and had seen that the house was in order and the plants still growing. Between phone calls and people coming

*and going, we talked for hours about things we did and the
people we met.*

Now that they were back in Western Australia, their contact
with police came to a halt. They called the Perth CIB to ask
them to liaise with Queensland Police, and soon after that
Sergeant Burke contacted them to say he had been requested
by Tony Murphy, the Queensland Assistant Commissioner
of Police, to file a report about the disappearance. Murphy,
who died in 2010, was later accused of corruption, and of
ensuring that anyone he 'protected' avoided being charged.
Described as a brilliant detective, we can only wonder what he
did with the Tony Jones report that he'd ordered. He certainly
does not seem to have investigated it. He retired in 1983. He
did phone the family to express his 'grave concern for Tony's
safety'. He was right to be concerned. 'There were no dealings
with police, other than our trip up to Mount Isa,' says Mark.
'There was one phone call from them, which my mother took,
just before Christmas. The officer in charge of the case later
became Superintendent. He said: "Look, Mrs Jones, don't be
like the woman who waited every day for her son to return and
expected him to come home, you just have to get on with life
and deal with it." Then at the end of the call he said, "Oh, he'll
probably turn up at Christmas like he said he was going to."
Mum was just completely distraught.'

That phone call came less than eight weeks after Tony went
missing. Realising the police had pretty much given up on them,
the Jones family turned to the media and asked them to help.
Brian writes: 'The reaction of the media was overwhelming.
I soon found myself rushing back into the city for interviews

with the local television channels and sending photos to the press in Brisbane. What amazed me with the journalists was the thoroughness of their interrogation; they were far more inquisitive than the police.'

Seven Network's *Today Tonight* agreed to interview Brian, and they arranged to fly to Brisbane for that. The media campaign was working, they realised, when a complete stranger approached Brian at an airport asking if they'd had any news of Tony. The family continued to appeal to the media for publicity. They approached *The Australian* newspaper, but according to Brian: 'The editor refused to publish a missing person story unless we came up with an interesting angle.' They eventually ran the story from the point of view that numbers of Catholic priests, mustered by Brian, were out looking for Tony. One positive sighting of Tony was produced via the public campaign – a driver came forward to say he'd given Tony a lift on 3 November from Cardwell and dropped him at Ingham. As this was before the phone calls home that night, the information didn't provide any new leads.

Someone who didn't see the publicity was a friend of Tony's, who called Beres to find out why Tony had not met up with him as planned to go roo shooting in Alice Springs. Beres was terribly upset by the call. Also upsetting was hearing on the radio, a few days before Christmas, a newsflash: 'Missing West Australia hitchhiker Tony Jones has been sighted in several towns along the Flinders Highway en route to Mount Isa.' Police had not informed the family of any new developments. Beres immediately rang Townsville and was told police were travelling to Mount Isa to check the sightings. Of course, the sightings turned out not to be Tony. Brian writes that the detective who spoke to the family 'was undermining our confidence in the police'.

The family continued to learn about developments only from newspapers, such as the story published on 21 December that read 'North Queensland detectives are convinced that missing Perth hitchhiker Tony Jones has been murdered.' On 23 December they published: 'Jones has certainly been out to Mount Isa. Jones spoke to two people in Hughenden, told them his name was Tony, and he was from Western Australia. It seemed definite he was out that way.' Brian writes: 'This was so infuriating; once again we found ourselves in the invidious situation of having to prove that Tony was dead.'

One possible reason for all the false sightings was that there was another hitchhiker in the area at the time who resembled Tony. On 13 November this young man visited the Hughenden convent. He had black hair and was 'Italian looking', so he may have resembled Tony in the darkened photographs from the newspaper, but did not look like Tony in real life. Brian writes: 'As time went by I began to realise that false sightings were a necessary nuisance in the search for a missing person.' He said that it was very difficult for the family having to learn about the sightings over the radio and in the newspapers. Brian continued to appeal to the media for publicity, but in January 1983 the producers of *60 Minutes* declined his request to film a story. It was to be another 33 years before his brother Mark would finally do a story with the same program.

The family did not receive any further contact from police until January of 1983 when police received an anonymous letter.

Signed, strangely, 'Lochiel', the letter said Tony's body was buried at the Fullarton River. Written in an untidy hand, the letter reads: 'I believe body of AJ.Jones x buried in or near Fullarton River bed within 100 yds west (then crossed out) southside Flinders. Hwy LOCHIEL'.

What does the strange note mean? Do the words 'I believe' signify the letter is from a so-called psychic who had a 'vision'? I have dealt with many such people over the years claiming to know where missing people are buried, and yet not a single one has been found by them. Their messages to me often start with 'I believe the body is buried...' Or is the note more sinister, and is a confession? The Fullarton River flows underneath a bridge on the Flinders Highway at Julia Creek, 190 kilometres east of Mount Isa. Eerily, as previously mentioned, murder victim Robin Hoinville-Bartram's body was found at Julia Creek. The name Lochiel is unusual – is it a place? There's a heritage-listed house in Brisbane called Lochiel. It's also the name of a Scottish clan chief. There are two towns in Australia called Lochiel, one in South Australia and one on the south coast of New South Wales, and there's a homestead in outback Queensland called Lochiel. It's in the middle of nowhere, north of Windorah and south-west of Longreach. It's almost 1400 kilometres from Cairns, so seems strange that the letter would be postmarked there.

In 1986 a friend of the Jones family found a rundown house on the Flinders Highway, not far from where Tony was last seen. Above the front door was a plaque reading 'Lochiel'. Police did investigate but reported there was no connection to the letter or the case. Brian writes: 'We felt sure the letter was genuine.' The family found it very startling that the letter referred to Tony as 'AJ Jones'. As Brian pointed out, most of the newspaper reports called him Tony Jones, and it was very rare for anyone to have included his middle name of John. This added credibility to the note, from the family's point of view. Was the note's author in possession of identification belonging to Tony? Police did search the area around Fullarton River for two days, with a team of 15 men, tracker dogs and metal detectors, but found nothing. Brian writes: 'We began to regret not being there at the search.'

Kevin decided to make a public appeal for the writer of the note to come forward, and it is poignant. He said:

An Appeal to Lochiel – Recently you gave information to the Townsville Police as to the location of the body of my son, Tony Jones. Unfortunately, a search of the area failed to unearth any trace of his body or belongings. Because we are extremely anxious to recover his body we are appealing to you to provide further information about Tony or his possessions or else confirm what you have already told the police. This would give some peace of mind and show you were genuinely trying to assist investigations. Your further assistance in this matter could relieve much long-term suffering. However, should my grief-stricken wife and family be afforded further anguish by way of a hoax we could only consider you to be callous in the extreme. I previously offered a reward of $2000 and am now prepared to increase that amount to $5000 for any information leading to the recovery of my son's body.

There were a few responses to the appeal, mainly from unhelpful psychics, but also an odd letter that read:

Dear Mr KF Jones, I do not want to get your hopes up and I do not want your money although I could certainly use it. I do not want it. This has been playing on my mind for a long time before I read in the paper about your son missing. If my son was missing I would pray to God someone would be able to help me find him. Would you write another letter to the Sunday Mail as soon as possible to say would or could your son possibly have been in Brisbane on November 16 last year maybe in a disturbed state of mind. Wearing jeans, thongs, and wearing a cowboy hat (not carrying it as stated in the Courier Mail the following Saturday) also carrying a knapsack. Would it be possible. This person could have been anyone. I will read your letter in the Sunday Mail and see what you have to say. I hope it is true for your sake. If so I will tell you what I saw.

Very frustratingly, the newspaper did not publish the reply from the family, urging the letter writer to come forward, for a month. The family never heard from the person again.

The Jones asked for a copy of the Lochiel letter to be sent to them in Perth, and waited a week. When it did not arrive, they called again, and police apologised and said they'd forgotten to send it. The family waited a further ten days, and when still nothing arrived, Brian phoned again. Police apologised and said they were unable to send the letter, as the original had been sent to Brisbane for forensic testing. Brian had to phone a further two times before they received the copy – five weeks after it had been received by police.

Years later, when DNA technology became available, the Jones family asked for the letter to be tested, but police claimed the letter had not been preserved properly and was unable to be tested. However, during the first inquest, police admitted that the letter had been lost. Mark still believes the letter might be of significance. 'There is information within this that has caused the family to take it seriously,' he says. 'We asked Townsville police if they could run tests on the back of the stamp to extract DNA using techniques currently available, but they told us such tests were not possible. The truth of the matter was they had lost the envelope. During the course of this current investigation we learned that the police had also lost the letter as well. If we are critical of Townsville CIB, there are good reasons for it!'

I asked Mark if the handwriting on the Lochiel note had been analysed. 'The police gathered a few samples which were shown to an expert, who simply said the sample was adequate, mostly because it was printed I think, though also a small sample. The problem is the expert said that the writing in the original Lochiel note had "attention to the writing process". We think it was written using the wrong hand.'

The family finally found some information about how Tony spent his time in Cairns, before he returned to Townsville. A young man named Dean Meldrum came forward to police after learning about Tony's disappearance. He told police he had spent a weekend with Tony, camping near the Kamerunga Bridge on the Barron River, north of Cairns city. Police did go to check out the campsite and found Dean's car. Beres wanted to speak to Dean personally, and despite police telling her not to, she went ahead and phoned his parents, who were conveniently in Perth. They put her in touch with Dean, and Beres asked him lots of questions to verify that it was actually Tony that Dean had met. Dean was able to confirm that Tony had been clean shaven at the time, an important detail to confirm accurate sightings, and that he'd been trapped in a fridge as a child, a story unique to Tony. Dean said Tony had an indigenous sister; also correct. Brian wrote that Dean told Beres that Tony had walked into his campsite about 5.30 pm and asked if he could camp with the group that night. Dean and his friends were happy to have him.

Brian writes: 'Tony spent the whole weekend sharing their food and drink, sleeping under their tarpaulin, fishing, yarning and lounging about.' His new friends drove Tony to Cairns on the Monday, where he went to the bank. They then dropped him by the side of the highway where he hitched a ride to Townsville. Three years after the phone call with Beres, Brian went to visit Dean to ask him some further questions about Tony. Dean said he was certain Tony did not have his rifle with him at the campsite. He said it would not have fit into Tony's backpack even if it had been dismantled. This is curious, because Tony sent home the empty rifle case in his luggage before this time. Dean's girlfriend remembers Tony wanting to stay at the campsite while the others went for a bushwalk into the mountains. She said Tony was really missing his girlfriend and was very homesick. Brian writes that the years following Tony's disappearance were especially hard for Tony's girlfriend, Natalie, who continued to visit the family for quite some time but eventually had to move on with her own life. Brian says:

'She will always be remembered as the dearest friend Tony ever had.'

After the Fullarton River search, police do not appear to have continued to actively investigate Tony Jones' disappearance. 'You could count on one hand how many calls we had from them over about the next decade,' says Mark in disgust. 'We jumped on anything and everything that came forward, but there just wasn't anything. The search at Fullarton River didn't bring up anything. There was a guy who came forward who reckoned he was working with Tony for a couple of weeks, but we knew he was elsewhere at that time. We (the family) followed that up; we rang the bloke and interviewed him.'

The entire family was involved with their own investigation, with even Beres interviewing witnesses. They would hold regular, big family meetings to discuss the next steps that needed to be taken. Older brother Brian was training for the priesthood at the nearby monastery and was just as involved as the rest of the family. It was a core group of Brian, Mark, Debbie and their mother who mainly took on the task of chasing down possible leads, but Mark recalls it was also any of the siblings who happened to be home at the time. It came down to the family to make public appeals for information, trying to find anyone who had seen Tony on the road between Townsville and Mount Isa. The thing that puzzled them the most was why anyone would want to hurt their brother, who was a very likeable, easy-going young bloke who got along well with everyone he met. Mark says:

The whole thing was surprising in as much as he knew how to handle people; he was just the sort of bloke you could meet and get to know very quickly, and it just seemed really odd to us that someone could knock him off. I mean, he had a bit of a thing about people who took themselves too seriously; he loathed bouncers and the way they'd throw their weight around. But as far as meeting fellow travellers and the sort of people you'd think might be generous in spirit and give him a lift ... some of the people we tracked down who had given him a lift had that immediate connection with him. There's one bloke who picked him up who asked Tony to put his backpack on the back seat, face down. Tony asked why, and the guy told him he didn't want somebody to be able to pull a gun out on him. Tony then told the guy he had a rifle in his backpack, broken down, and carried a starter pistol with him.

It's an unusual comment for the driver to make, and it makes you wonder whether he had had a bad experience previously that made him wary of hitchhikers. This driver came forward with his information not long after Tony went missing and the public appeals for information were made. He said he'd picked up Tony from Cairns and dropped him off in Townsville, but Mark says that couldn't be correct, as they knew Tony had taken three days to do that journey. The family had traced Tony's movements and tracked down the people who had given Tony his first two lifts.

Mark was recently re-reading the transcript from the first inquest into Tony's disappearance, and read that the man met Tony in Townsville and said they had a drink together. He said he was leaving early the next day for Mount Isa and that he could give Tony a lift the whole way. However, he claims Tony declined this offer, information that baffled police and his family, as they would have thought Tony would jump at the chance to get one lift the whole 900 kilometres to his meeting point with Tim. But at this stage Tony hadn't yet called home to Perth, and he didn't think Tim would be in Mount Isa for a few more days – he didn't know Tim was already there. Tony had also just about run out of money and his dole cheque was due a couple of days later, on the Friday.

The driver told police Tony had said to him he wanted to stay the night in Townsville, as he wanted to phone either his mother or his girlfriend to ask for some money the following morning. This story is confirmed, as Tony did phone his mother and also his girlfriend, Natalie, that night. Beres told Tony she had deposited some money into his bank account that day. 'It sounds like he did have plans to ring Mum and Natalie and ask for money,' says Mark. 'He would have probably only had four dollars on him at that stage, and no more money due for a couple of days, so I think had Mum not told him that the money was already there, he would have asked Natalie to send him some money. So, that's critical, because this driver wouldn't have known that – so this was pretty clear evidence to me that the guy he was talking to was Tony. He also said that Tony had this broken down rifle in his backpack, so everything fitted that it was Tony, except for the fact that this guy was sure he'd picked him up in Cairns. Now I think he's just got that bit mixed up. I think he picked up another hitchhiker, because he did talk about a number of other hitchhikers around that time.'

However, if Tony did have his rifle in the backpack, the information given by Dean the camper, that Tony didn't have it, would have been incorrect. Perhaps Tony was just very careful not to alarm his new friends at the campsite by pulling out a rifle, when he was quite anxious to have somewhere safe to stay for that weekend.

In May 1983, the Queensland government issued a reward of $20,000

> *for information from the public leading to the apprehension and conviction of the person or persons responsible for the suspected murder of Anthony John Jones who disappeared after last being heard from in Townsville on 3rd November, 1982. In addition, the Government will recommend to His Excellency the Governor that a free pardon will be extended to any accomplice, not being the person who actually committed the crime, who first gives such information.*

Tony would have turned 21 on 3 July 1983. The Jones' along with Natalie and Tony's other friends, gathered for a party, without the guest of honour. Brian wrote that it felt like a wake, not a birthday. November brought the first anniversary of his disappearance and Brian marked the occasion by organising two Requiem Masses, one in Perth and one in Townsville, not only for Tony but also to pray for all missing persons. Beres hung a large portrait of Tony in her lounge room and loved when people noticed it and started to talk about him. Tony's family travelled to Townsville on the first anniversary of his disappearance. They had no illusions they were going to look for their son. Mark says they had always known Tony was no longer alive: 'We feel very lucky that we knew what we knew. If we hadn't had the bank details, and even knowing where he made his last phone call from ... those things remove so many of the doubts. When we flew to Townsville, we all knew that he was dead, and we've always known that. It was seven years later that we found there were other leads to follow. In the meantime, we'd all gotten on with our lives and just accepted that there were no leads and nothing that anyone could do.'

It was not until 1986 that Beres felt able to sort through Tony's belongings. The pain of his loss was constant. Brian writes: 'Without a body, without a funeral, without some palpable sign of Tony's death there would also be an element of doubt. This is where the families of missing persons are so vulnerable. Every time there is an alleged sighting grief is suspected and other emotions are churned; the victim, it seems, is unable to rest in peace.'

As mentioned, National Missing Persons Week was started because of Tony Jones, in 1988, and it continues each year around the end of July/beginning of August. Even some police today are not aware that it was Tony's brother Brian who was instrumental in setting this up. Mark tells the story:

Brian was writing his book at around that time, and I guess out of that we got to thinking about what can be done to stop other people having to go through all this again. In the final chapter of his book he talks about his messages to the police and to the public, and talked about a few things he was pushing for like a national computer (system), which still hasn't happened. He had this idea of initially Missing Persons Day, to bring some awareness, as he realised after the initial story breaks then it can go quiet and it can be a bit of a struggle to get publicity after that. He thought that once a year this can open the door for people to get awareness for their cases. He spoke to a few people, including Ita Buttrose, asking what he could do to get this thing underway. Ita said, with a wave of her hand, 'Oh, yes, easy. And make it a week!' I don't know if she remembers that she was involved. I did a Tweet one day thanking her, but I'm not sure if she read it.

After that, the missing persons committee Brian was involved with got behind it, and he walked into the police station here and spoke to the big guys, and they said: 'Yes, sounds good, we'll be in that.' They got on board, and between them they put out press releases, and away it went. My cousin Garrett got involved too; he had a journalism background so he was able to help with all that. Now the Feds run the show.

Brian moved overseas not long after this; he was posted to China, and has not been involved with Missing Persons Week since the initial set-up. Cousin Garrett was involved for many more years. When the Federal Police took over they had a larger budget, and the people who were originally involved in starting the event gradually fell away, something Mark sees as a sad thing. 'It was never about being in police control, it was just something for the families. It's good in some ways, but in others I feel it's lost its way a bit. So, they were very surprised to hear from me when I contacted them to say the 25th anniversary was coming up, and they said: "No, it's only been going ten years" … I had to set them straight about who I was and when it all started.'

With police seemingly not doing anything to search for Tony, and with the family having exhausted their own efforts into finding out anything, the family began requesting that an inquest be held, to provide them with some answers. On the tenth anniversary of Tony's disappearance, in 1992, Mark,

Tim and Brian travelled to Townsville to speak to police. They went to Thuringowa police station and asked to see Tony's file. Mark said, in an understatement: 'I was a bit surprised at the state of the file.' The folder was almost empty. It was clear that police had not conducted a thorough investigation into Tony's disappearance, and Mark despaired at the thought of having so little to present to the coroner during an inquest. He says:

We'd been pushing for an inquest since the early years, about six or seven years in. Nobody's ever advised us. At some point we asked the police about it. Brian, Tim and I met up in Townsville on the seventh anniversary, and it was in my mind that after seven years of being missing, a person is officially dead. In 1992, on the tenth anniversary, I was speaking to the superintendent in Townsville and during that conversation he asked me what the coroner's investigation found. We said there hadn't been one, and he said: 'Well, there needs to be one, order it.' I followed it up a few months later, but eventually gave up on them doing it. It wasn't until 1996, when I moved to Sydney, that I wrote to the coroner and requested it again. They said yes, they'd go ahead with it. I don't even remember them taking a statement from me. I told the coroner they needed to get hold of Brian's book Searching for Tony, as we were pretty sure they'd lost all the original copies we'd given them. He agreed with that.

When we finally got the transcript of the inquest about ten years later, when John Mahoney was asked about the book in court, he said: 'Oh yes, it's on order, it will be arriving at the station this afternoon.' He never read it, despite knowing about it early on, and the coroner instructing them to read it and the family sending them copies. That was six years into the inquest, and they claimed it was just being delivered that day. I would hear nothing for months on end, and I would write to the coroner asking what was happening, and they'd write back saying police were still conducting investigations. The next year I'd get the same response. I had no idea what the police were doing. I got a call from them in about the second or third year, but no-one contacted me before that.

In about the middle of 2000 I wrote to the coroner and said I was moving to Perth, but would stay in Sydney if the inquest would be soon, as I didn't want to have to travel back for it, and he replied to say he couldn't see it happening any time soon, and I should go. A new guy started (with Tony's case, in the police) who'd been in the drug squad, and he got handballed the case; this was in 2001 and I'd just moved back to Perth. This was four and a half years into the inquest. He called me and got me to email him a statement, and he organised a DNA sample to be taken from Dad ... which they subsequently lost. Brian had a big dispute with them about that. They got a statement from Tim, and that was about it.

When they did eventually write and say the inquest was going ahead, I applied to them to have my airfares from Perth funded, but that was knocked back. I was in the middle of uni studies by then, so no-one from the family attended the inquest. I was furious, but I wasn't in a position to do anything about it. It was another three or four years before we got a copy of the inquest findings, and learned for the first time there were actual suspects. That reignited us to start again.

Coroner Ian Fisher delivered his findings from the first inquest on 20 February 2002, saying: 'I am satisfied that the missing person is dead. I find that he died on or around the 3rd of November 1982 at the hands of a person or persons unknown.' Due to a glitch in the law, the family were unable to obtain Tony's death certificate, as the coroner had not specified where Tony died. Wikipedia reports: 'The Queensland Attorney-General and Minister for Justice Linda Lavarch subsequently introduced new legislation in 2005, saying "the Jones family has suffered enough ... they should not suffer further by not being able to get a death certificate for their son."' The certificate was eventually issued in January 2006.

In 2007, the family obtained the transcripts of the first inquest and were horrified at what they read. The suspects introduced at this inquest were named Pickering and Douglas. The family had never heard of them. Apparently, neither had police. 'The coroner said: "What about suspects Pickering and Douglas?" and the police officer didn't even know who they were,' says Mark. 'He said: "Is that the guy from Longreach?" then he fumbled around and went on to say what he'd done about the guy from Longreach, and the next day he came back and said, "Oh sorry, that wasn't about the guy from Longreach, I don't know these other two." These were actually names given to the police during the time that the inquest was on.'

The names raised during the inquest were prompted by the publication of two identikit sketches that had appeared in local newspapers. One of the sketches was reported to resemble another man named Merv Stevenson. Stevenson was a former Townsville Police Superintendent around the time Tony disappeared, and had been accused of involvement in various criminal activities. The sketch was obtained from a witness in 1982 but was not published in the newspaper until 1992. The witness claimed to have been in the Rising Sun Hotel in Townsville when he saw a man he believes was Tony Jones drinking with an older man, who he believes may have been Stevenson. The witness recounted that Tony was talking about meeting up with his brother in Mount Isa. Tony is reported to have said the man was going to give him a lift to Mount Isa, and had kindly bought him beer and some food in Townsville. Stevenson died in 2002, apparently without ever having to answer any questions relating to Tony Jones, as police never interviewed him. Stevenson's son Paul does not believe his father had any involvement in Tony's disappearance, despite admitting his father did drink in the Rising Sun. In an odd twist, Paul is acquainted with the two men who feature prominently as suspects in the second inquest, as revealed in a *Courier Mail* interview with him in 2016.

The long delays by police in acting on the information they were given in the early days of the case led to frustrating consequences at the inquest. There were apparently four suspects: Douglas and Pickering, who also resembled other sketches provided by the public, plus a known criminal from Longreach, and the man whose sketch resembled Merv Stevenson. 'So, these names were given to police by the public, who had called to say this one looks like Pickering and this one looks like Douglas,' says Mark. 'I don't know where the coroner got those names, the police didn't know about them. It was just a sketch, and it just seemed so tenuous. The Longreach guy had a previous charge of a sex crime against a male, so it made that person look a bit more interesting, but prior to knowing that I just thought it was people calling in saying a person looks like a hand drawn sketch. What we were more interested in is the coroner asking about someone he called a suspect, and the person leading the investigation and preparing the brief knows nothing about it. And who was this other guy in Longreach he was talking about? We basically just wanted the answers. There was stuff in there that was redacted and we just wanted some of the blanks filled in. Both these guys [Pickering and Douglas] actually died during the course of the inquest, so they weren't even aware they'd been named at that time. That was just one part of so many questions that the transcript threw up.'

Brian Jones told *Townsville Bulletin* reporter Jessica Johnston: 'The documents highlight decades of police bungling, including the failure to follow up leads. And even the coroner's admonition to pursue these leads in 2002 appeared to have been neglected, some of the leads are now ten years old. Other information has been lost, ignored or never recorded. For months now I've been lobbying police to explore a few new lines of inquiry.' As it was abundantly clear that there had been massive failings on the part of police to properly investigate Tony Jones' disappearance, after the first inquest ended, the coroner directed police to go back and do their jobs properly. The police were ordered by the coroner to complete some of the things they hadn't done in preparation for the first inquest, but they still failed to rectify these errors by the time the second inquest began.

Brian continued, quietly, for a number of years to attempt to get some answers for the family by way of a second inquest. On

14 June 2009, the family formally asked the Attorney General for a second inquest. The request was ignored for 15 months. 'Brian was getting stonewalled,' says Mark. 'He was told it was part of operation something or other, so he couldn't be told what was happening. That's what got Brian going, that he kept getting fobbed off. Brian was really getting himself in a lather over the whole process. He sent the Attorney General a pair of his shoes along with a letter saying: 'Try walking a mile in my shoes and see what we've been through', and the media really latched onto that. I think that's why the second inquest happened. By way of making his point, he wrote to the Attorney General listing all the reasons why the inquest needed to be reopened. The AG got ambushed by an ABC journalist who wanted to know why he had ignored Brian's messages, so the Attorney General went on the air and announced a second inquest was underway. It took us all by surprise, especially me, as I didn't know Brian was even doing anything on the case. We started looking at some historical information and Brian and I worked on it together.'

On 18 September 2010, the Attorney General instructed the coroner to open a second inquest. The police assured the family the second inquest would not be like the first. 'They said that the state coroner and others were the best in the business, and this was our chance to push for change,' says Mark. 'He described the first inquest as an ad hoc volunteer system, barely official. He was the first bloke that I've spoken to in the whole time that could comprehend all the facts and ask intelligent questions, and I was pretty impressed with him, he seemed to be in our corner.' Brian was living in South Korea, and moved back to Australia a year into the inquest. Mark was hopeful the new inquest would give them the answers they needed. 'I thought, they'll do it right this time, they won't make us wait six years. I thought it would be over in a matter of months. When I met with the counsel assisting the coroner, he suggested we wait until the following January, when Brian was back. I wasn't happy about that, I said if we wait that long they won't do anything. Little did I know that was going to happen anyway, without a word from the coroner's office.'

When I first interviewed Mark, in 2014, he had been waiting four years for the second inquest to start. 'We keep writing to them, saying just get the bloody thing over and done with – enough already!' Marks says in frustration. 'We were clearly told it was going to be in that first January, so they clearly felt they were going to be ready by then, and now we're four years on from the start of it. If you don't put a time limit on it, and leave it open ended, then that's how you end up with a six year inquest where nothing gets done. If you make it three months, then everybody's got to concentrate on it for more than five minutes at a time.' The family's frustration at police only increased as the years dragged on without even a start date for the second inquest. Mark says:

There were some good people in authority. I'm not sure the police were any more interested in it the second time around, but they were doing what they'd been ordered to do. Having said that, one of the first things that came up was that an elderly grazier had written to the family in January 2011 to say that at around the time Tony went missing, he and a buddy of his, an ex cop, were driving on the outskirts of Cloncurry and saw a disturbance by the side of the road, in the salt bushes. They decided to investigate and found a clearing with some scattered belongings, maybe a campsite. There looked like there'd been signs of a struggle and some drag marks, maybe of a body … whether that was an active imagination I don't know, but amongst the scattered belongings was a letter addressed to Tony Jones, from his mother.

They gathered all the belongings up and took them to the Cloncurry police station, and told them: 'Hey, we think this it might be connected to the missing hitchhiker.' They left all the stuff with them. He's not too sure of the exact date; there was a search of the river in January and everyone in that area would have known about it, and they found the belongings a couple of months after that. For them to have stopped there in the first place, and then see what they saw at the site, like the drag marks, I'm sure they had this case in their minds already. One of the cops that he thought was there when he handed it in retired around that time, so it can't have been too much later. He's clearly an honest sort of guy and had a former detective with him, so that lends a fair bit of credibility to the whole thing. This guy tried many times over the years to find out what happened about that. He finally tried again, he rang Townsville police, but they didn't know what was going on. He actually spoke to the officer handling the case at the moment … she first said to ring Cloncurry and offered to put him through to Lost Property.

Mark pauses to have a wry chuckle. 'And that's when he gave up. He finally contacted us with the information and we passed it on the coroner. The police eventually, six months later, went out and did a search of that area, which had all changed very much, and they didn't find anything. We were waiting for days on end to find out the result of that search. We asked the coroner and they said: 'You'll get a police report sent to you about it.' To this day, we've never received that. We wrote to the coroner time and time again and they said: 'Yes, you'll have that by Christmas', but nup, never happened. Then earlier this year, the coroner retired. We only found out from a journo. But the belongings never turned up, and no-one knows anything about them. They reckoned the police station burned down and it was all lost, but I can't find any evidence about that.'

I put out the call on the AMPR Facebook page for long-time Cloncurry locals to contact me. I asked them all the same question – was there a fire in the Cloncurry police station? They all had the same answer. About ten years ago there was a fire in one of the cells, and someone was injured, but the whole station did not burn down, and it appears the damage was confined to the cell. There are no reports that any stored evidence was destroyed. Why was this evidence not sent to Townsville for further testing? Cloncurry police were specifically told it may be related to the Tony Jones case, so why was this not promptly acted on? Where is that potentially vital evidence today? Mark is weary of yet another mishandled lead.

'In 1982 they probably didn't have much in the way of computer systems, but you'd think when they got computers they'd have logged what was in their evidence room.'

In 2011, the Northern Region Crime Coordinator, Detective Acting Inspector Mick Walker, told the media that police were still investigating what happened to the evidence handed in to Cloncurry police. Inspector Walker said that searchers had covered an area of 400 square metres at the intersection of Quamby Rd and the Barkly Highway over a six-hour period, but found nothing. Perhaps if the area had been searched 29 years previously, when the information was first given to police, something might have been located. There's been at least four floods and three bushfires through the area in that time.

In 2010 the Queensland Government updated the original reward for information leading to the suspected killer or killers of Anthony Jones, and the location of his remains, to $250,000. To date, that reward has not been claimed. In February 2014 the Jones family reunited in Perth for a wedding. That year was to become a turning point in the investigation into Tony's disappearance.

Mark reflected on how the past 35-plus years affected them as a family:

The only rough spot is I had a huge fallout with my elder sister over it, the last time I was in Perth. That's the first time there's been any family eruptions. We got together for a wedding, and my sister asked me what the latest was. I hadn't brought it up; I was determined before the wedding I wasn't going to discuss the case. This was around when the news broke in the press about the leads. We were playing cards, and it came up again, and she was going on and on about how this had consumed our lives, meaning Brian and me. I guess she was more familiar with the time Brian had spent on it. I was sticking up for him a little bit, but she was lumping me in with it too. She just had this thing about me needing to get on with my life and get over it. It wasn't even me who brought it up, I hadn't mentioned it.

Then a couple of nights later she brought it up again. She felt it had been really invasive in Brian's life, and she probably had a point, to some extent. There's certainly been times in my life I've pleaded with Brian that whatever we did, we had to do for a greater cause than our own. But I was trying to tell my sister that this hasn't consumed my life – for the most part, for probably 28 out of those 32 years I wasn't even thinking about it, and for the rest of it I attend to things as they come up. I've spent a bit of time thinking about it, but I've had a musical career and a photography career in that time. It's not as if my life has come to a full stop, which she was categorising it as.

When this media campaign broke in February, on the Friday night I got an email from police telling me they were making a big announcement in the paper the next day. I forwarded that to Brian. I didn't realise Brian told Dad what was happening, and my sister thought that he'd had it in his mind that they were announcing they'd found his body or something, and that he was emotional. I knew nothing about that. It sounds like a bit of panic broke out in the family back home. She was not happy that we were referring in the media to Dad as being upset by it all, and he was doing some television interviews, that he didn't like us talking about it. It was a completely different take on the situation to my take on it. Dad's not really good at talking about what's on his mind, I understand that, but he also is proud of the fact that Brian and I have stuck with the task, and he's happy to help where he can.

In the early days Tim was a little bit upset that we were talking about it all the time, but I think he sees it differently

now. Brian and I had a big fallout when we had the seventh
anniversary get together. Tim and I thought he was running
the show, and I brought that up to him years later in an email
and cleared the air, and now we talk through any differences,
and we have worked closely together on it.

The announcement that police made to the media that day
took many people by surprise, including me. In March 2014,
Queensland Police executed a search warrant at the Hughenden
slaughter yards. Hughenden is a small town of just 1100 people,
523 kilometres from Mount Isa. It's 376 kilometres west of
Townsville, on the Flinders Highway, so it's fair to assume Tony
would have passed through Hughenden on his way to Mount
Isa. Detective Acting Superintendent Cheryl Scanlon said at a
press conference:

That location remains a place of interest in the ongoing
investigations into the suspected homicide. We have known
about the slaughter yards for some time but these things take
time consuming attention to detail in terms of gathering
information from people. For us to have executed a crime scene
warrant and for the first time detectives have been there, that
is of significance to the investigation.

Scanlon said police had sufficient grounds to search the yards
and the Grand Hotel and said both sites had a high degree of
relevance to the case. She said:

We have developed other lines of inquiry out of our further
attendance in Hughenden and the investigation goes on. They
become relevant in the investigation because it takes us along

the timeline of events that have been, up until now, difficult to establish the movements of Tony Jones. Part of the challenge for our team has been trying to establish where he has moved over those days so that is very much about where this investigation is going, to track those movements.

The *Courier Mail* reported that in 2014 Det Act Supt Scanlon said they were investigating 'several persons of interest' in relation to the murder of Tony Jones but would not provide further detail. She said: 'It is the biggest piece of collective information certainly in the last decade for this investigation. I am as confident as we have ever been that we believe Tony Jones has been the victim of a homicide. Our hope is sometime down the track we will have some answers for the family.'

Police also said they were interested in the Grand Hotel in Hughenden. They released this statement: 'Three witnesses interviewed by detectives have stated that they spoke to Mr Jones in the hotel in November 1982.' In the early 1980s the Grand Hotel was a very busy place. It's on the corner of the Flinders Highway, and there's a road sign pointing to Mount Isa – Tony's destination – right outside the front door. It's a very logical place for him to have stopped. It's about 15 kilometres out of town to the abattoir, and it's a lonely and desolate spot. Senior Sergeant John Mahony said: 'The people who know what happened to Tony in November of 1982 are 30 years older, their circumstances have changed and I urge them to come forward, to do the right thing by the Jones family, and by Tony.'

Suddenly, finally, things were happening. On 14 April 2016 the coroner held a pre-inquest hearing – six years after the inquest was ordered. The inquest date was fixed – 29 August to

9 September 2016. It took Mark by surprise, who had to start rearranging his life:

It was a shock when we found the inquest was on, because the dust had long since settled. I've been asking since the first scheduled date came and went, so I could just get on with my life. It's had an impact on my life, as it's affecting my decisions, like starting a new business or whether I move back to Perth. I know at some point I'm going to have to drop everything, focus on the inquest, prepare for it and be in Queensland ... it's a thing that hangs over you when you're trying to schedule other things. What has been different the second time is they have more respect for the state coroner than they had for the local magistrate in Townsville. At the first one, they had scant regard for the whole process from start to finish. The fact that for six years we were being told they were investigating – there are no signs they investigated anything in that time.

It's frustrating to Mark that the police mostly keep the family in dark about what they're finding out, as he believes only the family can confirm or dispel misinformation about Tony. 'This is why we are so galled by the police telling us to butt out and they'll handle things,' he says:

We said: hang on, you didn't want anything to do with it, we've done 90 per cent of the investigations over the last 30 years. Our hopes were very high when we found out about these fresh leads. It was only when they rang me and said: 'We've got three witnesses who spoke to Tony at the Grand Hotel in Hughenden and they're prepared to sign statements' ... I said: 'Are these connected with the original leads?' He said yeah, they fit in. I said, well, you've just crushed all our hopes, because if you're saying they fit in, there's no way Tony was sitting drinking in a pub when he was desperate to get to Tim, and he had no money. There were no phone calls home. It makes no sense.

I asked Cheryl Scanlon what description they gave of Tony, and she said she didn't have that with her. I asked if he had a beard and she said she couldn't give that information, that it would be a matter for the judge or coroner. I said, 'Well how come what you told me yesterday wasn't a matter for a judge or coroner? And more to the point, how could you not know whether the person sighted in the pub had a beard or not? Why are you so sure this is Tony, when you don't even know whether he had a beard or not? Now you're saying you've got a good lead, but you won't tell us what it is?'

The beard issue is a significant one. Tony's missing person photos show him with a beard, but on this last fateful journey across outback Queensland, a couple of days before he disappeared, we know he shaved it off, as he told Natalie on the phone. He would have been clean shaven at the time he went missing. The answer to this question may have indicated whether the witnesses were indeed going by a first-hand sighting of Tony the night he was last seen, or simply by the missing person posters. It's an issue that makes Mark angry. 'Who is going to know better than the family whether or not a description is accurate? Why keep that a secret from us? We played such a critical role in all those early sightings. The whole rationale for not telling the family was because it was this big covert operation – but we've got people ringing us telling us the story, it's public knowledge – what's your excuse now?

They contacted us saying: "We hear you're investigating lines of enquiry, we need you to not do that because it's got the potential to disrupt the investigation." But if everyone else knows about it, what's the difference?

'The beard was the vital thing that helped us determine a valid sighting from a non-valid one. All we're asking for is the descriptions, or at least a little bit of the descriptions, so we know what we're pinning all our hopes on. They just don't bloody get it. There was an Italian guy who was mistaken for Tony at the time; the police don't believe he's got anything to do with any of the original sightings. I don't even know how they could know that? If there were two or three people kicking around Hughenden that people thought looked like Tony, then why wouldn't someone else think that was Tony too? It's an insight into how memory works, that people are so sure that it's the person. No-one even said: "Oh, it looks a bit like him." It was always: "I've see the photo and I'm absolutely 100% convinced," and we know it wasn't.'

Mark's frustration with Cheryl Scanlon remains. 'She's still saying that she wants to speak to people who saw him in the weeks after 3 November. Weeks! *We* were up there then! It's ludicrous! It's just the one thing we've learned to do in 40 years is to think outside the square and think about pretty bizarre scenarios, especially ones that might have kept him alive in the early days, but I cannot come up with anything where a guy who's got absolutely zero money on him would be at the pub, and would not have gone to the bank over the next day. In three weeks of them travelling, and calling home to arrange their rendezvous, not once was he late with the calls. He was due to call his girlfriend on the 8th, his dole cheque was due on the 5th, if you plotted it all out on paper and saw how abruptly all those things ended, how you could think he was alive days or weeks later ... even the fact that her whole media campaign was around the time from the 3rd to the 11th. It's just ridiculous.'

I asked Mark about the dig at Hughenden, and he corrected me, telling me it was a search, not a dig. I said I had it in my head it was a dig for remains, and he said I had every right to have that in my head, as that's what the family had in their heads too. 'For two weeks, sleepless nights, thinking, "Oh wow, we're about to come to a very grisly conclusion to this whole thing", then two weeks later I said: "What's going on with the dig?" and they said: "There's no dig, there's no intentions of digging, but we'll let you know if we do." The only thing I've got to give credit to them for is they are at least now putting resources into this like they never have before. They've had four detectives working on it. I can't fault the resources, but I think they're barking up the wrong tree.'

I asked Mark if he was hopeful of an end to it all – of arrests being made, charges laid, finding Tony's body? 'No, not at all,' he replied. 'When these fresh leads were announced and police described them as "the best chance we'll ever have of solving it", I don't think we ever contemplated that possibility, from the first early months. I just don't know what evidence they've got. They'll need to match it with sightings. If you attach something to a case that's not valid, all you do is give the defence team a way to wriggle out of it. I got an email a couple of days ago from them saying they hope that there will be charges and it will go to court, and if that doesn't happen we'll press on with the inquest.

There's stuff that I'm wanting the police to give us, and they're saying that it will be a matter either for a judge or the coroner. They are sticking to their guns that this is something that's got the potential to lead to someone being arrested.'

But no-one has been arrested, years down the track from that interview, years after the Hughenden search.

Mark told me the family had long since given up hope that the Hughenden search would lead to anything, and they were frustrated that what they saw as a wild goose chase was simply delaying the inquest even further. 'In fact, the family have been begging the coroner to call a halt to proceedings and get on with the inquest,' he said. 'There will be nothing stopping the cops from pursuing the lead after the inquest, and it will give everyone a chance to see if the leads were valid in the first place. We certainly know the sightings in Hughenden in the days after his last call home are just utter nonsense. I'm just looking forward now to hearing why it was the cops chose to ignore our every plea for six months. To add insult to injury, the head cop has used the coroner's assistant to make some pretty amazing allegations against the family. So, bring on the inquest, I have some questions for Cheryl that will rock her world!'

In March 2015, Mark Jones posted these words on the Facebook page he created to appeal for information about Tony (https://www.facebook.com/missing82):

I would like to say thank you to the good people of Hughenden. A year ago the Townsville Police arrived in your fine town to ask questions about the murder of my brother Tony, which they believe took place there in 1982. We've heard almost nothing from the police since they took out search warrants on The

Grand Hotel and the abattoirs there. My family believe that it is highly unlikely that Tony was in Hughenden for a number of days as the police assert, and we would like to thank you all for your patience and sympathy. We are heartened that the police, after 3 long decades, are actively pursuing leads. We are disheartened that they have chosen to not communicate with the family or listen to our warnings about sightings in Hughenden back in 1982 that all proved to be false. In fact we have the name and address of one of the unwitting travellers mistaken for Tony at the Grand Hotel 10 days after we believe he was murdered. So, many thanks to you all and my apologies that you have had to suffer this attention and scrutiny which has reached bizarre levels at times. We hope that one day soon we will all know the truth about this investigation.

As the second inquest approached, Mark's involvement increased, as he contemplated uprooting his life. 'I'm thinking of moving to Hughenden and putting an end to this, because I feel like I have to deal with it. Dad's almost 90, and I don't think he thinks about it every day, but he thinks it's a complete wild goose chase, and for myself, I just can't properly move on while this thing's going on. I don't know how else to do it except to track down some of those witnesses who say they saw him drinking at the pub, or just finding something that completely discredits the sightings. The worst thing that could happen would be if they were to charge someone, and they got off. At least I take satisfaction in knowing that whoever the guilty party is, they've had to live with knowing one day they could get caught. If they get off, then you set them free and they no longer have to worry about it. But the biggest tragedy of that would be not having an inquest, and the inquest is an opportunity for us to push for better ways to do things, and it would be a shame to be robbed of that. My biggest fear for the last six months or so is that police will realise they've made a mistake, but they'll be too proud to come out and admit that, so it just goes on and on and on. The thought of that going on for another year or two is just not on.'

And yet, the inquest did take a further three years from when Mark and I spoke about this.

While police were preparing a new brief of evidence for the coroner, the persons of interest they were concentrating on remained a bit of a mystery. 'I haven't thought much about the person who did it,' says Mark. 'I've been detached from that. That's going to be interesting.'

On 24 February 2016, Mark sent me a bombshell Facebook message, telling me he was now confronted by this topic: 'Just thought I'd let you know, with little evidence of another missing person in north Queensland at the time, and a crumbling alibi for the main suspect, we think we might have Tony's killers … they were 17 and 16 at the time … is going to be a dramatic inquest!'

Preparations for the second inquest continued. In 2015, police asked the public to come forward if they owned a Voere .22 calibre bolt-action rifle. This is the gun Tony is thought to have had with him when he went missing. Several people did come forward to police, but none of the serial numbers matched Tony's rifle. In October 2016, the Channel Nine program *60 Minutes* presented Tony's story and interviewed Mark. This program proved to be explosive for Tony's case, because for the first time, the public learned the details about the Hughenden allegations. I spoke to Mark while he was being filmed for the program, to see how he was feeling about the show and also about the inquest. He responded:

The filming went pretty well, I think. This inquest is probably just going to be the start of a whole new chapter – a very bloody interesting one. They're just taking the low hanging fruit, good for them to get that out of their system before the real whodunit starts. You can't believe the strands and possibilities to this, Nic, I hope the media keep on top of it so others can follow it. On Monday the witness and I meet the Sixty Minutes crew at the slaughter house in Hughenden for some filming. Things are going to get very strange. It's too early, the sun is pelting through my windows.

I think it would have been quite a difficult task for Mark to visit the possible site of his brother's murder, standing on the spot where his remains may lie, but there was no doubt that Mark would approach it with the same grim determination he's demonstrated for decades now.

Just before the inquest, started Mark's anger towards police had softened somewhat and he acknowledged their efforts from 2014, at the Hughenden search, despite still believing they were concentrating on the wrong suspects. 'The police actually put an incredible amount of resources into this in 2014. But because they refused to listen to our pleas, the whole thing went up a blind alley for more than two years. It's staggering to look at the resources invested in this and just how little the police have progressed the case since hearing about all the confessions in 2012. Only now, in the last month or so, are they starting to look at the alibis for the two men. There are whole lines of inquiry missed by the police simply because they're so attached to the theories formed four years ago. I look forward to the day I can take you through the incredible layers and tangents that have emerged even in the past few months. Thank God the media are helping keep the bastards honest!'

I came back to working on this chapter in 2017. A great deal had happened. The second inquest finally began, six years after it was announced. Mark was very happy, believing he would finally be able to fight for some justice for his brother. Mark did end up moving to north Queensland, in 2016, so he could be closer to where the inquest was held, in Townsville. His new home has proven to be a beautiful inspiration for Mark's amazing photographs, and every time I see his work I am in awe. I can't help but think he must also have wanted to see what Tony saw, to walk where his brother's shoes fell. He takes a lot of photographs of the stars.

However, the latest inquest was to be another bitter disappointment for Mark and his family. It began in August 2016, was adjourned in September 2016, and resumed in July 2017. Nearly 40 witnesses were scheduled to give evidence at the inquest, which was set to run for three weeks. The inquest opened with the police stating they believed Tony Jones was murdered in Hughenden. The theory put forward to the coroner was that Tony hitchhiked his way to Hughenden, and on the night he went missing he was drinking in the Grand Hotel with locals. Three people came forward to police to say they saw Tony at this pub. They claimed a fight broke out, and Tony was allegedly killed with one blow by a local teenager. Another teenager allegedly assisted him to dispose of Tony's body at the Hughenden abattoir, by cutting it into smaller pieces and possibly burning it in the pits there. The teen who allegedly helped was a butcher at the abattoir, and best mates with the alleged killer. These two persons of interest were compelled to give evidence at the resumed inquest and the resulting revelations are explosive. They are currently the prime suspects in Tony's murder.

I'm going to make a tough call here – I'm not going to talk about these two suspects. No-one has ever been charged with Tony's murder. So, one day, *one day*, there just might be charges and a trial. I do not, under any circumstances, want any part of this book to hinder or derail the justice process for Tony. There has been far too much legal bungling already. Maybe in a future book I will be able to come back and say: 'Here's what happened', but at the moment, I won't. The book was also always about Tony's story, and his family, and their journey. So, that's what we'll focus on – for now.

The new inquest also looked at other suspects Michael Laundess and Andy Albury. Laundess was a petty criminal who had made admissions to fellow prisoners about killing someone, and Albury is a convicted killer serving a life sentence in prison in Darwin. I mentioned to Mark that the alarming thing was there was not just one possible suspect for Tony's murder but a string of people who had violent tendencies, and who were in the area at the time. With this many possible suspects, no wonder the investigation remains complicated and full of red herrings, even more than 40 years down the track.

Police previously named killer Andy Albury as a person of interest; however, in 2014 they released a statement saying: 'Whilst there have been media reports that Northern Territory prisoner Andy Albury is a potential suspect in the Tony Jones matter, there is no evidence to support those claims.' Andrew Albury is a scary bloke. He was convicted of the 1982 murder of a woman in Darwin, Northern Territory. Albury has claimed responsibility for another 13 murders, but his diagnosed mental illness means his information cannot be relied upon, and many police simply don't believe him. He told five police officers and his psychiatrist that he killed another woman in Mount Isa in September 1983. Police confirmed Albury was in town that night, and left at 8.30 pm on a Greyhound bus back to the Northern Territory. He also confessed to stomping to death a man sleeping in an Alice Springs riverbed in 1982, the same year Tony went missing.

In a letter to Chief Justice Brian Martin, Albury wrote: 'I have no wish to die. I am unstoppable – I love my work. I do not understand what the meaning of the word kindness is, it's never been shown to me so why in the fuck should I show it. This is not some sort of weird attempt at justification for killing – I do what I do by choice or urge. I will kill again, it's what I do for an occupation.'

Albury claims to have killed between eight and twelve hitchhikers in Queensland and other states. He said he disposed of them in mine shafts. Most of Albury's murder confessions have been disproved, although he was certainly in the right area at the right time to have come into contact with Tony. Albury seemed to target Indigenous people and had a hatred for Asians, neither of which applied to Tony. Albury was shown a photo of Tony by police in 2014 and said he did not recognise him. 'Albury was never really a suspect,' says Mark. 'At the top of our list was Laundess, who confessed to his cell mate that he killed a hitchhiker out there. My dad was beside himself that they were not investigating this man, and chasing these other people that he didn't think had any credence. I think Laundess definitely has to be checked out further. He's a violent, nasty man. He was in the area at the time. He admitted to killing a hitchhiker out there. How can you move on from that without investigating it further?

'When he first came up, a couple of years ago, the police report shows that the cell mate came in and told his story about the confession. They included some stuff about his drug dealing and that he's known for violence in several states, then they said they were calling for a full police profile on him, then it all stopped. We haven't been able to get anything more about him. We haven't discounted him for a minute. We don't know if they've eliminated him, and if they have, why? And if they haven't, why have they not investigated? They've just used this as an excuse to put a blanket ban on all discussions about the case. I understand they need to keep things secret, but why are we waiting 18 months for them to investigate one thing? This is the thing we're most upset about with the case.'

To make matters worse, Michael Laundess died in Perth in October 2015, before the inquest started, robbing the family and the court of being able to ask any questions of him. Laundess' brother did give evidence, and Mark commented to me that: 'The brother seemed to kinda like the idea that his brother might have been involved.' The fact that police failed to question Laundess adds to Mark's frustration. 'We told the police where to find him, you know, but they got there six weeks too late. They never located him in the four years before he died.'

The second inquest opened on 29 August 2016. Mark Jones appeared as a witness on the first day. He told the court:

We would hear about these sightings across the Flinders Highway and they drove us mad. The sightings weeks after Tony went missing made no sense. For the police to go to the media and suggest Tony was still alive destroyed the initial investigation ... they just didn't get that Tony couldn't be alive. If there were sightings of Tony days or week later it needed incredible proof.

Brian also gave evidence this day. The brothers were determined their voices would be heard this time around. When Mark described the day when Beres was told that Tony had not cashed his dole cheque, he said this is the moment his mother knew Tony was dead. 'That was like a dagger through the heart,' said Mark. Also on the first day of the inquest, Queensland Police admitted to poor communication with the family during the initial investigation in the 1980s and said a new team of North Queensland detectives were now looking into the case. They said police were keeping an open mind to any new evidence that may be raised during the inquest. 'There may have been failures early on in the investigation,' the barrister representing Queensland Police said. 'The Queensland Police Service will continue to keep the death of Anthony Jones as an open investigation.'

The coroner was told that the former lead officer of the case, Chris Lill, who has since retired, asked to be excused from appearing at the inquest for the first two weeks on medical grounds. Mr Lill also did not give evidence at the first inquest. Former prisoner Jason Barry told the inquest a cellmate, whose name he could not recall, had told him in about 2000 that he had killed a man in Mount Isa. Barry said: 'He stated to me he was out that way and said he had done a bloke in Mount Isa. Just basically that he buried them and they'll never find him if they ask about it.' Police located photographs of Barry's former cellmates and showed these to him, asking him to identify the man who had told him this story. He identified one of the men but when he was being cross-examined, he told the court he could not be sure it was the same man who confessed to him. Michael Laundess is believed to be Barry's former cellmate. As Laundess had died before the inquest started, his brother Brian gave evidence and said his brother may have been the one who sent the 'Lochiel' letter to police in 1983. But police lost the letter, so DNA could not be taken from the sample.

Journalist Samantha Healey wrote in the *Townsville Bulletin* in September 2016:

Mr Laundess said he and other family members believed the handwriting bore a resemblance to that of his late brother, and that examples had been provided to investigators. He said his brother had bipolar disorder and was not frightened of violence, but he said his sibling later told him that he had been checked out and was not 'on the police radar'.

The coroner stated: 'Brian Laundess gave evidence on 9 September 2016. His evidence was that Michael Laundess was working in north Queensland in late 1982. Michael has hitchhiked there and later told Brian it was a "hell of a trip". His brother had also spoken to him about the disappearance of Anthony Jones in the mid-2000s, and told him that he was a suspect in the matter. Michael Laundess told him that he was not involved, and the person who alleged he had confessed in prison had him mixed up with someone else. Brian Laundess also told the court that he had heard from his brother William that Michael Laundess had threatened Michael's wife with the comment, "Keep it up and I'll put you in a shallow grave with that other bugger." Michael had also told William between 1992 and 1994 that he had killed a man by bashing him with a stick. He also said that some family members considered that the handwriting on a letter referenced on the Wikipedia page was similar to his brother's.'

The coroner directed that a statement be obtained from William Laundess. The Wikipedia page mentioned was set up by Mark Jones and includes a photograph of the Lochiel letter. On 2 September 2016, prisoner Andy Albury was connected to the court by telephone from Darwin Prison to give evidence at the inquest. Albury refused to take an affirmation, before claiming the coroner had no jurisdiction over him. When asked about Tony, Albury said he knew who Tony was but he refused to speak to police about him. He said: 'I told them nothing. Jones will stay buried where I planted him. I'm not telling you anything,' then hung up the phone.

The two persons of interest connected to the Hughenden slaughter yards were discussed at length during the inquest.

Mark and Brian Jones presented a submission to Coroner Terry Ryan, asking for the slaughter yards and the council burn pits at Hughenden to be properly searched. They wanted ground-penetrating radar to be used to detect abnormalities in the soil under the burning pits. On the final day of the inquest, their submission was denied. It was a terrible blow, and a decision that is difficult to understand. Ground-penetrating radars are non-invasive search tools. They basically look like a lawn mower, but with no blades. The radar emits a radio signal into the ground and reflected signals are returned to the machine. The time it takes for the signal to be sent and received is measured and the depth of the ground can be worked out. In layman's terms, if the GPR is run over the surface of the ground and if the signals bounce off something unexpected, like a body buried under the earth, that will be recorded in the machine's data.

If it was a question of money, the Jones family offered to fund the search, and besides this, other Queensland missing person and homicide cases have received vast amounts of funding – why is Tony Jones less important? Counsel assisting the coroner claimed the submission was 'an attempt to get around a search warrant'. This is deeply insulting to the Jones family. It suggests that they are somehow in the wrong for wanting the property searched. Stephanie Williams said in court: 'Given that there is a lack of evidence … for a search warrant … and that there has been no consent by the property owner … to use Your Honour's power to direct such a search of the property would be an improper use of that power. It would be an attempt to obtain a search warrant through a back door.' It is a slap in the face to the Jones family. They don't want a back door – that front door should have been wide open to them, a very long time ago. Three witnesses, detailing three separate confessions, specifically naming the slaughter yards and burn pits, sounds like a really good reason to me to at least have a look.

A section of Stuart Creek was searched by police on 12 July 2017 after a witness claimed he saw a fresh mound of dirt there in November 1982. Nothing was found. However, police have still failed to do basic checks for the investigation. 'You know, they still haven't checked Tony's rifle against the guns handed in during the buy-back scheme,' says Mark. 'They did a check some years ago with all the states but gave them the wrong serial number – two, in fact. After we drew that to their attention they did a follow-up check, but not against the buy-back. The correct serial number of Tony's rifle is 257435 and the stock was stained dark red. He enjoyed roo shooting, and that's why he brought it on his trip.'

I asked Mark whether looking at Tony's final days, and dissecting statements and versions of events from the people his brother met, and having to hypothesise what may have happened has made him more wary of other people he meets in his own life. Mark considers the question carefully:

I don't think it has, but I'm analytical of people and the things they say, and the things that I read into … people's words. When I was in Mount Isa in 1992 with Mick Buckley, the private investigator, I met a Scottish chap up there and we became friends. He was really into analysing dreams and Jungian analysis, that sort of thing, and that took me on this whole psychological journey, and that's more responsible for me seeing the truth more clearly, and setting aside my Catholic upbringing and my trust in people, believing things that people tell me. At the time I was going through all of this stuff, I was managing a group of about 20 people and it brought about a big change in the way I dealt with them, being prepared to call them out on a few things. I don't let people pull the wool over my eyes. In a way, that's related to Tony, but in a very indirect way. It's a journey I probably wouldn't have gone on had Tony not gone missing.

Mark agrees that he's a very different person now due to Tony's disappearance. 'I was a brash, driven, 21-year-old at the time, completely self-absorbed and I think people like that need a bit of a tragedy or something to bring them back to earth a little bit. What I've been through with Tony has definitely changed the way I relate to people, my empathy towards people, people who are going through pain. It can't help but change you.'

Like many of the siblings I've interviewed for this book, Mark has dreams about his brother. 'For years I've had dreams where he suddenly appears, and there's some sort of explanation, and he tells me where he's been, so somewhere in the subconscious I've never really accepted [that he's dead]. It was six or seven years before I shed a tear over Tony. That's how removed I was from it. It was reading Brian's book, that's when I first shed a tear. The bits where Brian wrote about Mum being emotional, I couldn't even read that. I later read it on the plane on the way to Sydney for the launch of the book, then I cried for three days straight. For me, that book launch was like the funeral. I turned that into my moment of grieving. With a missing person, you just don't have that time when you come together with the family, and you all share it.

'We've certainly learned a thing or two about the grieving process. It's a really difficult thing for people who aren't directly involved in it to know what to say. They want to say sorry, but they don't want to admit that they think there's no hope, so they say: "Oh, he'll turn up", which no-one wanted to hear. We were struggling so much to get the police to comprehend the fact that it was that serious, so we weren't all that receptive or understanding of people who we'd tell the facts to, but they'd still say, "Oh, he'll turn up." It's a whole distorted thing – but that's the story of missing persons, isn't it? A distortion of reality. Apart from not having a body to bury, you don't have that moment when everybody comes and hugs you and shares that grief. When Mum died a few years later, it really was a funeral for two; it was an amazing outpouring of emotion that probably wouldn't have happened ...' Mark falters, overcome with emotion. 'I mean, obviously we would have grieved for Mum, but certainly the men in the family were probably not that good at expressing emotion, but we knew this is what funerals were for.'

Mark thinks if Tony had been found and they had been able to have a funeral for him, the open emotions expressed by the family would have been held more in check, but he thinks they knew what they'd missed out on, with Tony being missing, and not being able to hold a funeral for him, and they weren't going to hold back anymore.

Mark is quite a remarkable man; he's warm and funny to speak with, highly intelligent and has a gritty determination to get to the bottom of the incredible mess that's been made of his brother's case. Tony Jones is lucky to have him in his corner, along with the other members of this wonderful family. Under the surface of his frustration and anger with the police handling of matters, Mark does take the time to remember the brother that this has all been about, but it's a very private pain that does not very often see the light of day:

I feel like I deal with it in my own way. When I talk to strangers about, it's not so much that I try to be dispassionate about it; I guess I naturally am unless I'm in a particular environment. But I know if I can talk about it dispassionately, then it allows people to talk about it like a murder mystery on TV, we can just have a chat about it rather than have them think I'm going through something. And it is 40 years ago, it makes it easier for people if they see you're not in tears over it, makes it easier for them to talk about it. But I enjoy talking about the facts of the case, I guess that's therapeutic in itself, I don't really ever feel like I need a hug over it.

It's not something I generally talk about. If there's something interesting, I'll chat with my close mate, who was over here last week, because he's got a brilliant mind and it's always interesting getting his views on it. But I usually make sure we talk about what's news, then we move on. I'm really conscious that it's not the most cheerful topic of conversation. It trumps what everyone else is going to say. So, you have to be careful with it. But most of my friends probably don't know about it. It's not something I talk about readily. I just feel what I need is information about the case.

Brian says, about writing his book:

I have tried to express how we, the Jones family, have coped with our tragedy in the hope that it may benefit others, but I realise only too well that there is no right way or wrong way of dealing with a crisis; people simply cope the best way they can.

The Jones family have always been certain Tony was no longer alive after 3 November 1982 and they have faced some criticism from people who think they have given up hope of finding him alive. To this, Brian says:

Actually, it has been easier to cope with a 'dead' brother than a missing one. By believing he was dead (which was a logical conclusion) we were spared much of the emotional conflict between grieving and hoping. We were free to grieve his loss without constantly expecting him to walk in the door. We were also spared the self-reproaches that the families of runaway children often experience. To say, then, that we should not give up hope only aggravated the trauma ... hope must be based on reality, not imagination.

Brian says, in a plea to those who took Tony's life: 'Although we believe Tony is dead, we would still like to know what happened. We hope one day to give his remains the respect of a Christian burial. We know you cannot bring him back to life, but please let us know where he is hidden.'

As well as fighting for the truth about what happened to Tony, Mark is passionate about ensuring other families of missing persons are also supported and their cases not forgotten:

When I spoke at Missing Persons Week last year, I don't think I've been through such overwhelming emotion as that. I was just feeling it through my whole body, and I was constantly on the edge of completely dissolving in tears. I cried right through my speech. I just feel like I was feeling every single person's pain, who was going through it. Seeing what everybody else is going through is a trigger for me, watching other families talk about it. To see so many other people going through it, it's just horrible.

The families need to be involved, they need to do something, that's what I haven't been able to get the police to understand, you need to involve the families. That's what's so great about what they're doing in South Australia and NSW, having people liaise with the family and keep them updated, it's just so important. You can't let the grass grow under these cases; what should happen is as soon as the police run out of leads is it goes straight to the missing persons unit, and they take it up and liaise with the family.

Also, coronial inquests are taking more than ten or twelve years; that needs to happen as part of the earlier stage of the process, not something that happens later on. They give up on the older cases too early. Even in our case, we were getting leads after more than 30 years! Too many of them just get filed away, but the coronial inquest lays everything on the table; it picks up all the flaws, it picks up all the potential leads and they need to be done in that first year or two. With these old cases, there wasn't enough done, and not enough done to link these cases together like those Newcastle cases, to find a common theme.

As has often been the case with the missing persons in this book, there is another strange connection from one missing person to another. Anthony Eura went missing in 2006 from around Kununurra in WA. In 2015, Mark told me that Anthony is actually the brother of their foster sister, Bobbi. This means Bobbi has two missing brothers – both named Anthony.

In another bizarre twist, that I don't believe has ever been investigated, when I check the timeline for Anthony Eura's disappearance it was noted in the coroner's findings: 'Banking records from the Commonwealth Bank show that five withdrawals were made from Mr Eura's account at the BP Ord River Road House in Kununurra on 1 November 2006.' On the same day, Anthony was arrested by police in Kununurra for being drunk and was released at 9 pm. This is the last time Anthony was ever seen alive. In my first book, I detailed how Jamie Herdman was also in Kununurra on 25 November 2006, and made seven transactions in the town, including a $50 transaction at the BP Ord River Road House. Just 24 days after Anthony Eura made his five withdrawals there. Jamie Herdman vanished on 26 November 2006, and has never been found. Anthony Eura has also never been found.

Brian Jones eventually left the priesthood, married and had children. Tim finished the journey he began with his brother, but this time by car. Mark continues to campaign with Brian for justice for Tony. And still, the inquest remains adjourned. In limbo. It's taken me nine years, so far, to write Tony Jones' chapter. Every time I think we're getting to the finish line, something else happens.

In 2019, Mark Jones told me the reason the findings from the second inquest, that we were expecting by the end of 2017, have not yet been released is that there may be a legal issue with the entire process that will render the inquest invalid. In July 2019 the Queensland Supreme Court Justice Elizabeth Watson dismissed an application by the Jones family for a judicial review into Tony's case. The family had learned that Tony's inquest was held under the 1958 *Coroner's Act* and not the 2003 Act, and they were concerned that the inquest was therefore unlawful and that might impact any future criminal charges. Justice Warren stated the application had not been lodged in 'a reasonable time'. Mark wanted the inquest to be held under the new Act, which has updated and amended legislation. It's yet another setback for the Jones family, when all they want is justice, and to find out what happened to Tony.

It is beyond comprehension.

But maybe, if this all has to start again, they can petition the court to actually dig up the slaughter yards at Hughenden, and ultimately, we just might find Tony Jones. As I finalise this chapter the official status of the Tony Jones inquest on the Queensland Coroners Court website is 'Inquest Adjourned DTBF for findings'. DTBF is Date To Be Fixed.

In February 2023, Tony's father, Kevin Jones, sadly passed away. He waited so long for answers that never came. Beres died of leukaemia in 1990, no doubt an illness accelerated due to her intense grief. In March 2024 Mark Jones announced the sad loss of his sister Bobbi. Tony's last ever phone call was to wish Bobbi a happy birthday.

On 12 October 2023, Queensland Police called a surprise media conference and announced a $500,000 reward for information about Tony's murder. Once again, the Jones family had no idea this was happening. Mark said on Facebook:

I am so disappointed that, but for a call from the coroner's office just prior to the media statement by police today, there was absolutely no prior warning from the police about what was happening. They shouldn't be surprised therefore at the anger that we express about the surprise contents of their press conference. Any journos attending should ask the question: 'When did police last speak to the family?' Answer – three years ago. An inquest into a case like Tony's is a chance to fix some of the things that are broken – except that the state coroner has elected to hear it (now in its 13th year) under the 1958 Coroner's Act (now defunct), which does not allow him to make public findings about the failures of the police. This is a state that simply does not give a toss.

In full, the police media release sums up the ridiculously drawn-out history of what this family has endured:

Detectives from Townsville Criminal Investigation Branch are hopeful that the announcement of a $500,000 reward will bring in new information to assist investigations into the murder of Anthony Jones at Hughenden, west of Townsville, in 1982.

20-year-old Anthony Jones, known as Tony, was last seen on or about 12 November 1982 in the small township of Hughenden.

He last spoke with family at approximately 8:50pm on November 3, advising them he planned to hitchhike from Townsville to Mount Isa.

Investigations identified that the phone call came from a telephone box at Bowen Road in Townsville.

Tony failed to arrive to Mount Isa as planned and has not been heard from since.

Police have identified multiple witnesses that can place Tony as being in Hughenden on November 12, where it is believed he attended the Grand Hotel that evening.

Investigations indicate Tony may have been involved in an altercation at the hotel that night, prior to his disappearance.

On 19 January 1983 police received a handwritten letter under the name 'Lochiel' postmarked from Cairns, indicating Tony may have been buried in the Fullerton River.

The following day an extensive search of the area commenced and was cleared without any items of interest being located.

Over the following years, police investigations included approximately 60 statements and 270 inquiries completed by investigators.

A number of persons of interest have been investigated, and numerous land-based searches conducted in areas including the Fullerton River, Cloncurry River and Hughenden Slaughter yards.

At the time of his disappearance Tony was carrying a Voerre .22 calibre rifle with serial number 257435, a large blue backpack with aluminium framing and green sleeping bag, a green one-man tent, along with various personal items such as toiletries.

None of these items have ever been recovered.

In 2002, the Coroner ruled that Anthony Jones was deceased and had died at the hands of a person or persons unknown. Investigators believe Tony has been murdered.

In 1983, a $20,000 reward was offered as part of the ongoing investigation. In 1990, this was updated to $50,000. In 2004, it was further updated to $250,000.

In 2010 the inquest was reopened by the Attorney General, commencing in 2016 and concluding in 2017, with a date to be advised for the delivery of the Coroner's findings.

With active investigations underway, detectives from Townsville Criminal Investigation Branch (CIB) were approved to increase the reward on offer to $500,000.

Detectives will be conducting further investigations in Hughenden on Saturday October 14 and Sunday October 15, and urge any community members with information to come forward.

Detective Sergeant Brenden Stevenson of Townsville CIB said police are confident someone out there has the information needed for the matter to be solved.

'More than 40 years has passed now and in that time loyalties change, any information no matter how small or insignificant it may seem, could be the key to bringing closure for Tony's family,' Detective Sergeant Stevenson said.

'If you were in Hughenden or at the Grand Hotel on the 12th of November in 1982, you may have seen something that could be crucial to this investigation, it is never too late to come forward.

'We are also urging anyone with any information at to the whereabouts of Tony's rifle, or the identity of the person who posted police the letter from Cairns in 1983, to please contact police.'

The $500,000 Queensland Government Reward is for information which leads to the apprehension and conviction of the person or persons responsible for this murder. The

Government reward further offers an opportunity for indemnity against prosecution for any accomplice, not being the person who actually committed the murder, who first gives such information.

Clearly, this statement has errors. Even 40 years on, Tony Jones is still suffering the indignity of not only still being missing, without justice, but police can't even put out a media release with the correct date on it. TONY WAS NOT IN HUGHENDEN ON 12 NOVEMBER. By that date, he'd been dead for nine days.

We've now been waiting six years for the inquest findings.

I held back Tony's chapter from my first book, thinking *surely* the findings will be released by the time the second book is ready to be published. But, no. Here we are, still waiting.

Tony is still out there.

Justice is still not served.

His family still waits.

Brian writes that in Mark's last phone conversation with his brother he tells Tony he's going to see musician Dave Warner play at the local pub. Warner is, ironically, now a crime writer, with 12 novels under his belt, and he is also best known for his hit 'Suburban Boy', released in 1978. Tony would have absolutely known this song. I contacted Dave Warner and let him know about this connection, and he was deeply touched.

Is that how Tony felt? Just a suburban Perth boy, in desperate need to escape suburbia and find adventure?

I wake up every morning with no-one beside me
I wake up every morning and my mother will chide me

I'm just a Suburban Boy, just a Suburban Boy
Saturday night, no subway station
Saturday night just changing TV stations
I'm just a Suburban Boy, just a Suburban Boy
And I know what it's like
To be rejected every night
And I'm sure it must be, easier for boys from the city
I go to the football to cheer for my team
I go to the football to hear myself scream
I'm just a Suburban Boy, just a Suburban Boy
Sunday Session – I'm down at the hotel
Staring at girls that I don't know, well
I'm just a Suburban Boy, just a Suburban Boy
And I know what it's like
I've been rejected every night
And I'm sure it must be, easier for boys from the city

(Lyrics reprinted with the kind permission of Dave Warner)

If you have any information about the suspected murder of Anthony Jones please call Crimestoppers on 1800 333 000

CHAPTER SIX
Owen Redman

Owen Redman was last seen around Brunswick in Melbourne, in February 1991.
He was 25 years old.

When Dylan Redman answers his phone, he says, 'Hi, this is Dylan.' I thought little of it until he later told me he does that every single time, so that if his missing brother Owen calls him one day, he will know he's got the right person.

The Redman family lived in many different places around Australia. Owen is five years older than Dylan, and was born in Tumut, NSW. Dylan also has an older sister, Fleur. Their parents were working around the Snowy Mountains area when they met, then in Sydney, and a few years after Owen was born the family moved to Alice Springs in the Northern Territory. John Redman, a clinical psychologist, was teaching Indigenous children in the region. Dylan and his sister were both born in Alice Springs.

Dylan looked up to his big brother Owen. 'I was the annoying little brother but we shared a room, so the music he was into, I'd get into. I wanted to be involved in everything he did,' says Dylan. 'He'd play Dungeons and Dragons, stuff like that,' he chuckles. 'Owen was really intelligent and was always hanging out with the smart kids. My mother was quite intelligent as well, and Owen was a lot like our parents. He got along with everyone, but he was sort of a pacifist. I remember him coming home off the bus one day, and he had blood all over him. Mum and my sister were freaking out. Someone had picked a fight with him and he said, "Look, I'm a pacifist, I don't fight," but the kid decided to thump him anyway. I'm not sure what it was over. Owen had a pretty dry sense of humour. He was really into *Monty Python*, *The Young Ones*, *The Goodies*, that sort of silly English humour, and he was really into *Monkey Magic*, so if you didn't "get it" you'd be kind of going, *Is this guy being an idiot?*

The family continued to move around regularly. John was tutoring at the University of Queensland and the family lived in Brisbane for a time, and also Churchill in Victoria. 'I jokingly referred to us as gypsies, as we lived in so many places,' says Dylan. 'My wife lived in the same house all her life until we got married. I went to something like ten different schools, and so did Owen.' The family lived in Papunya, 240 kilometres north of Alice Springs and in about 1972 they moved to Darwin. Their house in Darwin was destroyed in Cyclone Tracy, so the family moved to Brisbane.

They continued their nomadic lifestyle, and in about 1980 they moved to Victoria. Their parents' marriage, always a little rocky, had started to seriously deteriorate. 'That's really where it fell apart,' says Dylan, who was about 12 at this time. 'I think there may have been some resentment of Owen by my parents, being the first born. It would have been hard being Owen. A lot of people said Owen was a super nice guy, but he also had a bad temper. I don't know if that's related to the things that happened in my family, like my parents' divorce and the fighting and custody stuff. Being the oldest, he had it tough, I think, towards the end [of the marriage]. But I look at family photos and we looked happy-ish.'

The couple divorced in 1983; Dylan and Fleur stayed with their mother, while Owen chose to live with their father. 'When I was living with my mum, she was quite conservative; she became a Christian when I was about eight, while we were living in Brisbane,' says Dylan. 'She took her faith and the Bible as a way of establishing order and understanding in the world, whereas my father was the complete opposite; he's a humanist, so Owen gravitated towards the humanistic way of thinking. My brother was interested in God and faith, but after living with my father he was turned against it all. It would have been tough for Owen; being older he would have seen that transition from free thinking, no religion in the home, to Mum going to a Pentecostal church.' Dylan shares his strong faith with his mum, who has since passed away, but he says it wasn't a natural path to take.

'My mum was pretty full on, and would make me go to church, and I would buck up against that when I was living with her. I know, now, that she was praying like crazy for me, and it was a series of experiences that led me there. I struggled against a lot of the ideas.' Dylan thought a great deal about the concept of God being his Father, and he wonders if Owen also struggled with the things his mother was encouraging them both to think about. 'Owen was very open to things, and never condemned my beliefs, never thought I was an idiot. He said, "Yeah, cool, I respect that, it's not for me necessarily but I don't despise you and I'm not going to put you down." He thought everything was relative. Mum was very forthright and upfront, and she'd bug him a bit; she'd tell him he needed God and that was it, she didn't sugar coat it. It could be a bit confronting.

'I think Mum and Owen were very much alike, but I think Owen was a lot more gracious, and they didn't always get along. Religion, from Owen's perspective, was hard because he'd been given it as *this is the way it is*. Fleur and Owen got along okay, but she was a lot like Mum, and at the time my brother and my mum were at loggerheads, because Mum would try to drag him to church, and he didn't want a bar of that.'

Owen went to school in Maryvale, from 1983 to 1986. After leaving school, he moved to Melbourne, and attended Latrobe University for a time. 'He studied something really boring at first, like commerce,' says Dylan. 'He realised that wasn't really him, so he went on to study drama and theatre and philosophy, but he dropped out. From what I understand, he didn't finish it, he wanted to work and make some money. He was pretty phlegmatic about it; he would have just thought, *Oh yeah, this is not for me.* It's not like it was a bad thing, he's just very laid back. We both are, but there's also this deep-seated seriousness, and to some degree, rage, sitting beneath the surface. I struggle with anger and I know my sister does too.'

Owen surprised his entire family one day by suddenly announcing he was married. No-one knew until after the ceremony, and Dylan remembers being in disbelief that it had actually happened. 'He said they got married for fun. He was 21 or 22. They went to the Dandenongs, and took photos, and I remember the way he told me he got married ... To be honest I didn't even think it was legitimate, for a while, I thought it was just a joke. There were only about three or four people there including the celebrant.'

Owen's casual and bohemian approach to his marriage was the same as he approached most things in his life – he didn't see it as a big deal. He liked going to Confest, an alternative bush campout festival in NSW. 'The group of people Owen hung out with were hippy-type people, living in Brunswick, getting into all the cool causes and stuff,' says Dylan. 'In the late 80s and early 90s Greenpeace was a big organisation. Peter Garrett was a big supporter of them, and Owen loved Midnight Oil.'

Owen had done all sort of jobs, like working in Taco Bill in South Melbourne, odd jobs, trying to put a band together, and he started selling Greenpeace subscriptions. Dylan thinks Owen's friends would have been really supportive of his working for the popular environmental organisation. 'He was compassionate and kind,' says Dylan, 'And he would have definitely believed in that cause, it wouldn't have just been a job. He was a passionate environmentalist. He would have been the sort of person who wouldn't wear leather shoes or eat hamburgers, he would have looked after the environment. I remember him criticising me about my clothes if I wore brand names, he was opposed to that. I'm not sure if he was completely vegetarian, but I remember him being really into eating falafels. I'm not sure if that was just because it was cool or hip or whatever. He ate lots of falafels,' Dylan says with a laugh, remembering how his brother introduced him to the popular Middle Eastern food. 'I was still living in the country, and I didn't know anything about those kinds of foods. I'd come to visit and we'd go out; he'd sneak me into pubs and see bands. He'd get carded [asked to show ID] and I wouldn't,' Dylan remembers with a grin.

'He liked all different types of music, liked experiencing all types of music and different things,' says Dylan. 'He had lots of acquaintances and friends who hung out at his house, they were all into music; in Brunswick he would have connected with lots of different artists and musicians.' Dylan remembers hanging out with Owen, listening to music and air-drumming along with the track; Owen was singing along and didn't mind that his annoying little brother was air-drumming. The memory makes Dylan smile. 'That's one of the reasons I started to play the drums, and I still do,' says Dylan. The brothers jammed along to INXS, Midnight Oil, The Police and Taco's 'Puttin' On the Ritz', from 1982. 'He liked Jean Michel Jarre and all kinds of stuff. I remember him playing me all this cool music of his, and me air-drumming to it. It was kinda nice, that was our connection. We went to the Corner Hotel, we saw alternative rock bands, but he was also into instrumental electronica as well. I remember, going to that Corner Hotel gig, Owen was walking down the road just roaring. I was embarrassed by it but at the same time thought it was awesome. He was very spontaneous. I think part of it was that I was pretty conservative and uptight and he was trying to loosen me up a bit. He and his wife, running down the road, roaring like lions and being silly.' It's a great memory.

If Owen had any grand dreams or ambitions, he didn't share them with Dylan. 'He approached Dad at one point with a business proposition, so I think he had goals and things he wanted to do, but he would have been limited by finances,' he says. Dylan thinks Owen might have wanted to move to the UK, or even to an Aboriginal settlement, but Dylan doesn't remember him ever talking about this. Owen made some demo tapes with his band, and Dylan thinks he may have wanted to make a record. He played guitar and sang with his band, and Dylan remembers him as being pretty good.

'I remember walking with Owen in Barkly Street in St Kilda where he lived … every time I go past that place now I think of Owen, it was so "him"; it was a second-storey flat and I'd go and hang out there. He was sharing a flat with a guitarist, and there were all these nice guitars around. As his younger brother, I really looked up to him. When we were walking down the street

I remember him saying, "Look, I'm really sorry for the way I beat you up a bit when we were kids, and I hope that you'll forgive me, I just want to have a good relationship with you"; he felt quite remorseful for the way he'd treated me. Out of everyone in the family, I know I was the closest to Owen.' That's Dylan's favourite memory of his brother, the day they talked and made it right between them.

Owen had disappeared before, but usually only for a few days at a time. Dylan says, 'In 1989 I was an exchange student in America, and I wanted to get in touch with Owen to say, "Hey, I'm heading off overseas, can we catch up before I go?" But we couldn't get in contact with him. We rang the number we had, but it didn't answer, he wasn't at the address; the only way we could get in contact was to go to Centrelink and put a note on his file from Dad saying, "Dylan's going overseas, do you want to catch up?" We didn't hear anything, then suddenly the night before I was leaving he rocked up to Dad's house. I've even got an old blurry photo of him on that night. It was like nothing had happened, no apologies or *sorry I disappeared*. So, he'd done it before, but it was more that he'd changed addresses and didn't tell us. Dad's always been pedantic about getting my address and phone numbers since then, because he's afraid I'll do the same.'

Owen and his wife had an unusual marriage, often living in separate share houses. Dylan describes them as a very bohemian couple and very untraditional. His wife said Owen would sometimes take off for a few days and then reappear, so it was a month before Owen's wife contacted Dylan and John to tell them she thought Owen was missing. She later told Dylan the marriage was coming to an end, and it had not been a good relationship. Owen's bad temper made his home life strained and tense, and she knew it was time for her to leave him. This was shortly before Owen went missing, and he and his wife were living apart. It was February 1991 and Owen was 25 years old. After the phone call from Owen's wife, Dylan and his dad drove out to Brunswick, where Owen had been living with a group of guys. Owen had left all his belongings behind in the house and his flatmates told Dylan and John they had no idea where he was.

Although not initially very worried, thinking his brother had simply taken off again for a while, Dylan did have some concerns that no-one had seen Owen for a month. After their visit to Owen's flat, John and Dylan went to St Kilda police station to report Owen as a missing person. They collected all Owen's belongings – these are still at John's home. Owen left everything behind – money, clothes, passport – and he didn't collect his wages from Greenpeace. Dylan phoned his mother and his sister to let them know Owen was missing. 'I don't think Mum dealt with it very well, but she reconciled it to being Owen's choice,' says Dylan. He goes on:

Before we knew Owen was missing, I remember the phone ringing a few times. At the time I was living with Dad. I used to answer the phone by just saying, 'Hello', and apparently, I sounded a lot like my father. People would mistake me for him when they called and would start talking to who they thought was Doctor Redman. But when Owen went missing, the phone would ring and I'd say hello, and I'd just hear a pause; they'd wait for a moment then hang up. There were three or four calls like that.

When Dylan found out Owen was missing, his first thought was that Owen had been doing the hang-up phone calls. He felt Owen hadn't spoken because he wasn't sure whether it was Dylan or his dad on the other end of the line. Dylan thought Owen may have been calling to let them know he was leaving. Owen's relationship with his father was sometimes strained, and Dylan feels that Owen may have hesitated to speak with his dad. 'I wish I could have been there for him, and helped him, rather than him disappearing, but I couldn't,' says Dylan sadly. 'I wish I'd answered, "Hey, this is Dylan," and then he'd have talked to me.'

Dylan, like many siblings of the missing, wishes he'd stepped in to help his brother before he chose to leave. 'I could see the signs. His wife said he had withdrawn from his usual group of friends, he wouldn't go out anymore, he'd stopped drinking. It was almost like he was trying to get his act together and then make the big move. But I'm wondering if that's just me trying to rationalise it, and say he hasn't committed suicide, he's not dead or been murdered. I don't think he's the sort of guy who would have been murdered. He wasn't into anything bad, no hard drugs or anything.' But interestingly, Owen knew one of Ivan Milat's victims, and he stopped hitchhiking after that person disappeared. So, could Owen also have been one of Milat's victims? Ivan Milat killed at least seven backpackers between 30 December 1989 and 18 April 1992. Two of his victims were a young couple from Frankston in Victoria. Chillingly, the couple had been on their way to Confest near Albury, the same festival Owen enjoyed going to.

'He lived a fairly meagre lifestyle; he didn't have much. He didn't drive, but I think he had a licence. If you went to his house you wouldn't see lots of stuff, he was more into people and having a coffee, talking to people, he was very conversational, a relational person. It's funny ... he's a very serious person, and I can relate to that as I can be a very serious person too, sometimes I make jokes just to disarm myself ... but Owen could also be easy going and flippant. It was like Dr Jekyll and Mr Hyde. I'm less so, now, I've calmed down a lot, but when I was younger people would look at me and wonder what was going on.'

I suggest that marriage has mellowed him, and Dylan agrees, saying his lovely wife Lisa is a very chilled-out person, who calms him down when he gets agitated. He says:

Owen could get really cranky about things. It was very passive-aggressive behaviour. I've struggled a bit in my own life, and I think if I wasn't a Christian, if I didn't have a great network of friends and church people around me, there may well have been a time when I thought, stuff it, I'm going, and just taken off. Owen didn't have the benefit of having a church community around him to help him. Even Fleur, my sister, has said she feels like that sometimes, that she could just leave everything behind and go. When life throws you a curve ball, I have to admit, sometimes I think I've had enough of this, I'm going to move to Wales!

But I realise you can't just do that. We've built a nice life here, but it's easier to say I've had a gutful of this, I'm just going to reinvent myself. And I hope that's all it's about, with Owen. He's said, that's it, I've had enough, I'm reinventing myself, I'm going to start all over again. That's my gut feeling. For all I know now he may be married or have another partner.

I can see Owen living somewhere in the country and having this laid-back lifestyle, being isolated and growing their own stuff. It was within his world view, his experience of the world, moving around a lot and trying new things and not settling down.

Dylan thinks that rather than ask for help, Owen would have tried to work out any personal problems he had himself. His wife said Owen tried to fix the problems in their marriage, but it just didn't work. She has since remarried, but she had an extremely difficult time trying to obtain a divorce from someone who was missing.

Dylan feels that dealing with Owen's disappearance has always been his responsibility, despite only being a teenager when his brother went missing. He wishes more effort had been put into finding Owen early on, but concedes he was the one closest to his brother, and was himself very young at the time. 'My sister feels he might be lost and screwed up, but even if he is, he's still my brother and I still love him. Maybe that would present a whole bunch of different challenges in itself if he's mentally ill or addicted to drugs, but I honestly don't think he is. I think he's a bit different, a bit out there, but it doesn't mean that I would reject him. At the end of the day, it's his choice.'

In the police media appeals about Owen, it was suggested that he may have been using the names Owen Moore or Stuart Moore. These names Owen used, Dylan thinks, for fun, as part of a performance. 'He toyed around with a stage name,' says Dylan. 'He liked acting, he did act in a few movies. I thought Owen Redman was a pretty good stage name, but I think he was looking for another one. I have friend who, without my permission, has gone to see clairvoyants – I don't put any faith in any of that – but all the psychics have all said that he's dead. The police reopened Owen's case, and said to me, "By the way, we did get a letter in 1993…"'

Dylan was horrified that it had taken police so many years to let his family know. 'They then went on to say they had thought the letter was bogus. It said, "Owen's in Western Australia, in Carnarvon, he's not in a good way." Dylan had also considered the possibility that Owen had sent the letter himself. I asked Dylan whether sending a letter like that is something Owen would do if he was alive. Or if he decided to disappear and start a new life, would he cut off all contact with friends and family forever? Dylan doesn't know. After finding out about the letter, Dylan immediately wanted to jump on a plane to Carnarvon, and was all set to track down his brother, but police stopped him shortly before he left, telling him they'd discovered who the author of the letter was. It turned out that a relative of Owen's former wife had gone to a psychic, and this information was what the psychic had said, so the person wrote the letter as if they were someone who knew where Owen was. It was a crushing disappointment for Dylan. 'I think that's why they seemingly haven't put as much time into Owen's case, because of this wacky letter,' says Dylan.

He says a few people contacted him over the years with possible sightings of Owen, but when Dylan took these sightings to police they berated him for taking too long to inform them. 'One lady said she saw him in a shopping centre in Geelong. I asked her to contact the police and then I eventually passed it on to them, but after months of waiting to hear back from them they finally said I should have given it to them sooner, and I'd gone through the wrong process. But how am I supposed to know that?'

Like most families of the missing, suddenly having to deal with police is a totally new experience, and one for which they are unprepared. In 2005, Dylan was invited to attend National Missing Persons Week and was featured on the big screen during the football. He remembers being interviewed by various media sources who asked him about Owen, and when one reporter asked him how he felt about Owen being missing, Dylan broke down in tears. 'It was really embarrassing,' he says sheepishly, but it's clear he feels deeply about his brother:

> *The thing that makes me feel desperately upset is if he would feel like no-one cared, that no-one would be looking for him, that no-one would be interested. It's sad to think that he wouldn't realise we were looking for him.*
>
> *Maybe he thinks I don't care. Or maybe it's embarrassing. When we were kids we'd get angry and just run off, and then going back to people and apologising was very humiliating and embarrassing, and perhaps from his perspective, coming back would be like that, but a billion times harder. Or maybe he just thinks we don't care. There's been plenty of stuff in the media and it's been on national TV.*

Dylan says the police officer who organised the Missing Persons Week appeal at the football, and also organised an age-progressed image of Owen, was a fantastic officer. There have been four different police officers who have handled Owen's case in the last ten years alone.

Dylan's Christian faith and strong network of friends from his church have helped him cope over the years since Owen went missing. His church friends would recognise the times he was struggling and take him aside for a coffee and a chat. 'If I wasn't a Christian I think I'd struggle to find any hope in the situation,' says Dylan. 'I've felt abandoned at times, as I am a fairly independent person, but I know there's this ever-present, all-knowing, all-powerful God who's got me in the palm of His hand, so even when I start to feel cheesed off with life I know that God's in control, and it's okay. It sucks, it's not fun and I don't enjoy it, but I can get a hold of it and think that God can help me understand other people, empathise with people. This situation [Owen being missing] isn't positive in any way, but God can help make it positive.'

As I have spoken to the families of the missing for this book, all of whom have had varying degrees of faith and who have been happy to talk about that, it's been interesting to note that most of them have *not* been angry with God for the situation they are all in, having a missing sibling and the pain that has brought to their lives.

'God hasn't inflicted this pain on my family,' says Dylan. 'We all have free will, free choice. If I was going to be angry at anyone it would be Owen. Sometimes I am. It fluctuates, just like grieving. I never actually had the opportunity to grieve for my brother, so I haven't gone through all the stages of grief. One of those stages is feeling angry. Mum died in a car accident in 2011, and I remember going through all those stages; actually, I think I did feel angry at God over that one,' he says sadly.

'But I can't be angry with God. I'm His child, but at the same time, parents can't control their children, control their actions, it comes down to kids making good choices. Mum's crash was a tragic set of circumstances. But I'm not angry at God about Owen. The main thing I want to do is make it into something positive, trying to find something positive in all the mess. That might be being a support to other people who have missing family members, we can say, Hey, our situation sucks but we're in it together, you're not alone.'

I asked Dylan if it felt strange that God knows where Owen is, but Dylan doesn't. He considers the question carefully. 'Being a high school teacher, I ask my students to do certain tasks. Sometimes they'll ask me why they have to do it when it seems like a waste of time. I tell them that they have to trust that I'm asking them to do it for a very good reason, and I won't always explain every tiny little thing I ask them to do, all the time. Sometimes they have to trust that I care about them, my heart is huge and I want to make sure they get the best they can from me as a teacher. I liken that to God. God loves us unconditionally. He let His son die on the cross for us, and we can trust Him. I trust Him, therefore I've got to trust that even though I don't know where my brother is, and that's frustrating, at the end of the day God knows where he is and exactly what's happened but perhaps there's a reason why I haven't found out. Maybe God's protecting me. Owen's made a choice and God isn't going to force Owen to come back. I think if he was buried in a shallow grave somewhere, God would have sorted it out so that someone would find it and there'd be some closure there.'

In 2014 Dylan decided he was going to walk to Tumut, his brother's birthplace. It seemed to be a good way to raise awareness about Owen still being a missing person. 'I'm not trained in media but I've been sending out press releases about Owen for years,' says Dylan. 'I was feeling really helpless one day. I thought, *Why do I have a brother who's missing?* I need to do something a bit crazy, but spectacular. I thought I'd do something ridiculous, a bit unusual, something I've never done before and see if that would provoke media focus. I saw Samuel Johnson on TV, who had ridden around Australia on a unicycle for his sister, who has cancer, and thought, *Well, if he can ride a unicycle, I can walk, I like walking.* So, if I can walk for myself, then I can walk for my brother. As soon as I thought of it, I knew I had to do it. I put it on Facebook and asked people to support me, but instead there was a flood of negative people. Or realists. They told me I was crazy, that I couldn't do it. I was annoyed, as I expected everyone to say that it was a great idea and that they'd walk with me! If I saw something like that I'd be, like, *Yes! I'm walking with you!* I think if they'd all had missing brothers, they would have taken time off and walked with me.'

Dylan's wife, Lisa, was a great support on his trip, which saw them in one of the coldest places in Australia in the middle of winter. It was freezing. 'She would drive the car about 5 kilometres ahead, hop out and take a couple of photos. But then it was too cold for her. We'd bought her thermal pants but she didn't wear them, she didn't think it would be that cold,' Dylan says with a laugh. 'I thought the fact that we were on the Snowy Mountains Highway would have given it away.'

Dylan actually developed hypothermia during the last leg of

his walk, and sadly didn't make it all the way to Tumut. 'I only had 22 kilometres to go, but I just literally couldn't walk any further. We got to this ridiculous hill just outside Adelong and it was, like, one degree. I had some water and a muesli bar and I thought right, come on, so I made it to the top of the hill but then sat down in the car and all will and desire just went out of me. I started shivering like crazy and felt really yuck and that's when I realised I had hypothermia. We drove the last part of the walk and we parked on a hill overlooking Tumut, next to the hospital where Owen was born, and I wished that Owen would somehow just be there, but then the harsh reality kicked in and I just wanted to sleep. But I want to go back there one day and walk those last 20 kilometres from Adelong.'

Dylan was buoyed by the comments and support from his friends about his walk, and delighted to have proved the doubters wrong, but was disappointed not to have completed it. Much of the walk was done around Dylan's suburb in Melbourne prior to the trip to Tumut, as Dylan was unable to get permission to walk the entire distance beside the highway. I told Dylan I thought that if Owen knew what his brother had done – trying to walk to Tumut – he'd be sitting back in shock, saying, "I can't believe you did that for me."

Dylan says, 'Mmm, that was the hope. I sort of felt a bit hopeless, as I didn't get any response, but then again, I didn't get much mainstream media response. I sent out a lot of emails but I didn't really know who to call. It's not a very attractive kind of cause. It's not cute little kids or animals.'

I tried to help Dylan out before his walk by sending out media releases to regional and larger newspapers in the hope that they'd pick up the story but I, too, found it difficult getting their attention.

Dylan has given police a DNA sample, in case Owen is found one day and they need to confirm his identity, but his parents declined to give samples. Dylan's father does occasionally still bring up the topic of Owen's disappearance with Dylan, but those times are few and far between as the years go on.

Lisa, Dylan's wife, has been a great support and comfort to him, dealing with the loss of his brother. 'She's good at listening,' says Dylan. 'She doesn't know *what* to do, and tells me that, but I tell her sometimes doing and saying nothing is the best thing. She's the best. I have a friend who constantly gives advice and now I don't even call him when I'm upset as I just want to talk. But Lisa is really good; if I'm struggling with something she won't offer advice, she'll just listen. We go for walks together and I'll bounce ideas off her. Sometimes she'll get angry if she knows I've been upset, and I'll have to calm her down; she's not angry at Owen or anything; in terms of him she just listens and doesn't try to offer advice.' I think that's very important for the partners of these siblings of the missing, as the pain of having a missing person is a truly unique feeling that you can't know unless you experience it first-hand. The ability to listen is a very valuable skill.

It's been more than 30 years since Owen Redman was last seen by friends and family, yet his loss still affects Dylan constantly. When we spoke, I had the feeling he was restless, with a touch of wanderlust, and he has since resigned from his teaching position in search of something more in his life. Shortly after our interview, Dylan travelled to Cambodia with members of his church to teach impoverished children new skills. He's also exploring his love of drumming, photography and music much more, and so many of those characteristics are exactly the same as Owen had; a need for more in his life.

So, life goes on for Dylan Redman, but thoughts of Owen are never far away. I think Owen would be proud of his little brother, and the great things he's doing in his life. Dylan continues to chase up possible information about Owen, but it's getting harder. 'I've had that lead from Geelong so I'm thinking I might go and investigate it further; put up some posters and talk to the local media. I'm afraid to have hope anymore. Afraid to get my hopes up then have them dashed again.'

In 2017 Dylan and Owen's father John had a stroke, and then passed away in January 2020. Dylan and Fleur are on their own now, still looking for Owen.

Owen Redman is the kind of person who, even after spending a couple of hours on the phone with his brother talking about him in great depth, I still don't feel I know. He's quite an enigma, and every time I'd ask his brother Dylan a question, thinking I knew the answer, it would often come back as, 'No, he wasn't really like that.' Owen is an intelligent and complex man, and I really hope he's out there, reading these words.

Owen, it's not too late to reconnect with your brother. He's waited every day of his life since 1991 for the phone to ring. Please call him. He'll answer it, 'This is Dylan,' hoping that it's you on the other end.

If you have any information about the disappearance of Owen Redman please call Crimestoppers on 1800 333 000.

CHAPTER SEVEN
Andrew Anderson

Andrew Anderson, aged 21, was last seen in October 1990 in Valla, near Nambucca Heads, on the mid north coast of New South Wales.

Many of the stories you've read in this book start off with very happy, carefree, often idyllic childhoods. This is not such a story.

Barbara is the eldest child in the Anderson family and was born in Sydney. Both her parents were nurses before deciding to move to Nambucca Heads, on the NSW North Coast, when Barbara was six months old. After leaving nursing, their father worked for a company selling venetian blinds. Thirteen months later baby Shane came along, and he and Barbara remain close today. Andrew was born in 1969, then Scott came along 18 months later. All the boys were born in Macksville.

Big sister Barbara doted on them. 'It was expected that I'd look out for my younger brothers, in a big way,' Barbara says. 'Mum was the eldest, too, and had to look out for her own brothers and sisters, so that's what she instilled in me. And I did it, all through school and high school; if something went wrong, I had to be accountable to my parents for what my brothers did. I'd be the one to get into trouble because I hadn't looked after them. My parents were very hard on me. My father was a very big man, and he had this belt … honestly, it was four inches wide and very long, and when we got a flogging, the belt would come out. We copped a lot of that, we had a very hard upbringing.'

Despite this, Barbara says she loved her childhood, particularly when the family moved out to the farm. In 1973 they bought a piece of land in Valla, 10 kilometres north of Nambucca, and relocated an old house to the site. Over the years the family added extensions to it. Barbara loved living there, despite the lack of mod cons. 'We had an outhouse – we never had a septic,' she says. 'My brother had to do pan duty, when he was only about ten. There was a hole dug right down the back and that was his job, to empty the pans. We never had a bath or shower in the house; I used to bath the boys in the old laundry tub. The shower was a 44-gallon drum on top of the toilet, just cold water; that was the shower for years. We never had hot water; any hot water we wanted we had to boil in the old copper. At that stage Dad was selling earthmoving equipment, so he travelled from the Queensland border down to Newcastle. He was away a lot. Our first, and only, holiday was going with Dad to a sales conference in Rockhampton, so all our holiday photos are of us kids standing in front of these huge earthmoving machines.'

Sadly, Barbara has lost many of her childhood family photos – her mother destroyed them, for reasons unknown. Her mother also did not take photos of her children when they grew older. Barbara recalled this, and some other childhood memories, with bitterness. 'We weren't allowed to have any play time until I'd spit and polished all our black leather school shoes. I had to do the ironing, but I wasn't allowed to do Dad's work shirts. I had to wash Mum and Dad's cars. We all had jobs, but a lot of it was thrown back on me. I was a slave. We weren't game to say we were bored, or they'd find something for us to do. There was never any money. Dad worked long hours and was away a lot; we never had a phone, so when he went away there was no contact with him.'

Despite this, Barbara does fondly recall playing with her younger brothers. 'Having three younger brothers, I played Tonka trucks with them, and as we got older we got the old paddock bashers, flog fuel from Mum's mower and put it in and drive the cars around, dust flying – that's how we all learnt to drive. Andrew really loved Valiants. I loved that part of my life, the things we used to get up to. We built cubby houses, we'd swim in the waterhole, we saved up our pocket money and bought an aluminium punt boat and we'd row around the billabong. We'd roll down the hill inside old tractor tyres. I loved it, absolutely loved it. The highway was in front of us and the railway was behind us, so it was noisy, but we got used to it. We could also hear the ocean from the house. I had my own bedroom, and the boys all shared another one. We grew up living next to our three cousins and we'd all catch the bus home together. If there was trouble the driver would just order all the Andersons off the bus, all seven of us,' Barbara laughs.

The cousins all looked out for one another, and everyone knew everyone else in the surrounding district. Barbara says:

Valla wasn't very big in those days so when we wanted to go to the beach, we just went over the railway tracks. We just walked a couple of Ks into town to visit friends. If friends came out to the farm and stayed, they'd have to help us do our jobs before we were allowed to have any time to ourselves.

As we got older, Mum and Dad would go away visiting family and they'd leave me to look after the boys, often for three or four days at a time. I was only about 12, still at primary school. I had to get them out of bed, get them dressed, make them breakfast, make their lunches ... if one of them was sick I'd have to stay home and look after them and get the other two off to school on the bus. I'd then have to get them tea when they came home, get them bathed and in bed. It was hard. But I did it, right up until I left when I was 17. That was my responsibility; I was like a mother to them.

I nearly burned the house down once, trying to cook chips for my brothers. I can remember my brother running down the paddock to my aunty and uncle's house to get them to come and put the fire out on the stove. When Mum and Dad got home and saw the burned wall, we all got a flogging.

Barbara recounts this story in tears, reliving the horrible feelings she had as a child, but soon recovers with a sniff and a laugh. 'I'm in counselling now,' she says. 'I have been for years. I don't resent them. As an adult now, looking back, it would have been hard with Dad working the way he was, trying to provide a home and a roof over our heads.'

Barbara remembers little brother Andrew's childhood with fondness. 'Andy was good at school, in primary school. He got himself in a bit of strife in high school, all the boys did. He wasn't one to start a fight, but if there was a fight, he'd go in to defend someone. He wasn't a troublemaker. He was soft, compassionate and caring; he had a lot of feminine ways about him. As he got older, a lot of people thought he was gay, as he had a feminine side. Not like Shane and Scott, they're "what you see is what you get"; they're rough, tough blokey-blokes. But Andy was a bit of a mummy's boy; he and Mum were close. But I was also close to him. That's probably why Mum resented me, and said a lot of the things she did in the years after Andrew went missing.'

'Andrew *loved* duck eggs,' Barbara recalls with a smile. 'Growing up, we had chooks and ducks and geese, we had two pet emus, we had lambs, goats, potty calves – we were self-sufficient. Andrew would have two or three duck eggs at a feed. And Weet-

Bix – he started off with five Weet-Bix, then went up to eight, then ten ... Dad used to say: "I worked hard for that food, don't you waste it!" But Andrew would eat the lot. He went up to 12 Weet-Bix, and Mum had to get him a special bowl, the size of a fruit bowl. He ended up having 16 Weet-Bix every morning! He was so thin, but he was tall, and we were all very active.'

When Andrew was a teenager he didn't have much idea of what he wanted to do with his life when he left school. 'He was casual and carefree,' says Barbara. 'None of us never really had a lot of mates, just the people we grew up with, and Andrew didn't really have a best mate. I don't think Andrew ever brought a mate home; he'd rather clear out and go and see his mates, because of the way Dad was.'

Andrew left school after year 10 and went to work in the sawmill at Bowraville. He worked very hard and really enjoyed the work, and his boss thought he was fantastic. 'He'd come home covered in sap. After a while, you can't get that stuff out of your hands,' says Barbara. Andrew worked his way up at the sawmill to head benchman because he was a quick learner, and so good at what he did.

Their brother Scott also went to work at the mill, and they all continued to live at home. 'As soon as we'd get our pay, Mum would have her hand out, wanting board,' says Barbara. 'She took about half of it.'

When she was 17, Barbara left home. 'I was very keen to leave – very, very, *very* keen.'

She had started a truckie's base station, broadcasting from the house, at just 15 years of age. Her father had started the VRA – Volunteer Rescue Association – at Nambucca Heads.

Their website states the intent of the VRA is: 'Rescue from motor vehicles within Nambucca Shire. Rescue from rail, aircraft accidents, rescue from inland waterways. Lighting at emergency scenes. Searches for lost persons. Traffic control and event safety, and incident co-ordination. Domestic rescues. Industrial rescues.'

Little did Dan Anderson know that his own son would later become one of the lost persons his organisation dedicated itself to finding. As a result of her father's involvement, Barbara learned radio operations and used this to assist truckies by giving them road updates. She absolutely loved it, and still keeps in touch with many of the people she met via the CB radio. When Barbara was 17 she 'met' a truckie over the radio and seized the opportunity to leave home to be with him. She explains why she was so desperate to get away from her family:

The situation at home was that I was getting beaten. My brothers were, too, by our father. We were starting to become independent, become our own people; we had our licences and jobs and friends, and the jobs around the house weren't getting done like they used to be. We were getting a bit slack and not pulling our weight. But then, Mum was taking half our pay packets.

We'd talk back to Dad, stick up for ourselves, and Mum would blame us for things, and that would set Dad off. We'd all get a flogging. I had black eyes; it was getting serious. The boys started to fight back. My brother pushed Dad over once, and then cleared out for two days. I had to stay at home until I got married; I wasn't allowed to live with my fiancé before then, and the week before I got married, my father got me in the kitchen and started kicking me, over and over.

I saw my fiancé as a chance to get out. I did love him, but that was my chance, as I had nowhere else to go. I felt bad about leaving the boys there at home; Andrew was living in a caravan down the back and the boys were in the house. I think Andrew didn't leave because he was a mummy's boy. He just took every day as it came, didn't plan for anything. He was so soft and gentle; he was so caring. He'd always come and give me a hug, and you'd feel the love in the hug.

After Barbara left home, the only family member she kept in touch with was Andrew. The home had no phone, so she could not speak to her other brothers. Barbara was no longer on speaking terms with her parents after a disagreement; Barbara had been involved in a car accident a couple of years previously and had been badly injured. She was awarded a compensation payout, and when the money was awarded to her, her parents demanded half. Barbara's new husband told them firmly they were not getting a cent, and as a result Barbara and her parents stopped speaking. Her parents sent her several letters via a solicitor demanding the payment, which was refused. She didn't see her parents again for more than a year, but Andrew had regularly visited Barbara.

Andrew had a few girlfriends, and when he was about 17 he was living with one of them in the caravan on his parents' property. He'd built an extension onto the van, like a small flat. Barbara recalls the girl as being 'absolutely gorgeous' and recalls she wasn't from the local area; she wasn't sure how Andrew had met her. The relationship eventually dissolved, and they amicably went their separate ways. Years after Andrew disappeared, the girl would still visit Andrew's parents. Barbara remembers one time Andrew was in the caravan with his girlfriend. Under the van was a hen nesting on eggs, and Andrew knew there was a fox in the area. Andy heard the fox under the van and ran outside, stark naked, brandishing a shotgun. The commotion roused the rest of the family, who all ran outside to find Andrew, in the nude, chasing the fox with a chicken in its mouth, down the paddock. This is one of Barbara's favourite memories of her brother, but she recalls this story with tears. She misses him terribly.

It was around this time that Barbara thinks Andrew started to become involved with the wrong people:

Andy would hang around with some mates who were older than him, who had a bit of influence over him. That's when Andrew got a bit sidetracked and caught up in their stuff. He was about 17 and had just got his licence. They were into drugs, and he was easily influenced. He'd never done that before. He smoked a bit of hooch, and the other guys were growing it, and he was helping them grow it. I had a feeling at the time this was going on, but I didn't find out until later. It did worry me. I tried to warn him off one guy; I said, 'What are you doing mixing with him?' But he'd tell me he was a mate, and it was okay.

When his aunt and uncle moved to Cabramatta in Sydney, Andrew would travel down to visit them frequently. This was about a year before he went missing. Shortly before he went missing, he was spending more and more time in Sydney. Their grandparents moved to the family property in Valla, from Sydney, and although Barbara was still not on speaking terms with her parents, she would visit specifically to see her grandparents, and to see Andrew. 'My kids adored Uncle Andy,' says Barbara. 'They loved Shane and "Uncle Stott", too, but Andrew was always there, and the kids would run up to him.'

Andrew turned 21 in March 1990, and at the time was living part of the time in the caravan at home and sometimes with mates in Nambucca Heads. He was still working at the sawmill in Bowraville. Barbara was living with her husband, not in contact with her parents and was not able to see her brother as often as she'd like, so was not immediately aware that Andrew had gone missing. She realised that it had been months since he'd contacted her, so she asked her mother where he was. Her mother told her she had not seen Andrew in some time. Barbara says:

I knew when Andrew went missing that he hadn't just packed up and moved away. I knew there was something wrong. I knew straightaway. I said to Mum and Dad, 'Have you heard from Andrew?' and Mum said he was fine, that he'd gone away to Queensland or whatever, he'll be back. They said he'd gone on a holiday and not to worry about him.

It took me about 18 months to convince my parents to report him missing. I'd tried myself to contact Missing Persons Unit, but because I wasn't his next of kin, they wouldn't take the report from me. They said it had to come from Mum and Dad. I'd beg them to contact Missing Persons but Mum always said no, that Andrew was fine. I asked them if they'd heard from him at all, they said no. Mum said the last time she'd seen him was October 1990.

Barbara didn't believe for a moment that Andrew had simply gone on holiday; she is certain he would have called in to see her and told her in person what his plans were. He would have also told his aunt in Sydney, who he was very close to, and his cousin Mark. Barbara started to have suspicions of her own, knowing there had always been violence in the house. She has not voiced these concerns, until now.

'I had a feeling,' she says. 'I wondered if they'd had something to do with it? Or maybe there was an accident.' However, Barbara was having troubles of her own, coping with her marriage falling apart and three young children. It all became too much for her, combined with her brother's mysterious disappearance and her parents' unwillingness to report him missing, and Barbara had a nervous breakdown. She found herself in hospital, with no support from her family.

Finally, after 18 months, their parents reported Andrew to police as a missing person. Barbara did not give up her campaign to force them to do something to find Andrew. Despite her own fragile mental state, Barbara searched tirelessly for her brother and begged people to help her. 'I wrote letters to everyone – *The Midday Show*, John Laws, Ray Martin, magazines like *New Idea, Women's Weekly* – I sent his photo to all of them. I was going on the possibility that he did go away on holiday or started a new life.'

As well as suspecting her own family, Barbara was concerned about the marijuana-growing mates of Andrew's, and whether they may have harmed him. By this stage, some of them had convictions for serious violent crimes. Andrew's parents said he left the farm in his early model white Ford Falcon sedan, but it was later discovered that the car had been sold by one of Andrew's mates, who claimed Andrew had owed him money. This man has been extensively investigated by police as a suspect in Andrew's disappearance.

Despite her belief that her brother had come to harm, Barbara still held out the faintest hope that he might still be alive:

One day I was shopping in Woolworths and there was a guy going through the checkout next to me. He looked like Andrew. I must have been staring at him and he started to look back at me; I was thinking, 'Oh my God, it looks like Andrew!' I started to leave but I thought, bugger it, I'm going to say something to this guy. I went up to him and said, 'Look, please don't think I'm rude, but you look so much like my brother.' He said that was cool, and asked where my brother was. I told him my brother was missing. He felt terrible. He'd originally felt good that he reminded me of my brother, until he heard that. He said, 'I'm sorry I'm not your brother.'

I'd drive down the street, looking at every person walking along, trying to find him. I'd go to Macksville and Nambucca, walk down the streets, looking for him in crowds. I was just possessed. I was obsessed with wanting to find him. That's how I became.

Barbara went home to her parents' farm and discreetly searched the property for any sign of Andrew being there. 'Growing up, we had an orange Leyland P76. I remember one night, at about one o'clock in the morning, I saw lights out where the car was parked. I remember being so scared that I got on my hands and knees on the floor and crawled into Mum and Dad's room, woke them up and said there was someone outside. The next day, the car was gone. About two years later, the boys came and got me and said they wanted to show me something. We walked down the back of the property and there's the P76, in the scrub, with tree branches all over it. So, I did think it was possible that Andrew was hidden somewhere on the property too.'

Even after the Andersons finally reported Andrew as missing, his father, Dan, remained unconcerned. He and his wife still maintained to police that Andrew had just gone on holiday. Barbara tried to find out from her parents what was being done in the search for Andrew, but her father would just tell her to ring the police. The Andersons did go to the Missing Persons Unit open day in Sydney, where Barbara's father introduced himself to police saying, 'Hi, I'm Big Dan.' He told them all he'd started the VRA in Nambucca Heads. 'He was no saint, though,' says Barbara. 'He got up to stuff. He liked to big-note himself.' Their original police contact in Missing Persons Unit in Sydney sadly passed away, so the case was taken over by another police officer. Barbara says police did try to investigate, but kept coming up with nothing.

'Roger Climpson did a piece about Andrew on his show.[1] There was also an American show[2] on TV that included a minute or so of photos of Australian missing persons, and Andrew was on there too.'

'I had to do all that because Mum and Dad wouldn't do

---

1 *Australia's Most Wanted*, hosted by Climpson, 1997–1999.
2 *Cold Case*, which aired from 2003–2010.

anything. I just wanted to find my little brother,' Barbara says, her voice breaking with emotion. 'I wanted to know where my little brother was.'

Barbara felt that when the police investigation ceased, she had to keep going, and for years kept trying to get the media interested. I have had Andrew on my website for more than 18 years now. Most of the cases on my site have multiple photos and several news articles to give a better picture of the circumstances surrounding the disappearance, but Andrew's page only has a few lines, and just one black and white photograph. It was all I could find.

'That photo is one I took of Andrew nursing my son when he was six months old, it was in early 1990. When I look at that photo, I see a very proud uncle.' Heartbreakingly, Barbara no longer has this photograph. The police took the print and never returned it, and she cannot find the negative.

'I think he was wearing a Billabong singlet top in that photo. When the SES went looking, a while after he went missing, they found that shirt. It was among the evidence we had to go and identify. They found it in one of the areas they used to grow the marijuana. There were ammo tins, food, a blanket from home, a cane knife that was Dad's, and clothing, football socks. Mum always bought the boys football socks for Christmas, and Mum and Dad identified them as belonging to Andrew. They took cadaver dogs through, as they thought there'd been foul play. That was out near Thora, halfway between Dorrigo and Bellingen.' The picturesque locality is around 40 minutes' drive from Valla. Barbara gave the police other photos of her brother when he went missing, but she does not know what became of these.

I often feature Andrew on my AMPR Facebook page, where it is seen by hundreds of thousands of people. The last time I posted his photo, Barbara was contacted by several people, all claiming to know what happened to Andrew:

One lady contacted me, and said her friend had heard about a conversation directly from a man who confessed that he'd murdered Andrew. That's all been given to the police, and police have interviewed them all, but some of them were too scared to say what happened; they were fearful of what this man might do to their families. But that man's dead now, so all those witnesses don't need to be scared of making statements any more. I want the police to go back and talk to all those people again. They didn't want to do anything, they said, 'Oh, we can't go back,' but I said, 'Look, the situation's changed, this man is dead!' That's why I asked you to put the photo up, because I thought with that man now dead, it might be in people's minds, and they'd be prepared to come forward and say what happened. I also had a lady contact me with information that Andy's body was in 'treacherous country' at Thora, but that statement had already been given to police. A bloke I went to school with told me he'd run into a guy who had a thumb in a jar. He told my friend that it was Andrew's.

There was a coronial inquest into Andrew's disappearance in 1997 which lasted for a week. Barbara was startled to be called as a witness, as police had told her she'd only need to provide a statement. She was asked by the coroner when her last contact with Andrew was, and whether she had identified Andrew's recovered belongings that were being held at Macksville police station. She identified a shirt that was found as being the same one Andrew was wearing in the photograph she had given to police. Two persons of interest were named by police at the inquest, one of them being the man who sold the car. Andrew also reportedly owed money to another man for a stereo he had bought. The stereo, a microwave and a television were all seized by Macksville police under the suspicion they were stolen goods, and that Andrew had stolen them. The items were eventually returned to Andrew's parents.

'I told Mum and Dad I wanted something of my brother's, as I had nothing,' says Barbara, 'So, I got the microwave, and I had that for years and years. What really annoyed me, though, was there were so many people who knew stuff but weren't involved in the inquest. The police just skimmed on the outside, and didn't delve any deeper, they didn't say they wanted other people to come up as witnesses. They only had people who had heard stuff, but no-one that really knew definitely. One guy at the inquest said he'd heard that Andrew was in the bush, and had done this and that, and had heard Andrew was on his hands and knees, and that someone had shot him in the head. That made that thought go through my head, Andrew begging for his life and the man standing over him laughing. That scenario went through my mind for years and years. There was another rumour that the man was going to cut off Andrew's ear to show everyone that he'd done him in. I've heard lots of little bits and pieces of stories over the years.'

Ultimately, the coroner found that Andrew Anderson was

likely deceased, and a likely victim of homicide by persons unknown. Barbara's parents sold their property and bought a smaller home elsewhere. 'I always thought they were trying to distance themselves from the house … if Andrew was buried there,' says Barbara ominously. The property has never been searched by police or SES in the hunt for Andrew, which is curious considering it was his last confirmed location. 'Mum was always resentful of me, didn't understand why I was upset, she would say, "He's *my* son, what are you so upset about?" She said it quite a few times. We didn't speak properly for years.'

To get through the difficulties in her life, Barbara says she's lived for her kids. Barbara was married a second time, which only lasted six months. After the marriage failed, she concentrated on her children and devoted herself to their upbringing. Then Barbara met Al, who she regards as the love of her life. However, Barbara has continued to face tragedy in her life since Andrew disappeared, with her much-loved partner Al's death. Her grief at his loss made it almost impossible for her to continue her campaign for information about Andrew.

'I did go through counselling when we lost Andy and my marriage broke down, and the difficult childhood I had was brought up – I know it was hard on me,' says Barbara. 'When I started getting messages on Facebook from people about Andy, I said to them that it was just too much for me, could they please contact the police. It's been more than 30 years. I won't ever give up on him, and I said to my daughter Stacey that if anything ever happens to me, and I pass away, if anything ever comes up with Andrew, will she follow through with it, and she said yes.' Tragically, that will never happen. Barbara's life of tragedy has continued, with the death of her beloved daughter Stacey from breast cancer in November 2022.

In October 2015, on the day I finished writing Andrew's chapter, I messaged Barbara to let her know it was finished; I wanted to send it to her so she could check it was accurate. She messaged back to say that her father had just died. She, understandably, has mixed emotions about this – he was a hard man who hurt her terribly throughout her life, but he was still her dad. Her mum also passed away in June 2020. 'I've lost my aunt and uncle; my cousin Mark was killed in a car accident not long after Andrew disappeared; his younger brother Glen hung himself; my grandparents have died – all of them not knowing,' says Barbara. 'I imagine them all up in heaven, with Andrew, catching up with each other and looking down on me. We may never find his body. I've got nowhere to go and visit his grave.'

Barbara will never give up searching for her little brother, who she says didn't deserve whatever violence befell him. 'He was so soft. In the end, he was easily influenced, or trying to keep in with the crew, the cool crowd. I don't know why he got tied up with them, whether he owed them money, or they had something on Andrew. Maybe he knew something and threatened to go to the police. I just don't know. But I know there are people out there who know what happened to him. I really wish these detectives would investigate all this further and get statements from all these people. They should. Now that [the main suspect] is dead, they've got nothing to be scared of. Just tell us the truth.'

So, what really happened to Andrew Anderson? Did his

choice of friends ultimately lead to his murder? Was it his thumb in that jar? Is he buried in the bush at Thora? Or does the answer lie closer to home? Did Big Dan take secrets to the grave with him? Or did he die never knowing what happened to his boy? Surely, Barbara has endured enough pain. Surely someone can tell her what happened to her brother?

If you know what happened, please come forward and tell police what you know. You can remain anonymous if you wish. Call 1800 333 000.

CHAPTER EIGHT
Jamie Howe

Jamie Howe, aged 29, was last seen around the Leichhardt and
Glebe areas in Sydney on 27 March, 1987.

There are big families. Then there's the Howe family. One of an astonishing *eighteen* children, Jamie Howe grew up in a large, proudly Catholic family, with lots of brothers and sisters. The kids were Brian, Peter, Gavin, Martin, Judy, Bobby, Dorothy, John, Kathy, Jenny, Gregory, Barry, Adrian, Vernon, Jamie, Elaine, Roslyn and Alan. Tragically, Roslyn died as a baby. The family was so large that 11 of the boys formed their own hockey team in the 1980s, and the Winfield cigarette company used them to promote their catchphrase, 'Anyhow, have a Winfield', changing the first words to 'Any HOWE'. Their mother, Mollie, was a nurse before she married, and their father Jim was a technical officer with the Postmaster-General's department, later Telecom, then Telstra. Jamie also later worked for Telecom.

The family lived in Forest Lodge, a small suburb near Glebe, in inner city Sydney. Arundel Street is filled with beautiful terrace houses that now sell for millions, but back in the sixties and seventies, when Jamie Howe grew up there, it was a very different story, with the Howe family having to somehow find room for 19 people. The suburb dates back to 1836, and Arundel Street holds great historical significance for Sydney. In 1794, Arundel Street was where Parramatta Road crossed Orphan School Creek, just 24 years after Captain Cook landed at Botany Bay.

Jamie went to Marcellin College in Randwick, a Marist Brothers school. 'He was very good at school,' says his sister Judy. 'He was very popular. He was well behaved at school, but not so much after he left. He did well in the Higher School Certificate.'

Elaine is two years younger than Jamie, but their birthdays are only one day apart. 'I considered myself his birthday present,' she jokes. 'When he was at school he'd get into trouble from our father, because he didn't do his homework. We got on really well. Growing up, he was my closest sibling. As teenagers, we mixed in the same circles, and we were both leaders in Young Catholic Students, he was the president for a while. We went to the same parties, we knew each other's friends really well. After we left school, we moved in different circles. I got married and had kids, and he was single and hung out with our brothers a lot more. He was a groomsman at my wedding.' The photo of Jamie that appears on his missing person posters was from Elaine's wedding.

'I'm the lucky one – number 13 in the order,' says Adrian in jest. 'When we were kids we had tons of happy times. We used to have adventures with each other and play in the streets.' Adrian laughs as he recalls one particular memory. 'As kids, we picked up this stray dog. We weren't allowed to keep it, so we were searching for somewhere for it to stay; we'd take scraps to it every day, and hang out with it. We tried to put it into a cubby house that we had, and a shed, but nowhere was suitable. We went to this block of flats near our house, and we knew it had a little storage room. We'd always be exploring buildings – the streets were our playground. We were left to our own devices a lot. We had some meat that was pretty off, and we took it for the dog. This fellow who lived in the flats saw us and chased us, and we bolted for our lives. I was going okay, but my friend and Jamie were behind me. The guy caught us and asked us what we were doing. We told him about the dog, and he found the rancid piece of meat in our bag, and he must have thought we were street urchins, down there eating the meat ourselves.'

Vernon loved their childhood together: 'We'd go and play handball up against the wall in the carpark up the road. We'd play pinball with our hockey mates. We'd go to Jubilee Oval, where we played hockey and touch footy. We got on our pushbikes with hockey sticks and pretend the bikes were horses and the hockey sticks were swords, and we'd joust with one another. A little bit dangerous, but it was fun. We rode billycarts, that we made ourselves, down the steep hill. We'd go around to the factories collecting bottles, because they were worth five cents each. That was mainly me and Jamie. Our living conditions were crazy, but we had some of our friends sleep over because it was like a party; it was fun sleeping at the Howes' house. Mum and Dad would tell us to go out and come back when it was dark. We had a free rein. But we didn't do anything wrong … much,' he says with a laugh.

Adrian and Jamie were three years apart in age, and were always very close. 'Our family were all in little groups, so you hung out with the ones in your age band,' says Adrian. 'So, me, Vernon and Jamie were pretty tight. Jamie was very outgoing, happy and cheerful as a child. He liked to follow his big brothers, as he wanted to be like them. He liked to be part of the family's forays, and share their morals. He was a nice kid, had plenty of friends. We played lots of different sports together.'

Elaine recalls Jamie as being a sweet and sensitive boy. 'Growing up, we'd plan birthday parties together, and how we could save up our money, what we were going to cook and who we'd have there. But we never had a birthday party. That was so typical of him, he was always dreaming.'

Adrian remembers fun times at Christmas with their extended family. 'My father was one of 14, so we have lots of aunties and uncles in the country. At Christmas we'd take a train trip down there with no parental supervision, then we'd all get picked up at the train station by various people and be taken off to one of the cousins' places. Jamie and Vernon went on this train trip, and a few of the others, and we'd take over a compartment and lie on all the seats so no adults would come in there. It was about a 24-hour trip. Me, Vernon and Jamie were all taken to the same family farm and we'd spend six weeks there with our cousins. They were really good memories. I actually can't think of any bad memories; we never clashed.'

Growing up in a house with 16 brothers and sisters was a challenge for the Howe kids. 'It was noisy,' says Judy frankly. 'And so crowded. We had good times and bad times, the usual arguments in families, but they all played together. Dad was strict and Mum was a softie. They had their rules, and we had to stick to them.' Judy remembers when Jamie was confirmed into the church. 'I was Elaine's sponsor, and Barry was Jamie's sponsor. I remember it was lovely just seeing him on that day, giving him a little gift and seeing how happy he was. He was just such a sweet little boy. He was very sweet as an adult too.' Elaine has posted the most beautiful photo of herself and Jamie on Facebook: a black and white photo of an adorable little blond boy and a pretty little girl in pigtails, with identical Howe smiles. Among the comments are Elaine saying, 'He was my best mate when we were kids,' and sister Dorothy saying that she misses him and she's glad they can share their feelings. She says, 'I love to see his photos, but it's also very sad.'

All the Howe kids started playing hockey from about the age of six. Jamie also played rugby league and cricket. He played hockey all his life, and it was one of his great loves. The Glebe Hockey Club website says that Jamie played 249 games for them. At the time of his disappearance Jamie was coaching the under 11s junior team, the five to nine year age group. 'He was very good at it,' says Judy. The 1977 Glebe Hockey Club newsletter mentions Jamie was selected in the Sydney Colts A side to play in the NSW State Championships. The whole family was involved with the club, and still is to this day. In its almost 90-year history, Glebe Hockey Club has elected just 39 life members. Four of those are from the Howe family.

Death struck Jamie's life more than once before he was out of his teens. Jamie had a childhood friend, Michael, whose family were all close to the Howes. When he was about 18, Michael tragically drowned in a backyard pool. 'That was devastating for Jamie,' says Elaine. 'There were another two boys from the youth club who we were close to, who grew up with us in Glebe. They took a drive to the south coast and went missing. They eventually found their car, that had gone over a cliff. They only retrieved one of their bodies. Soon after, another of Jamie's friends from hockey died when he was struck by a car. Within a couple of years, he had four close friends die. They were massive events.'

I mentioned to Elaine that, particularly in relation to the two boys in the car, Jamie would have known exactly how it felt to have someone you were close to go missing, and it seems unlikely he'd deliberately choose to do the same thing to his friends and family.

After leaving school, Jamie remained living in the area close to his family. He shared a house in Leichhardt with one of his brothers and a friend, and got a job with Telecom, as a linesman. 'He didn't like sitting in an office,' says Judy. 'He loved being outside, so he enjoyed being a linesman. He loved going to the beach, and playing hockey.'

But Elaine says Jamie never really settled down. 'He'd get excited about things, and then lose interest,' she says. Several of the family became teachers, and Vernon wonders whether that played on Jamie's mind. 'I ended up going to uni and getting a good job,' he says. 'I don't know whether he was ever jealous of that. Sometimes I think, maybe. But I think he just wanted a steady job.' Elaine has a different perspective about what Jamie was really like. 'He was an idealist,' she says, after a moment of reflection. 'Everybody loved him, and he was lovely to everybody, but he was a bit quiet, and insecure. Vernon and Adrian were better at sports, better at school, really popular … Jamie was popular too, but he was a bit quieter and although he was good, he was not quite as good as them at sport and school. I don't think he was envious of them, and he certainly didn't articulate that, but I think he felt a bit inferior to the other boys. Those two in particular.'

Vernon echoed this word for word when I spoke to him. 'I think he looked up to me. A lot of people thought we were twins because I was small and he was big, even though he was 18 months younger than me. When we were younger I was faster, I got into rep. hockey teams – he did, too, but I got into bigger ones. I played higher grades than him, but then he started playing high as well. I was very lucky that girls liked me and I had a lot of girlfriends … He did too, but for me, it was really easy. When I was at school I got really good marks and he wasn't bad, he did okay, but he was average. I was more low key than him. Life was a bit harder for him. I think our father got more cranky with him than me; I was the goody-goody but Jamie talked back, he was strong willed. I never had a problem with him, though. We had a bit of a push-around maybe twice, once when we were only 13, and one other time he wouldn't give me a turn on a pub Pong machine. But that was it. I felt a bit uncomfortable because he was struggling financially and I wasn't. I didn't mind shouting him things here and there.'

'He was popular with women, and he was quite a nice-looking fellow, he had the blond, curly hair,' says Judy. 'He had quite a few girlfriends, some of them longer term. He had one serious girl, but that was over quite a few years before his disappearance. At the time he went missing, he wasn't in a relationship.' Judy believes Jamie would have made a good dad. 'He was always really good with little kids. All his nieces and nephews loved him. He was a bit of a magnet for small children.'

Adrian says that their relationship was as friends as well as brothers, and that applied to the whole family. 'He was well liked by us all. He would come to my place and help paint, or whatever,' he says. 'The same with the rest of the family, he'd often go to someone's place after hockey and have a barbeque. We used to hang out on weekends and after work. His friends were my friends, too.'

Vernon remembers he and his brother once dating the same girl:

There was this really pretty barmaid at the Toxteth who I started dating. I had to go back to the bush, but I came home on weekends to see her, she was really pretty. A month or two later I got a phone call from Jamie, to tell me he'd been taking her out. I said, 'Well, it doesn't bother me, because I've got a girl out here in the country, and I can't have two relationships, so enjoy.' It was nice that she liked both of us. Then when I did get back to Sydney, she wanted to go out with me again. In the end she moved to Melbourne, and I think that hurt Jamie a bit. I was a player before I met my wife, in about 1983. But he had plenty of girls too.

Jamie was a regular in the pubs around Glebe, and would often drink too much. He began to have problems caused by his drinking. 'He might have got into fights because of it,' says Judy. 'The hockey players used to go to the Toxteth pub in Glebe. Although I never actually saw him drunk, other family members would tell me about it. Some of them were concerned. I'd hear it through the grapevine. You wouldn't look at him and think, *That guy's a drinker.* He definitely wasn't an alcoholic; he was able to get up and go to work every day, and play hockey. He didn't drink every day but when he drank, it was sometimes to excess.'

Elaine was not really aware of Jamie's heavy drinking. 'I never really saw that side of him,' she says. 'I don't ever recall seeing him crazy drunk. Looking back, there was a time when he was splitting up with his girlfriend and we were at a party, and he could get a bit mean if he'd been drinking, but I think he was just upset about the breakup.'

However, Vernon saw a different side to Jamie than he showed his sisters. He saw Jamie get into trouble when he was drinking:

There was one night when Jamie got into a fight. He was drunk, and in a different part of the pub that we normally don't drink in. He used to approach girls a little bit differently to me, because he'd be a bit more forceful; if a girl walked past he might grab her arm. I think he did that to this particular girl, and her boyfriend was there. The boyfriend told him not to, and Jamie got into a fight with him. Jamie ended up on the floor with the bloke on top of him, belting him. Our brother Greg, who was a bit of a bluer, went out there to help Jamie, but one of their friends smashed a glass and told Greg to stay out of it. There were two-bit crims, in the other bar.

These 'two-bit crims' would be talked about again, after Jamie's disappearance.

One night after a drinking session at the pub, Jamie drove a Telecom work vehicle home. He had an accident in the car, and because he had been drinking, he was responsible for all the damage to the vehicle. This caused him considerable financial hardship, as he was paying back the money he owed for years. Jamie's wages were being garnished in order to pay his debt, leaving him very little to live on. He frequently struggled to find his rent money. Jamie's money issues were compounded when he developed an interest in gambling.

'I think he was gambling to try to get himself out of a hole,' says Adrian. 'A few of the brothers were into card games at the pub. They were a bit like the first poker machines. Lots of the young men would gamble some of their money away, but Jamie got himself into trouble with that as well. There's a temptation to try and win your way out of debt, but you get yourself in a bigger hole.'

Vernon, however, doesn't think Jamie's gambling was a serious problem. 'People said he had a punt, and he did, but every time I saw him punt it was very minimal, like trifectas and stuff like that, which don't cost much. Back then, there weren't that many meetings to bet on, not like today. It was harder to be addicted. I didn't see him gambling much, so I don't think it was a big issue. He only played the pokies every now and again. He might just put $5 in there, in 20 cent pieces; we'd do it together for a bit of fun. He'd never win. I just did not see him as a gambler.'

'He was hopeless with money,' says Elaine:

He was really generous with money, as well. He'd always be the first one to buy people a drink or loan them money. I never experienced him gambling. I had no idea his situation was so bad; he hid that from me, and he would have felt ashamed. It would have reinforced those feelings of inferiority and not living up to expectations. He never asked me for money.

Judy also says Jamie never asked her for money nor told her of his financial difficulties. Jamie did, however, owe money to other family members. He owed money to the brother he was sharing a house with, and this brother covered Jamie's rent for him on more than one occasion. 'Jamie would have felt bad about it, but he probably couldn't help himself,' Judy says. 'But he had a conscience.'

Jamie and his brothers and their families planned trips to Canada and New Zealand to play hockey. Adrian recalls he and Jamie were roommates on the trip to New Zealand. Jamie went on the Canada trip just a few years before he went missing. 'It probably wasn't a great idea to go on that holiday,' says Adrian, fearing it contributed greatly to Jamie's financial stresses. 'I knew he was broke,' says Vernon, and remembers Jamie having yet another car accident around this time. 'I lent him my car to drive to work one night, and he wrote it off. It wasn't insured. He'd been trying to get money to go to Canada for the hockey trip and he said, "Look, I'll give you that money for the car, I just won't go to Canada." It was an old car and it didn't cost that much anyway, so I told him not to worry about it. But that might have been on his mind. I didn't want him to *not* go to Canada.'

Jamie's income had been severely restricted by the work vehicle payments, so he needed a bank loan to afford to go on the trip to Canada. Judy says, 'Our brother Peter was a bank manager, and organised the loan for him, but that was not repaid, so when he disappeared Peter ended up getting that written off. The two major financial problems he had were the bank loan, and having to pay back the money for the vehicle repairs. I think his total debt was around $10,000. To him, that might have been overwhelming, who knows? But even at that time, it wasn't insurmountable. He was working, and had an average wage.'

The police statement later presented at the inquest refers to Jamie's loan for the Canada trip, and states Jamie struggled to meet his repayments, so the loan had to be restructured. Peter told police he believed Jamie was under financial pressure at this time.

Adrian says that after Jamie went missing, the family asked around and realised the true extent of their brother's debts:

You'd see someone you hadn't seen for a while, a friend of a friend, and ask them if they'd heard from Jamie. I remember one particular time I asked this fellow and he said, 'No, I haven't seen Jamie, but I want to see him because he owes me money. If you see him, can you make sure he comes back and pays me?' I saw another guy that we grew up with, who told me Jamie owed him money too, and he wasn't Jamie's best mate or anything, so it was even more people than we thought. We didn't go around to all his friends asking, 'Did Jamie owe you money?' We didn't even ask within the family. If he'd borrowed money from friends, chances are they've said, 'Oh, well, we'll just write that off' or they'd wait until the next time they saw him.

Elaine believes Jamie would have hated being in this position, of owing money to many people. 'He would have been anxious, and covering up,' says Elaine. 'He was naturally sensitive, so it would have been affecting him, for sure.'

Judy, too, thinks Jamie would have hated owing his family money:

He would have felt terrible. He definitely would have felt ashamed and embarrassed, he was that sort of person. Peter would have believed Jamie was going to pay the bank loan back. He might have spoken to Jamie about it, but I can't see that he would have come down on him. He would have been more concerned about him personally.

Elaine sees a difference between the brothers and sisters in her family, with the brothers keeping certain things between themselves. 'The boys in our family are kind of like that – there's a cone of silence, they don't dob on each other. They protect each other. Often the girls wouldn't hear about what was going on in their lives. If anyone had told me Jamie was having financial problems, for sure I would have tried to help him.'

Vernon says there were so many members of the family that if everyone had been aware of the problems Jamie was having, they could have all contributed just a small amount each and probably fixed it.

'None of us had a lot of money,' says Elaine. 'I was young and married with little kids, so I wouldn't have been able to fish him out of serious problems by myself, but it would have taken very little from all of us.'

Adrian believes Jamie's debts were far worse than anyone realised. 'I think he borrowed money from *this* person to pay *that* person, to pay *this* debt,' he says. 'I think he got himself into a bit of trouble with a bunch of people, not just the two official debts. I think he owed quite a few people money. He found it hard to make ends meet. He came over to my house one weekend and was helping me do some painting and renovation. I asked him if he was going out and he said he just didn't have the money to do it.'

On the day Jamie went missing – Friday 27 March 1987 – he was last seen by a workmate, who gave him a lift home from work when he finished, at about 4.30 pm. Where exactly Jamie was dropped off is unclear, as this workmate was never interviewed by police as far as the family are aware, and he is not mentioned anywhere in the inquest documents or police statements. The police statement says this workmate's name is unknown, but the family knows the man well, so it appears they were never asked by police if they knew him.

According to the NSW Police missing person appeal, his work colleague dropped him at a bus stop at Ashfield, although this is further west than Jamie lived and Ashfield is not mentioned in the inquest documents. Jamie had never owned a car, so usually travelled by public transport, and occasionally received a lift from colleagues and friends. Elaine believes Jamie was actually dropped off at his home in Leichhardt. The work colleague who dropped Jamie off that day was the friend of a hockey player from their club; Vernon says he's a really nice bloke. He agrees with Elaine and thinks Jamie may have been dropped off on the corner of Elswick and Marion streets in Leichhardt. We know on that same afternoon Jamie withdrew $50 from an ATM at Broadway, about 5 kilometres from his house in Elswick Street, Leichhardt. After withdrawing the cash at Broadway, Jamie vanished.

He was due to coach the under 11s hockey team the following morning, a Saturday. When he didn't turn up for this, the alarm bells started to ring among some members of the Howe family. Jamie loved coaching, and had never let the kids down. When they realised Jamie didn't arrive for training on Saturday some of the family, at their usual Saturday night get-together, discussed the situation around the table.

'There were disagreements about what to do,' says Judy:

We had a lot of people with a lot of different opinions, but majority ruled. Some of us wanted to go to the police and some of us didn't. They thought maybe he'd gone off with a girlfriend or something, and would be embarrassed to have the police turn up. Maybe he'd gone for a night out and spent the weekend with a girl, because he was very popular with women. I don't know whether he'd done that before, but it wasn't beyond the realms of possibility for him to do something like that.

Some of us thought we should give it a few days before we did anything. So, we asked around, all the hockey players and different people, but no-one had seen him, and after a few days it became obvious that he was missing. I was one of the ones who wanted to go to the police straightaway. Another sister felt the same; we were concerned from the start. But the rest of the brothers probably knew him better than we did, and they said give it a few days.

The crunch came on the Monday, when he didn't turn up for work. That's when my father went to the police. My parents were very worried. At the time I was really worried too. I just didn't know what to think. I thought maybe he'd had an accident, or something's happened to him ... why hasn't he turned up? It seemed to me to be so out of character. He was so family oriented. Even if he'd gone off with a girl, not to contact somebody, and not to turn up at junior hockey, or senior men's hockey later, and not contact anyone to say he couldn't make it – that immediately rang alarm bells for me.

Elaine was not at this family meeting, but says if she had been, she would have insisted they did more than wait.

Their brother Adrian was also very concerned from the start: 'He wasn't the type of person to go missing,' he says. 'I was really surprised. There was always a lot of contact with a lot of people, lots of contact with his family. He was very regular; he went to work every day, he didn't have irregular patterns in his life.'

'The last time I saw him was at hockey training on the Wednesday night,' says Vernon. 'I think we were in the same team that night. After training we had a beer at our hockey club, which was just an archway under a railway bridge, and then I went up to the Toxteth Hotel. The weekend before I'd lent him $20, and I was really broke, so I asked him that night, "Have you got that $20?" He said, "I haven't, really," but his friend said to me, "I'll give it to you." So, he gave it to me, for Jamie. That was the last time I saw him. Jamie was very thankful and polite, and said to his friend he'd make sure he got it back.' Vernon doesn't think the exchange was embarrassing for Jamie. 'We used to have a culture of lending each other money and shouting drinks at the hockey club or the pub. So, it was no drama if someone said, "Can you lend me $20?" And $20 was more then than it is now. He was fine that night. We trained hard. We met up at the pub, he got a lift up there. He was in a good mood. On the Saturday, I was supposed to play hockey with him that afternoon, but he didn't turn up.'

Vernon answers with an adamant 'Nope!' when I asked if he was immediately concerned about Jamie when he failed to show:

Because sometimes people don't turn up to their sport. I know I did it, if I'd been out with someone the night before. I just thought he was hung over, or with someone having a fun time. I didn't have any concern at all. I was living in Newtown with my other brother and I went around to my parents' place on the Monday, and Adrian's wife said, 'Vernon, where's Jamie?' as soon as I walked into the house, assuming I knew where he was. I asked, 'What do you mean?' They said he hadn't been heard of since Friday, and I said I didn't know, that I hadn't seen him. I knew he hadn't turned up for hockey, but I wasn't worried about that. After a couple of days, I didn't know what to think. I still thought, Oh, he'll turn up.

Elaine also became aware her brother was missing on the Monday morning. Jim and Mollie used to babysit Elaine's children, and when she dropped them off on her way to work her father asked her if she'd heard from Jamie over the weekend. 'Dad said nobody had heard from him. He said, "It's okay, he'll be fine." I said, "What do you mean, no-one's heard from him?" Something must have happened. I asked Dad if he'd rung the hospitals and police, and he said, yes.'

Jim Howe reported Jamie as a missing person to Annandale police on Monday 30 March and formally completed a written missing persons report at Annandale police station on Wednesday 1 April.

Older sister Dorothy went to the house Jamie shared, but didn't find anything out of the ordinary. If Jamie did return home after being dropped off that Friday, he would have found something that might have shocked and distressed him so much, it prompted his disappearance. Pinned to the front door was an eviction notice. The notice stated they were $900 in arrears with their rent. The brother Jamie lived with told police that nine weeks before Jamie went missing, Jamie asked him to give him his half of the rent money and that Jamie would give it to the landlord. This obviously didn't happen. We can imagine the panic that Jamie must have felt seeing the notice, and realising it was his fault, and that he had no way of fixing the situation.

The money he withdrew from the ATM that day was his last $50. Was he going to give it to the landlord to try to delay the eviction?

'He would have gone home, seen the eviction notice, and thought, "Holy shit, my brother's going to go through the roof,"' says Elaine. She believes that Jamie likely went home before or after going to the ATM. 'What's strange is his glasses were at home,' she says. 'He didn't have very good eyesight, so he would have had trouble reading the ATM without them. That makes me think he went home.'

Judy says Jamie didn't go anywhere without his glasses. He certainly would not have been without them for his day at work, so this means Jamie must have returned home after work, as they were found inside the house. The police report said there was no damage to the front door, so Jamie must have been able to gain entry fairly easily, even if the locks had been changed.

The family members I spoke to all have different ideas about what they think happened to Jamie at this point. Adrian believes the eviction notice was the straw that broke the camel's back, and tipped Jamie over the edge:

What I believe happened is the day Jamie disappeared there was a notice on the door to say the boys were locked out because of the rent issue, or it may have been a notice of eviction. My impression is that was the critical incident, that note on the door, and that prompted him to disappear. Maybe he thought he'd put the rent money on a sure thing at Randwick that day and double his money, and then he'd be out of trouble. Then he loses and finds himself in a bigger hole because he owes money for the rent, to the bank, to his work, to his workmates, his friends, his brother ... maybe other brothers as well.

If Jamie borrowed $200 here and there, they're not going to go and tell the others he borrowed money from them. So, he would have thought, 'I can't go and see that person or that person'; he's shamed into not finding a solution.

My way of thinking was that he did run away and commit suicide. I figured he jumped off The Gap³ or something, into the ocean. That's what I assume. If you go into the ocean, you can disappear without anyone finding you. I always assumed he'd go somewhere like that. As kids, we used to go there all the time, we went to Bondi a lot too. The Gap would be the obvious place. He probably caught a bus. It was a place he knew quite well. He was a bit of a risk taker, he wasn't scared of things. I can imagine him just thinking 'Well, I'll do it and everyone will be better off, and I'll be better off.' I can imagine him doing that kind of thing rather than taking an overdose of drugs, or hanging himself or some other way. Something quick and final.'

Elaine doesn't believe Jamie took his own life:

I thought he'd taken off, that was my first gut feeling. Maybe interstate, and developed a new identity. But then when I found out he hadn't taken his glasses or any of his things, and

---

3   The Gap is in Watson's Bay, a cliffside location north-east of the city that is notorious for suicides. It's about 15 kilometres from Leichhardt, where Jamie lived.

no-one had seen him I wasn't so sure. One of his childhood mates lived on a farm out of Sydney and I thought maybe he'd gone to see him, but he hadn't heard from Jamie. Nobody had.

I had a police officer friend at the time, and they knew Jamie quite well, and they were looking through all their records as well, unofficially. They couldn't find anything. They checked his date of birth against anyone with other names as well. There was no evidence that he'd set up a new identity with any combination of names that we could think of.

So, the longer it went on, the more I thought he'd met with foul play. I never once thought he'd committed suicide. I think it's pretty hard to get rid of your own body. It didn't make sense to me. If he jumped off The Gap, I think someone would have seen him do it. It was a Friday afternoon, not two o'clock in the morning, there would have been people around. He'd been through bad things before and never self-harmed. It was really upsetting for him when he broke up with his girlfriend.

Vernon agrees with Elaine:

I didn't think it was suicide, as I didn't see any signs at all, and I didn't see any reasons. I didn't think it was intentional murder, because there was nothing he'd been doing wrong. I just thought he'd had some accidental death and someone hid the body. Hit by a car, or got in a fight and they went 'shit, this guy's dead'. That's the only thing I can believe happened. I don't think he moved away and is alive. I still think that today; it seems more realistic.

Yeah, he was broke, but lots of people are broke, and he had a big family circle and lots of friends who could have helped.

Vernon thinks the family and friends Jamie owed money to wouldn't have cared about the debts, and like Vernon would have told Jamie not to worry about it. 'They would have just told him to pay it back whenever he could.'

Vernon is certain Jamie didn't go to their regular pub after finding the eviction notice. 'If he went to the Toxteth on that Friday, after work, I would have been there,' says Vernon. 'I hadn't made plans to meet him, but he had lots of other friends; I wasn't expecting him to be there, but he often was. He caught buses, but if he had money he'd catch a taxi. We'd get there in the afternoon, after work, and we might leave at 6 or 7 and go home for dinner, or we might go on to the wine bar or club. Or we'd go and play cards or Trivial Pursuit. That's what Jamie did, we all did. Get a feed, go home.'

I asked Vernon if he thought Jamie was planning to gamble his last $50 the day he disappeared. 'Put it this way. If I had $50, I'd buy a couple of beers, then I'd try to win money.'

Judy also thinks it's possible he used that money for gambling. 'Maybe he was trying to win big and get himself out of trouble,' she says.

Vernon doesn't agree that Jamie would have put a large amount of money on a horse. 'I've never seen it. I've never seen him throw money around.'

Bizarrely, police did not speak with any of Jamie's workmates when investigating his disappearance. It fell to the family to try to piece together his last movements. 'My father did a lot of investigations,' says Judy. 'He was the one who contacted the workmates and the hockey players. He was so concerned. He used to go and see the police all the time. He believed they were doing all they could to find Jamie, but Dad died before the inquest was held. We found out that nothing my father passed on to police was ever put into Jamie's file. All it said was that he had gone missing. It was terrible. I don't know what my father spoke to them about, but he used to go and see them regularly. He organised advertisements in newspapers; that ended up being pretty awful because he got lots of crank calls. He'd tell us what he was planning to do next, and we'd all talk about it and tell him what we thought.'

The Salvation Army used to run a Family Tracing Service. It began in the 1920s and by the time they ceased operations in 2018 they were conducting 2000 searches a year. On 19 May 1987, Jim gave the Salvation Army a typed page of information about Jamie. He kept a handwritten copy of this document, and Peter provided a copy of this document to police when making his statement for the 2009 inquest. It's titled, 'James Leo Howe Relevant Features'. It's touching in its detail, and it's clear Jim is a proud dad. Jim describes Jamie's physical features and also says his nose is

> ... *broken to one side. General appearance – athletic, neat, casual dresser. Religion – RC (non practising). Sexual preferences – Single heterosexual. No regular girlfriend. Personality – Quiet & agreeable. Generous and considerate to all members of large family and friends. Lived all his life in Glebe district where he is well respected and popular. Social activities – Graded player with Glebe District Hockey Club where he has been an active member since childhood. Coach of a junior team at the above club. Plays indoor cricket, social cricket, social tennis & touch football. Social drinker (beer) and*

cigarette smoker. Does not use illegal drugs. Has no criminal associates or connections. Living conditions – Shared rented house with his brother Gregory at 168 Elswick St Leichhardt. Work history – Has been in constant employment since leaving school – the past four years with Telecom Aust. Circumstances of Disappearance – Between 4pm and 4:30pm on 27th March he was driven from work to a bus stop in Liverpool Rd Ashfield, from where he apparently journeyed by bus to Broadway where he withdrew $200[4] from the Commonwealth Credit Union (Ready Teller) and since that time and date his movements are unknown to his family, friends, place of work or other acquaintances. Beginning 29th March 1987 contact was made with some fourteen hospitals, morgues and police to no avail. On April 1st details of his absence were given to Annandale Police Station for listing Jamie as a missing person. There is no evidence of his intention to disappear and the fact that he did not return home after work to pick up clothing, personal effects & papers, or to even change and shower seem to indicate whatever happened was unplanned.

The large group of Howe brothers and sisters frequently got together to discuss their missing sibling. 'It was horrible,' says Elaine. 'Especially that first year. Mum and Dad went through some terrible situations in their lives, with people in the family, but Mum always said Jamie going missing was the worst thing that ever happened to her. Having no resolution to it.'

As the months went on the Howe children would try to support their devastated parents. 'We used to have regular visits

---

4   This figure of $200 differs from the amount in the police statement, which was $50.

with them,' says Judy. 'A whole crowd of us used to turn up on weekends. We'd have dinner there and we used to play cards and board games like Trivia Pursuit, as a family. That's when we'd talk about Jamie, when we all got together. We'd ask our father what was happening, and he'd say the police were investigating, they were trying to do this or that, or there was an article in the newspaper.'

Vernon remembers the time as a bit chaotic, with his family all having different ideas about what to do. 'There are so many people in my family, and they were all saying this and that, and I was just sitting back waiting for him to come home. There was not much I could do. They once talked about going on TV and talking about missing persons, and they asked who in the family would do it and I said I would, but it never happened. That was within a year of him going missing. They wanted to get public awareness about it and see if someone knew where he was. Three of us were going to do it, a morning show or something. The older sisters, especially Judy, were the ones who were trying to get people to investigate as much as they could.'

Judy says that she approached the ABC, which was running a show about missing persons and interviewing family members, and asked if someone from the family could appear. 'They took down all the details and stated that they would consider my request and get back to me if it was successful. They never got back to me.'

Jim and Mollie were devastated by Jamie's disappearance. 'My father was stoic,' says Vernon. 'But my mother went into a sort of trance state for a while. The Christmas after he disappeared, we were supposed to go to the family in the country, and she wouldn't leave. She didn't want to miss Jamie's call to say Merry Christmas. They asked me what I thought had happened to him, but they didn't talk to me about what their idea was.'

Vernon struggled to understand why Jamie would be a missing person. 'I just thought it was weird. It wasn't his personality. When he went missing, I was never really sad, I was just bewildered.' Vernon says he doesn't feel any guilt over Jamie's disappearance, because he had no idea it was going to happen, but he felt a sense of great unease. He can't believe Jamie would cut off all contact with their parents:

I felt really uncomfortable for a while because I didn't see any signs. Did I miss something? I'd go around to visit my parents every now and then, but Jamie was around there heaps. He lived really close to them in Leichhardt. He was a real family person like that.

A friend of ours at the pub used to say, 'Come on, you know where he is,' and it used to be really annoying, that people thought I knew where he was. People knew we were close. They thought I was protecting him from something. Because we were close, people thought that I knew what was going on, where he was. It was so out of character for him to disappear and not contact anyone.

That's why people believed I must have known something, because they thought he must have still been in touch with someone in the family. It was a couple of weeks before I thought something was wrong. I just thought he'd taken off. I knew he

*had money problems, but I'd always said to him, 'The family
can help you out if you're in trouble' because there was so many
of us, and we all had jobs.*

Time went on, with no sign of Jamie. The family assumed that
the police were investigating his disappearance, but that seems to
not have been the case. Jim led the family's own enquiries. 'Dad
was the head of the family, and I had my own family,' says Adrian.
'So, I left it to him, and Judy was pretty involved too. I was there
if they needed me. I don't think the police these days – unless it
was a missing child or something – would do much more than
they did then, other than run it through their databases. There
was no sign that he'd met with foul play; I don't think anyone
came forward who said he owed a lot of money to a bad person.
So, I can understand the police not doing very much with it.
Having said that, they didn't revisit it very often, and when they
got enquiries from the family, it doesn't seem like they did too
much. They probably just thought, "He's a man, he's allowed
to go missing if he wants to, he had a few problems, so maybe
he's just disappeared for a day or a week or a year." I didn't really
know how much the police delved into it. I probably know more
now than I did back then.'

Judy also trusted that the police were doing their job. 'I didn't
really think too much about the police at the time,' she says:

*We didn't really ask exactly what they were doing. We just
thought they were doing everything they were supposed to
be doing, like talking to people; it was only later that we
discovered they hadn't interviewed anyone. I've since heard
this was usually the case back at that time. There was*

nothing in the file to indicate they'd done even the barest of investigations, other than speak to my father.

They certainly didn't interview any other members of the family. At the time, there were 17 of us they could have interviewed. But you put your trust in the police, and we didn't question it. I don't know why. I remember at the Easter Show, the year after he went missing, in the Police Pavilion they had a missing person flyer of Jamie. That made us think they were doing whatever they could. But putting up the flyers and putting his photo in newspapers during Missing Persons Week in 1988, 1989 and 1992 was all they did.

The family had a few contacts and were able to check organisations such as Medicare and social security agencies to see if Jamie was active. All queries drew a blank; there was no activity after the date he disappeared. The family say police did not investigate these avenues until 2007 as they prepared for the inquest. 'As far as I'm aware, no-one has been interviewed by police,' says Judy. 'They should have interviewed his hockey mates, the ones he used to go drinking and gambling with. If you went into a police station at the time, there was a board with missing person flyers on it, but that was it. We didn't even find that out until we went to the inquest in 2009.'

In early 2007, Dorothy's daughter Katie contacted the Missing Persons Unit. They agreed to review Jamie's case and take a DNA sample from family members for comparison with the unidentified persons database. DNA samples could be forensically matched to any human remains that had been located or might be located in the future. However, no further action was taken at that time. Katie then contacted Balmain police to get things moving again, and asked them to contact her mother, Dorothy. Consequently, Detective Senior Constable Pia O'Donohue was assigned to the case on 7 November 2007.

Detective O'Donohue and her team carried out database searches and contacted other government agencies from January to July 2008. She first contacted Dorothy around April 2008 to advise that the case was still open and investigations were ongoing. Late in 2008, Detective O'Donohue contacted Dorothy again and took a DNA sample. Dorothy gave a police statement in September 2008. John, Peter and Greg also gave police statements between October 2008 and May 2009. There was no further contact with Dorothy until May 2009 when Detective O'Donohue advised Dorothy that she was preparing a brief for the coroner and would submit it on 19 June 2009.

In 2009 Police issued another appeal for Jamie as part of the inquest preparations, but I have a copy of the poster and it simply says, 'Circumstances: James was last seen on 27 March 1987 at Ashfield.' Police required a written request from the family if they wanted an inquest, and their reasons why. The family provided this, and the inquest was finally held on 17 August 2009.

Bones were found at Kurnell, in Sydney's south, in 2007, and Judy believes a skull was sent to the USA for DNA extraction, along with Dorothy's DNA sample. Judy wrote a letter to the NSW Coroner asking for the cause of death of the remains found at Kurnell. The coroner replied that he was unable to give her the information. Police were also testing more than one set of remains to see if they belonged to Jamie. 'There were a couple of possible matches,' says Judy:

One of them had to be sent across to America, but we never heard anything about that. I asked my sister a few weeks ago about that, and she still hasn't heard. We just presume there was no match. They said, 'If we do find a match, we'll contact you.' I guess they didn't find a match, so they didn't contact us.

Judy feels guilty that she didn't follow up on the results of this test but I assure her that it is not her responsibility to chase the police; her family should have been kept informed. The DNA was tested in 2009, so it's disappointing that no contact has been made with the Howe family since that time.

The police statement from Jamie's inquest does mention that tests on human remains located at Towra Point in October 2006, identified as 'Body number 145', returned a 'slight chance' of a match with Jamie, but not enough DNA was unable to be extracted for an exact match. Towra Point is at Kurnell, but interestingly the unidentified bodies found in the sand dunes were found in October 2007 – has the police report recorded an incorrect year, or is this a different body? As far as I am aware, these remains have still not been identified, although there was much speculation at the time they were discovered as to who they may belong to.

Interestingly, remains of more than one person were found at Kurnell, buried in the sand dunes; there were possibly three people. There was speculation that the remains could have been one of three missing couples from the Sydney area in the late 1970s and early 1980s. DNA testing ruled out the remains being those of missing Juanita Neilson, underworld hitman Christopher Dale Flannery, missing person Lynn Woodward or Peter Mitros. The NSW Homicide Squad has since released more information about the remains: two of the victims are male, one aged between 24 and 46 and the other aged between 24 and 40. The third victim might be female but they are still unsure. Carbon dating has identified the bones as being from the period 1962 to 1981 – too early to be Jamie.

'They did say the skull was about the right age,' says Judy. This would indicate the remains were not those of the missing couples, who were all aged between 18 and 21. Jamie was 29 when he went missing.

'They said they couldn't rule out that the skull was Jamie, that's why they sent it for DNA testing,' says Judy. 'They weren't able to extract sufficient DNA to be able to match him with other remains. So, that's why they sent it off to America.'

At that time, America was one of the few places capable of extracting mitochondrial DNA from remains. This form of DNA is passed down through the maternal side of the family. It is often easier to extract this type of DNA from remains that have been degraded, for example, by being exposed to the weather, or are aged.

It was also thought the Kurnell remains could have been the victims of underworld criminal Neddy Smith, who reportedly disposed of his victims in sand dunes near Botany Bay. Smith was convicted of two murders, the last in October 1987, and was sentenced to life in prison in 1989. He died in 2021.

Jamie was last seen in March 1987. One of Smith's favourite pubs was the Iron Duke in Alexandria, which is just 4 kilometres from Jamie's regular pub, the Toxteth in Glebe. On the day Smith committed the last murder to give him his life sentence, he was heading to the Australian Youth Hotel in Glebe – just 2 kilometres from the Toxteth. Smith spent a lot of time in inner city Sydney pubs in the 80s, and it's almost certain he and Jamie would have been in the same pubs at the same time. But there's no evidence to suggest they knew each other, or ever met. None of the contacts I have asked, who know a great deal about the Sydney underworld, have ever heard Jamie's name. I made some enquiries among journalists very familiar with the underworld, and while Jamie did frequent pubs known to be meeting places for criminals, there is no evidence to suggest that Jamie was involved with them in any way.

Adrian does think it's possible Jamie interacted with these underworld figures, simply because they all used to drink at the same pubs. The Toxteth Hotel had a definite reputation as a hangout for local crims – the 'two-bit crims' his brother was warned about previously.

Vernon says: 'When you walked into the main bar of the Toxteth, that's where we all stayed. Then there was a pool table, then you walked out to the lounge bar; that's where the crims hung out. That's where Jamie was the night he got bashed, but he shouldn't have been out there. We usually had this mutual respect for each other. We never got into confrontation. They were two-bit crims, not big time.'

Adrian agrees with his brother. 'The main pub that we used to go to was the Toxteth, and there were villains there, back in those days,' he says. 'People who were connected to bigger and bad crimes. We knew them because some of them went to school with us, and they were associates of our associates, and we knew them because they were just in the pub. So, there were people there who were into violent crimes, and drugs, and gambling; so, we did know those people, but we didn't really associate with them. To my knowledge, Jamie didn't at all, and I think I was close enough to him to have known. We knew them to say hello to, but we didn't hang out with them. Maybe we'd sometimes sit in the same group as some of the heavies that hung around the Toxteth. This was the inner city; there were crims all around the place. But he wouldn't have borrowed money from someone like that. It was more likely family and friends. I guess if you were desperate enough … maybe he gambled with someone. I think, though, that if he'd run up a big debt with a bookie, the bookie would have found someone else in the family and said, "Look, your brother owes us money, do you want to talk to me about it?" Even if he got up a big debt, I can't see it being a *really* big debt.'

However, a strange part of Jamie's story is a statement from another of his brothers, Martin, who has since passed away. 'Martin said Jamie had come to see him, and was worried about something,' says Judy. 'Jamie said something about going to Kurnell, around that time. Martin said he thought Jamie was frightened, but he didn't say of what or who. Other people have dismissed what Martin said, and he was very sick at the time. The other brothers thought that Martin had it all mixed up. But he said, "I had important information at the time, and nobody asked me about it." Nobody had ever asked him any questions. At the time of the inquest, the whole family was advised, and anyone who wanted to go could have gone, and four of us went – me, Elaine, Peter and John. Martin would have gone, but was just too sick. Who knew how much Martin knew? But no-one ever asked him. Because none of the other brothers knew about it, they said it was unlikely that it occurred. Maybe it was just Martin thinking about the case and thinking about Kurnell.'

Elaine believes that Martin's story was that Jamie was heading to see him on the day he went missing, and was going to ask to borrow money. Martin told her he'd agreed to give him money, but that Jamie never turned up. 'I can't imagine why Martin would have fabricated that,' says Elaine. 'It was weird that he didn't ever say it before, but nobody asked him. The police had never been in touch with him. It's odd that he sat on that information for so long.'

Vernon is baffled by the story. 'I don't know why he thought that Jamie was involved with criminals, because I was always with him, I would have known,' he says. 'So were other brothers. There was a time I was living in Condobolin for four years, but I came back to Sydney every holidays and saw him, we were very close.'

Martin had a terminal illness at the time he told others about this event, and he passed away shortly afterwards, in 2009. This was the same year as Jamie's inquest. As I mentioned earlier, four members of the Howe family were elected life members of the hockey club, and Martin was one of these four. His wife, Margaret, was another. Their daughter, Helen, and Vernon are current life members. In Martin's biography from the hockey club website he's remembered as 'a straight-forward chap, what you saw is what you got. He made a difference in this world; he made a substantial difference to the lives of those around him and was a great contributor to the Glebe District Hockey Club affairs for close to 50 years. He was an honest hardworking man, who made a contribution when and where he could. He had a never-say-die attitude to the game, his astute reading of the game; his reliability and his optimistic approach, even in the direst of circumstances have inspired many a team mate.'

He does not seem like a man who would invent wild stories about his missing brother. Significantly, Martin worked at the Caltex Oil Refinery in Kurnell until he retired. This is just a kilometres from where the human remains were located in the sand dunes at Kurnell. Did Martin believe these remains were of his missing brother? Did he know more about what happened in the area he worked in?

The NSW Coroner conducted an inquest into Jamie's disappearance in 2009. Before the inquest, police collected statements from Dorothy, John, Peter and Greg. Greg provided his statement on 26 May 2009. Greg's witness statement reads, in part:

> *My brother James Leo HOWE was reported missing to Police on Friday 27th March 1987. As far as I am aware he was last seen by a work colleague that afternoon and he was dropped off by that work mate at a bus stop in Ashfield and from there I believe he travelled to Broadway and withdrew $200 from an automatic teller machine. James was the fourth last child out of eighteen children. There is 7 years between James and I. We were all pretty close growing up ...*

I was about 32 years old when James and I decided to move in together. We moved into 168 Elwick Street Leichhardt. James and I have an agreement that James would give me half of the rent money every week and I would pay the rent. I cannot remember exactly how much the rent was. This happened up until about 9 weeks before he went missing. From about 9 weeks before he went missing James was asking me to give him the rent money and was telling me he was paying the rent for us. I remember the day he went missing, there was a note on our front door saying that we were $900 in arrears. I thought that James may have seen this note and taken off up the pub. I know that James wasn't very well financed. I know he had had a car accident at work and Telecom was taking money out of his pay and he wasn't earning much. He would never really say anything about it. I think he was embarrassed about it all. I told him once that he should go and see a finance company but he didn't act on that, that I know of. He didn't talk about his financial situation too much, other than mentioning he was broke.

James was a very likeable bloke. He got along with people. He was involved in hockey a lot, right up until he went missing. He liked to go for a few beers and liked to put on a few bets. I don't know whether he had any gambling debts. He seemed to be chasing money and would put on a bet hoping to get a win. James wouldn't talk much about his work. I know he didn't like his supervisor much but it seemed like he was friends with other workers. The day that James went missing I came home from work about 2pm and saw that note on the door. I used to get home before him and then go up to the pub. I left the note on the door when I left to go to the pub so that he could see it. I just thought he was up at the pub when he didn't come home. I didn't tell anyone that night James didn't come home as I thought he was just up at the pub and didn't think it was a big deal at the time. I remember that he didn't come home that whole weekend.

Then during the beginning of the next week I started to ask around and call family to see if anyone had heard from him. I thought he may have taken off because he hadn't paid the rent. There was nothing unusual about the house the day that James disappeared. All his clothes and belongings were in his room. There was no damage to the house and no door locks had been forced.

I think it was about a week later that my dad reported James missing to the police as we thought he was just going to turn up. About a week later Dad came over and packed up James' things as I had to move out. When James' things were being packed up there was nothing that seemed out of place or unusual. Everything was how he had left it.

I didn't see much of James as I was working so a lot of the time I wasn't there. The last time I saw James was probably the morning that he disappeared or maybe the night before, I'm not too sure. There was nothing unusual about his demeanour before he disappeared other than he was frustrated that he had no money. He was not on any medications that I know of. He didn't have any illnesses that I know of. He didn't have a girlfriend that I know of ...

I don't know of any incidents or anyone that he may have had a run in with or owed money to. I do remember that a couple of months before he went missing he asked for a loan to get some dental work done. He asked for $800 but I never gave it to him. It now seems to me that he owed about $800 to someone as that seemed like a lot of money for the dentist.

Greg's statement and memories are particularly valuable, as he lived with Jamie. It was the same day the note was placed on the door that Jamie disappeared, which seems to be a huge coincidence. Greg also gives evidence about Jamie owing large sums of money to unknown people, and when all these statements are put together it feels like Jamie owed money to quite a few people, which he concealed from his siblings.

Peter's witness statement, given to police on 13 January 2009, also talks about the large sums of money Jamie borrowed, but he stated he never knew Jamie to gamble, which differs from his brothers' statements. It reads, in part:

In May 1985 Jamie came away with my wife Rosslyn and our two children and another brother, Martin and his wife and their two children ... for a hockey trip and holiday. Jamie was very close to all of his siblings. I remember that Jamie had to borrow some money to come away with us. He borrowed money from the State Bank of NSW which I was the bank manager at the time. I believe it was at least $5000. I believe that Jamie got into some difficulties trying to repay this debt. I remember restructuring his repayments during 1986 to assist him.

I think these difficulties were made worse when in 1986 he had a car accident while he was working for Telecom and damaged the company vehicle and he was held liable for the cost. I believe Telecom were taking the cost of the vehicle damage out of his wage which put him under financial pressure. I don't remember him ever complaining to me that he was under financial pressure but I knew that was repaying money. Other than that, financially I know that on the day he went missing Greg went home after work and there was an eviction notice on the front door because of non payment of rent and apparently Jamie was getting the rent money from Greg who thought that Jamie was paying it but he hadn't been which is why the rent was overdue. Which seems to indicate to me that Jamie was under financial pressure.

I socialised with Jamie particularly after hockey and at family functions. I cannot remember Jamie ever gambling or being involved with drugs ...

Jamie was a very likeable person, he was outgoing and was an extrovert. He would always be involved in family functions. He was always honest and reliable ...

His disappearance is out of character for him and I thought that he may have taken off because of his financial strains but I thought if that was the case then he would have contacted one of us, however he hasn't.

John gave his witness statement to police on 5 October 2008. It reads, in part:

I would describe Jamie as being very likeable, he was a bit of a worrier and was an emotional fellow ...

Jamie went overseas around this time ...

I can recall that Jamie borrowed the money to go overseas and that he owed this money to the bank. Around this time I remember he borrowed my brother Vernon's car and he had a car accident and he may have had to pay money back for this. So, I know that he owed a bit of money. Jamie also used to like to have a punt on the horses. I am not sure how involved he was with gambling and how bad it was.

John talks about the accident with Vernon's car, but we know Vernon did not ask Jamie to pay for that. John went on to say that Jamie hinted to him he'd like to move into the house John had bought with Vernon, but didn't actually ask to move in. This conversation made John believe Jamie was having financial difficulties. John's statement continues as he tells a poignant story:

The last time I saw Jamie was the Thursday before he went missing. I was at the Toxteth Hotel with just our brothers having a few drinks as usual. It would have been after work. I remember that during the night I could feel someone looking at me. I turned around and saw Jamie was staring at me. He was sitting down with a couple of people and was about 5 metres away from me. He was sitting with his elbows on his knees and he was just staring at me with a weird stare. He seemed to be worried or angry and I remember that he didn't look happy. This is the last time I saw Jamie and this look that he gave me stays with me as it was unusual for him to have that sort of look.

I feel guilty now that he is still missing and that I did not do more to help at the time he went missing. I know that Jamie was in financial strife but to me he did not seem depressed at the time, however thinking back now I know that things weren't going well for him and he didn't look happy the last time I saw him. I can't imagine him just leaving his family as we were all very close. He would always be at every family function and be one of the first ones there.

Dorothy's statement shows her great affection for her little brother:

He always dressed well and always looked nice. He had nice golden-coloured skin. I would describe James as having a happy nature. He was very friendly and always polite and well spoken. He enjoyed his family ... I don't think he was left with much money at all after trying to pay back his debts. I know that James did like to have a bet on the horses and a drink but I would not say he was an alcoholic or that he had a gambling problem. He may have tried marijuana but I am sure he didn't have a drug problem.

When he was living with Greg I think Jamie was concerned and worried about not having enough money to live on, or pay the rent. I wouldn't say that he was depressed though. When I saw him at lunch he was always straight. He would go out with the boys but when he was with the family he was always proper and was never argumentative with anyone.

I remember that he had a great relationship with my mum and dad. I know that they loved each other. I would see James every couple of weeks ... he was always happy to see me and we would always have a good chat.

When speaking about the family's response to Jamie going missing, Dorothy says:

> ... *some of the family thought that he may have just run away because of his debts, some were worried that he had committed suicide or that he had been murdered. The fact that he just disappeared was just so out of character for him that we thought the worst.*
>
> *We pieced together James' last movements on that Friday 27 March 1987 ... I do know that he had his work bag with him and his Telecom work clothes ... at some stage he must have gone home as Greg found his work bag and reading glasses in James' bedroom. All his clothes were still in his bedroom.*
>
> *I remember going to Greg's house and there was nothing that looked like it was out of place or out of the ordinary.*
>
> *Dad passed away in 1990 and since that time we never heard any more about his case. We thought that we were never going to get any answers so we didn't pursue the matter with the police. Our mother passed away in 1996.*

The coroner's findings from Jamie's inquest are pitifully brief. The police statement says, in point three, that Jamie was reported missing on 27 March 1987 (Friday) to a probationary constable at Annandale police station. This is incorrect – this is the day Jamie was last seen, but we know his disappearance was not realised until at least the following day, and his father reported him missing on the Monday. Point four says that in 2007 Senior Constable O'Donahue was appointed officer in charge of investigating Jamie's disappearance. This suggests that absolutely nothing was done by police between 1987 and 2007 to investigate Jamie's disappearance.

'It was a shock,' says Elaine. 'We'd been lied to. It was a joke. How would they know he was dropped off at the bus stop or ATM if they didn't interview anyone? From two pieces of paper in his file, that was apparently enough evidence for him to say he's committed suicide. It's all just supposition, and I don't think there was any evidence that it happened. It's outrageous.' Elaine is upset that the coroner told the family it was likely Jamie had committed suicide:

There was no evidence for any of that. I was frustrated and angry. And I didn't really understand what was going on until after the event. Talking and thinking about it afterwards, I don't think we were prepared enough. We were only told on the day of the inquest. They said we could ask questions but none of us did, as we were not ready. None of us challenged what the coroner said, like none of us asked why they didn't talk to his workmates. It was very upsetting. They said in those days there wasn't any real missing persons unit. The assumption was that if someone went missing, it was of their own volition, and they didn't investigate if they were an adult. They also didn't have resources to do a proper investigation.

Judy wrote a letter to the coroner after the inquest to ask for more information, and asked why the police had not re-interviewed anyone in 2009. The coroner replied: 'After 22 years, experience suggests that interviewing family members, friends, workmates, or Salvation Army staff is unlikely to throw up information that will reliably throw new light on James' disappearance because memories fade so much.'

I beg to differ. I interviewed four of Jamie's family members for this book, and they all provided me not only with accurate memories, corroborated by all of them, but they also recalled exact details, names and important conversations. I would suggest that had police interviewed the workmate who dropped Jamie off that day, he'd recall things very well simply by being aware for all these years he was the last person to see Jamie before he disappeared. I believe he's probably gone over that car trip in his mind a thousand times over the years.

Judy is also very angry about the lack of police involvement in Jamie's disappearance. 'We naïvely thought that when we went to the inquest we'd find out something,' says Judy. 'But we didn't find out anything at all. We were really disappointed. We weren't really able to ask any questions during the inquest. We probably should have taken a lawyer to help us, as I thought afterwards of things I should have asked. It was over very quickly. We were shown the file, and there was nothing in it. The police officer read out the statement of the things that had been done, and one of the things was they'd searched the databases in 2008 and found nothing. The police officer who attended the inquest did interview a few members of the family, briefly, but there was no proper investigation, no follow up. It wasn't very well done, wasn't very searching. They just asked our opinion about what might have happened. She selected four people from the family to talk to. Four, out of 16 brothers and sisters. None of his friends, his colleagues, the hockey club members; they didn't talk to anybody like that.'

Another source of frustration and anger, which I share with Judy, came from our attempts to access the coronial documents I have included in this story. Judy first made an application for the documents in early November 2017. She didn't receive them until September 2018. Aside from this being a ridiculous amount of time to receive a fairly small number of basic documents, the response from the coroner's office was very distressing to the Howe family.

In June 2018 Judy rang the coroner's office for an update on her request, and was told Jamie's case was 'low priority' for them. This was extremely upsetting for her to hear. In August 2018 I suggested to Judy that her next enquiry might mention that Jamie's case was being featured in my book, in the hope that this may speed up the process.

She wrote to them: 'Please note that my brother's case is being featured in an upcoming book, which will be documenting the obstacles my family has had to overcome, including this one. It's very unfortunate that this is one more hurdle that we have had to face in the very long search for answers. I am sad the public and other families of the missing will have to learn what a very hard road they have ahead of them, and have to hear that, in effect, their missing person is a "low priority".' I don't know if this had any effect but the documents were finally received within a few weeks after waiting nine months for them.

Weeks without Jamie turned into years. 'For the first couple of years, I couldn't read a newspaper properly,' says Judy:

All I did was scan the paper for information about Jamie.
I am an avid newspaper reader, and I did this every day. I

wasn't aware of any other news items. Or I'd watch a TV show about missing persons. I'd walk down the street and think I'd spotted him. I followed people quickly trying to see if it was him. And I was always looking in crowds. I don't do it anymore, but for years I did. Probably other relatives of missing people have done the same. My brothers and sisters probably did too.

For years and years, it was uppermost in my mind, daily. It gradually stopped. But I still regularly think of him. I used to dream of him. I dreamed that he turned up. He was just like he was when he left. He explained why he went away and he was sorry that we were all worried. We all forgave him and said it doesn't matter, that he was back now and that was the main thing. He just said he had to get away. I'm the only person who still lives at the same address that I did when Jamie disappeared, and I had these thoughts that if he ever came back, the only person he'd be able to contact would be me. I'd open the door and he'd come in and I'd have to grab him and make sure he didn't disappear, and contact other people without him knowing.

Vernon dreamed about Jamie too:

There was a period there where I had these constant dreams about him. It was quite a few years later. They were so realistic. He was very happy and friendly and I said to him, 'Where have you been? Welcome back!' That happened quite a lot. I'd wake up in the morning and get ready for work and think, am I meeting Jamie tonight? Oh, oops. They were that realistic. We were in city situations and country situations.

But I didn't feel sad when I realised it was just a dream, I thought at least I'm still thinking about him. But I don't think we'll ever find him.

Vernon wonders what happened to Jamie's body. 'If his body was disposed of, it was done very well. If he committed suicide, which I don't believe, how can you do it and disappear? If he did, why? I just don't believe it. I saw him two days before, and there was nothing, no signs. I think he was unlucky and he came to some harm, and they got rid of him somehow. Someone knows something. I've told Judy what I think, and it was emotional. We don't talk about it much anymore.'

Adrian has also thought a great deal about what could have happened to his brother. 'There's a thousand ways you can meet your end,' he says:

Maybe he did get beaten up by someone; but it's more likely, knowing Jamie and knowing his circumstances and the kind of person he was, he'd feel remorse and shame, a sense of helplessness, with no-one to ask or turn to – he'd already asked a number of people and ended up owing them money, so he couldn't turn to them again. Being the age he was, being a risk taker, he might have been drunk and depressed and felt it was the last straw ... that day he was down to his last $50 and he had to pay money back to people, and he said, 'I just can't do it.' He'd have to face people.

Maybe he'd arranged to pay people back that weekend and they were going to come and see him. I can see that path. When he went missing I jumped to the conclusion pretty quickly that it was a suicide. That's still my view. I didn't think he'd gone for a swim and disappeared, because he would have told someone where he was going.

As a young male, he was risk taking, to a certain extent. Young males tend to do things half-heartedly. It's fairly rare that you get murdered. And the reasons people are murdered, he had nothing to do with – he wasn't a drug dealer, he would have had more money if he was. He just smoked a bit of grass occasionally, but he wasn't really into all that stuff. He played a lot of sport, and that doesn't fit with that lifestyle. He wasn't a thief, he still went to work up until the day he went missing, and he only had fifty bucks in the bank, so to me it all pointed to suicide. I didn't really tell people that because I didn't want to upset them. I didn't express those thoughts too often. He didn't display anything at the time to make us concerned; he didn't seem suicidal.

He did have troubles in his life, and you don't know how deeply those troubles affected him. But in retrospect, you think maybe they did affect him. I think he would have had a sense of shame, because he couldn't solve his problems. There's that whole male thing about not asking for help and not telling people that you're in trouble. I think he was very conscious of how people thought of him. It played on him that he couldn't get himself out of the situation he was in.

Jamie's parents never recovered from his loss. Judy believes the constant worry about Jamie's disappearance contributed to their father's death, just three years after he went missing. 'My father died of a heart attack, and he was definitely under stress because of Jamie. He was thinking about him right up until the time they both died,' she says. 'It was always uppermost. They'd moved back to the country, but my father always kept in touch with police. Mum died in 1996.'

After the death of their parents, it was left to the many Howe brothers and sisters to continue to look for answers. 'We all get together, still,' says Judy. 'We've always been close. You don't need a lot of other friends, because you've always got someone in your family. We have a family gathering to watch the grand final every year, and family Christmases, weddings, that sort of thing. My parents have now gone, and several of my brothers have died, and a sister, but for the first few years we really missed Jamie at these family events. When Mother's Day came around you'd hope Jamie would turn up, and the first Christmas we were really hoping. When we get together we do theorise and talk about Jamie, every now and again; whoever's there gives their opinion. We wouldn't talk about it every time we met, but it would come up at different times. It got less and less as time went on. But even today, like when you contacted me about this, I contact my brothers and sisters and we discuss it again and bring out the theories for the next six hours, then it goes away again. We've all got different theories, too. Some of them think he probably committed suicide, some think that he was murdered, some think that he possibly just disappeared because of his problems to start a new life elsewhere. To start again from scratch.'

Judy thinks it's possible that Jamie did just choose to disappear. However, she doesn't believe he could or would have stayed away for so long. 'I don't think he committed suicide. I might be in the minority there, though. I just can't bring myself to think that, because of his personality. Even though he might have felt shame and might have been under stress, I don't think he would have done that. But who knows. I think suicide is the least likely scenario.' Judy remains unsure about what she thinks has happened to Jamie. 'I fluctuate,' she says:

I know he had a lot of problems, financial problems, and I accept that, but it's hard for me to believe he committed suicide. I know it's hard for a lot of families to accept that when it happens. But for one thing, it's pretty hard to hide your body when you commit suicide. And there was no indication that he felt suicidal. Obviously he didn't write a note, and nobody said he was suicidal. All his clothes were still there. He didn't take anything. He had clothes in the washing machine. He just had a wallet on him and the clothes he was wearing. He didn't take his glasses.

The overall majority of the family think he's dead. They think he must be dead, or he would have come back, or contacted us, because of the nature he had, and how close he was to the family. But I have heard of people coming back after 30 years. It might be just too hard for him to come back.

One of my sisters is interested in family history, and we found out that one of our great-grandparents also disappeared. She tracked him down – he'd moved to New Zealand and had another family. Everyone here thought he'd died. So, it can happen.

One of the most bizarre theories about what happened to James Howe has come not from the family but from an American stranger who makes YouTube videos. It's a story so weird that it's been difficult to write about, as I don't fully understand it myself.

I was contacted out of the blue by a woman who had happened across a strange YouTube video about something called Sodalitas Vulturis Volantis. A Google search of this leads you into some pretty out-there territory. But, basically, the YouTube video was about how a man in the USA had uncovered some documents that seemed to list participants in an ARG – Alternative Reality Game.

One of the names on the list is James Howe.

The creator of the video seems to suggest that all the people on the list, including Jamie, were abducted by a secret organisation, Ciccada3301, to 'play' this game. It's really the stuff of science fiction films. The list has Jamie's entry as: 'Asset – Howe, James L. ID: SVVJ2787' (this is basically the date Jamie went missing – March 27, 1987). 'Location – Ashfield Australia. Inducted: July 7, 1987. Class: 32.PSM.Intel. GL.TK+2' (no idea what that means). And most bizarrely, 'Status: Boisterous.'

According to Wikipedia, Ciccada 3301 is an organisation whose goal is to recruit highly intelligent individuals from the public to join them, and these people are chosen by their ability to complete puzzles, and code-breaking and alternate reality games posted online by Ciccada 3301. The *Washington Post* in 2014 called the group and their activities 'one of the top five eeriest unsolved mysteries of the internet'.

But what has a current internet-based group recruiting geniuses got to do with a missing Telecom linesman, who liked to have a punt and a beer, from 1987? The information posted in the documents about James is easily available to anyone on the internet, both on my website and the NSW Police

Missing Persons Database, which can be publicly accessed. Significantly, the NSW Police site says James was missing from just Ashfield. Not Ashfield, Sydney. Someone unfamiliar with Australia might list the location as 'Ashfield, Australia' – as in the document. Also, after looking at the case more closely, it would seem that Jamie probably went home to Leichhardt before he disappeared.

Another missing man on the list, Italian Filiberto Pennisi, appears on the Doe Network website, a quality American resource I have used many times over the years. James also appears on the Doe site, but his profile page is currently inaccessible. Also on the list is Petrus Beentjes, from the Netherlands, who is on Doe as well. Another name on the list is Donald Mohrbacher, missing since 1967. Donald's profile appears on an American website called Find the Missing. Has someone trawled the pages of the Doe Network and NamUs websites, put together a list of missing persons, then claimed they have all been taken for this fictitious game? These are people, not just names and photos on the internet. They are real people, dearly loved and missing, not to be made into characters for a game. It's shameful.

Another curious twist to this story is that the Howe family are currently searching for another missing person. Eighteen-year-old Zac Barnes was last seen in November 2016, in Thornton near Newcastle, NSW. He had been in a car with friends, on his way to a train station, when he suddenly jumped from the vehicle and ran into nearby bushland. He has not been seen since. Zac's grandfather is Gavin, Jamie's third eldest brother. Zac actually went missing the day I interviewed his aunt, Elaine. Journalist Dan Proudman interviewed Zac's mother, Karen, in March 2017. Her words about Zac are eerie when compared with the words her father's siblings have said about her missing uncle Jamie: 'Along with the support has also come the theories, the rumours and the nasty comments. Mrs Gudelj has taken them head-on. "Is there drugs involved? I don't know. Was he an addict? No, he wasn't. But he probably experimented, he is an 18-year-old. Did he drink? Yes," she said. "He did owe money, but it was only a small amount. And it wasn't gambling. It was definitely not enough money to lose your life."'

For the Howe family, Jamie's disappearance remains a mystery, but they hope that one day it will be solved. 'The coroner's report didn't have an open finding, but they did say it was likely he'd died,' says Judy. 'But they were unable to say where or when, or identify the cause or manner of his death. So, I guess it's open. It annoyed me that they even said it at all. After a certain number of years, he was declared dead so that they could finalise his superannuation. One member of the family wanted to have a memorial and a farewell to Jamie, and use the superannuation money for that, but I objected; I said the money should be kept for Jamie in case he ever turns up. But that probably didn't help the other members of the family who wanted some closure. It didn't really cause any problems, though. I just felt that if he does turn up, he's got a few thousand dollars to get him going again. My mother kept most of Jamie's things, but I've got a few little personal items. We kept his clothes for ages but we eventually gave them away.'

I asked Elaine if she's in the 'I don't know' camp when it comes to what she thinks has happened to her brother. 'Pretty much,' she says:

I went to a couple of clairvoyants after Jamie disappeared. One of them said Jamie owed somebody money, and they held a knife to his throat and accidentally killed him. That story fuelled a lot of the ideas in the family about what happened to Jamie. Another one said that he moved to Melbourne and got a new identity. I think that's possible. But by the same token, I think he was really close to Mum and Dad and his nieces and nephews, he had that commitment to the little kids' hockey team; for him to just take off and never, ever let anybody know that he was okay, I think that's really out of character for him.

Vernon has reflected about his brother many times over the years. 'Things have always gone through my head. There are lots of different theories. We investigated a lot of things and we couldn't work anything out. The one thing we all agreed on was there was no reason for him to be murdered, or in trouble with criminals. No reason for him to commit suicide. That's all feasible, but I just don't believe it. Some bad situation must have occurred.'

Elaine says she believes most of the family think that something has happened to Jamie, but not at his own hand. 'I think the prevailing theory is that he owed somebody money, and somebody's knocked him off. It may not be underworld, but maybe dealing in marijuana on the side and Jamie's owed them money, and they've roughed him up a bit. I don't think anybody has got any real idea.'

Vernon says he does see Jamie as having been aggressive, and described him as a fighter. 'He didn't stand down. Some of my other brothers were like that too, and some of the rest of us were quieter.'

Judy says her brother's disappearance has changed her moods. 'I guess I get more anxious, probably. Or angry about different things. Like finding out the police had not investigated, that made me angry and I felt I had to write off about it, even years later. Then I get to a stage where I don't do anything again.' She still relies on her family to get her through the pain of losing her brother. 'I became a bit obsessed with talking to my children about Jamie. They've been a great support. They listen to me. My husband was also a great support before he passed away. He knew Jamie well. He didn't really talk about it from his own perspective but whatever I wanted to do, in the search, he supported me.'

Judy's happiest memory of Jamie is playing cards together. 'The last time I saw him was probably a week before he went missing. He was always so lovely, that's how I remember him. We'd have family card nights and Jamie would always make cups of tea. I was 12 years older than him, so we weren't confidants, but we always had a lovely relationship. He had a lovely personality, he was very likeable. Very charismatic.'

Elaine agrees. 'It's such a long time ago now, but it's still upsetting. We think about him and talk about him often. Every now and then it really comes to the forefront of my mind. My son reminds me a lot of Jamie. They're both idealistic dreamers, bad with money...' Elaine laughs. 'But also charismatic and lovely, everybody loves them. Similar looks as well. It helped having so many brothers and sisters, we all supported each other. Especially my sisters Judy and Dorothy, we used to talk a fair bit about it and we wrote poetry about it. There's a big chunk missing out of our lives, and out of our kids' lives. He used to see my children a lot, and they remember him. It does feel like he's missing from family events, but he's not the only one missing anymore.'

A few of the siblings have since passed away, such as Martin. I asked Elaine how important it was to her that Jamie is one day found. She is almost overcome. 'Very,' she manages to say. 'It would mean the world. Just to have that closure, one way or another. I hate not knowing. I feel bad that I didn't do more at the time.'

Like all those close to a missing person, Adrian feels keenly that he can't say any final goodbyes to his brother. 'There's no closure. You can't go to a funeral and say farewell. Having this book written about him, telling his story, is a legacy for him, so that he hasn't disappeared off the earth completely.' Adrian says there's a sadness when he thinks of Jamie. 'I kind of compartmentalise it, and stick it in the back drawer where I don't go and visit too often. You've still got the guilt too; maybe if I'd done more at the time. A way of finalising it for myself was to say that he's committed suicide. If it turned out that he was alive, and he turned up, then that would be a bonus. If he's dead, then I don't have to go every day looking through the streets to see if I can see him, or searching through the missing persons lists. Maybe he would have had his own family. We miss him at family functions. He was particularly close to Vernon and myself, and Elaine. He was a good brother and a good friend.'

Elaine says: 'He was a dreamer. He would have loved to have got married, had kids, had a house. He wanted the everyday life that everybody has, that he saw his siblings achieve.'

Vernon says again how well liked Jamie was. 'I see people now that I haven't seen for a few years and they always ask, "Have you heard anything about Jamie?" It feels good that they ask, good that they remember him.' Vernon says that recalling his memories of Jamie, even the ones like Jamie getting into fights, is not a painful experience for him. 'I get a tear in my eye, but it's good to remember,' he says. 'I like talking about him. I'd tell him things, he'd tell me things. I always found him to be true and genuine.'

There are so many different theories about what happened to Jamie Howe that day, and as well as I feel I know him after interviewing those who knew him best, I don't know the answer. The family does mostly agree that he is no longer alive.

I have researched the underworld connections with investigators who know every in and out of those criminal figures, and found nothing to suggest Jamie was one of their victims. Most of the family cannot believe that Jamie took his own life, but in my experience with many suicides of missing persons, the signs are not always there. Would he have left his glasses at home? If he was upset about the eviction notice, then possibly he forgot them when he left the house. If Jamie upset the wrong person and they harmed him, it's an extremely well-guarded secret, as there are no rumours that I have uncovered, and there usually are.

If we go by the theory that Jamie was dropped home from work that day and found the eviction notice on the door, he would have known it happened because he had failed to pay the rent and spent the money elsewhere, and knew he'd have to face the others to explain why. He went to the ATM and despite it being Friday and pay day, all he had to his name was $50, and a mountain of debts in front of him, including to the bank, to his employer, and to more family and friends than is probably known. And most significantly, to the landlord, who was not as forgiving as his family and friends about the money owing. Maybe he saw no way out of the mess he was in. He had a wonderful, supportive, loving family, but he'd already borrowed so much from them, maybe it was just too hard to ask one more time. Nevertheless, to this day we don't know if Jamie is alive or dead. He may have committed suicide, died through misadventure or started a new life elsewhere. We just don't know.

This is a giant, beautiful family, who are all still intertwined in each other's lives. Peter sadly passed away in 2019 after a long illness. I have seen their family photos and comments on their Facebook pages, and delighted in their jokes, encouragements and open expressions of love to one another, that they all display, all the time. For Adrian's 60th birthday a huge number of the family all took a cruise together, and there's a marvellous photo of them all on board, proudly wearing their matching 'Adrian's 60th!' T-shirts. I can't help thinking Jamie Howe should be in that photo too. Certainly older, with more than a smattering of grey through the blonde curl, still with his cheeky grin and squashed nose that didn't detract from his good looks. He should have been on that cruise with his wife and kids and maybe grandkids, having a ball with his siblings and celebrating his close brother's birthday. It's a terrible, terrible shame.

If you have any information about what happened to Jamie Howe, please contact 1800 33 000. You can remain anonymous if you wish.

CHAPTER NINE
Sandrine Jourdan

Sandrine Jourdan was last seen on Tomlinson Road, Caboolture, Queensland on 13 July 2012. She was a 37 year-old mum of three.

This is the story of a beautiful, complex, intelligent, talented, accomplished, much-loved woman and mother, who was there one minute and gone the next. It's also the story of her fiercely loyal and loving family, who refuse to give up the search and will continue shouting her name from the rooftops until they find her.

Sandrine Jourdan's family grew up between France and Australia. Her older sister Christine was born in Australia; Sandrine was born in France. The children grew up near Marseilles, but lived all over both countries. Their mother met Sandrine's father and they were married in Australia. Christine was one year old when they moved to France. Fabienne is the eldest (Sandrine's half-sister), then Phillip, Christine, Sandrine, Bernadette, Diana and Zach. It was not a happy childhood, with the house being run according to the strict rules of their stepfather. Eventually, Sandrine's mother, Sylvia, decided she could no longer stay in their marriage and moved her children back to Australia.

Just getting to Australia was no mean feat. Mum Sylvia sold everything they owned and sister Christine was working two jobs so they could afford all the airfares. Sandrine was 15 when they came to Australia, in 1989, and recorded the event in her diary notes:

Arrived in Australia with my mother – the strength of all of us, my eldest brother Philip – guardian, my elder sister Christine – our dearest, my younger sister Bernie – our drive, our younger Diana – our fire and our youngest brother Zachy – our love.

The family moved to Deception Bay in Queensland. It was a few months before the children could start school in Australia, as they didn't speak any English, but they quickly settled in well at the local high school. Sandrine was an excellent student and was very popular, especially with the boys. 'They used to call her Elle,' says Christine with a laugh. 'Short for Elle Macpherson.' Sandrine was beautiful and curvaceous, and her French accent won her many admirers.

Sandrine met Michael when she was 16, in 1991.They had three children – Jessie, Sam and Nakita. As well as being a doting mother, Sandrine kept herself constantly busy. She worked in shops, volunteered in hospitals, schools and nursing homes, helped her sister with her dog grooming business, studied arts and languages and eventually found her passion gaining qualifications in horticulture. 'If you showed her how to do something, she'd have a go at it,' says Christine. 'Michael had a bricklaying business and she even used to go out to jobs as his labourer. My ex-husband employed her as a concrete labourer and reckons she's one of the hardest workers he's ever had.'

Sandrine loved working outdoors and in nurseries. She also loved art, and was talented at drawing and painting, taking many classes. 'She absolutely loved painting,' says Christine. 'Our whole family have posters and paintings that she did, everywhere through our houses.' Sandrine's Facebook page shows her beautiful artwork, and she spoke on there about how much she was enjoying creating it:

I've decided to put my stuff up from now on and share with you guys some of my inspirations. This one is 'at one'. Thank you, guys, for giving me confidence. It makes me want to keep going on this painting. I have been struggling with (it) in the last couple of weeks. You guys are gems! The painting is 'natural balance'.

When Sandrine's relationship with Michael ended in 2008, she was in emotional turmoil. No-one realised, not even her close family, but her life was spiralling into a dark place. 'She attempted suicide at this time,' says Christine, 'But she denied it. Then she attempted it again while she was in hospital. The first time was a car accident. She was going too fast and aimed for a telegraph pole, but changed her mind at the last minute and rolled the car. While she was in hospital after the accident, she tied a few of her bra straps together, of all things, and tried to strangle herself. She was in hospital for quite some time until they diagnosed her with split personality and severe depression. She told us it was bipolar disorder, and it wasn't until we read the medical files she had amongst her paperwork that we realised what was going on.'

Christine hadn't seen any signs of mental illness in Sandrine before her breakdown, other than often dramatic mood swings. 'She would get very angry, then five minutes later she'd act like nothing had happened, she wouldn't remember. That was when I said, "Sandrine, you need some help, you cannot remember saying this to me?" We'd have an argument about the fact that she'd just done that, or said this, but she wouldn't remember.'

Before the car accident Sandrine had not received any treatment for her illness, and her family had no idea things were as bad as they were. 'We knew she was struggling, but she was so headstrong that she refused help, and she had to do it on her own. That was the way she had to do it.'

Sandrine was hospitalised for nine weeks. She promised her family she would never try to take her own life again, and after one of her friends suicided she declared she would always be available to help anyone she knew who was having suicidal thoughts. Sandrine realised she needed help and agreed to her treatment readily, attending counselling sessions regularly and taking medication.

When Sandrine became unwell Michael had taken their children to live with him in Western Australia. As she began to recover, Sandrine started making arrangements to see the children; they would either fly back to Queensland or Sandrine would fly to Western Australia. Sandrine's only concern was that her children were happy, and if they had chosen to live with their father at that point, she was okay with that. The children told her that when she was better and had her life back on track, they would come back to live with her. Strangely, around this time Sandrine was becoming fearful for her safety. She told her children she would be contacting them from a blocked number every Tuesday at a specified time. For Sam, it was 3 pm, Nakita was 4 pm and Jessie would be on a different day. She told them they could not contact her, but that she would contact them. Sandrine would often use public phone boxes, but she was still able to receive calls on one of her phones. Every Tuesday, without fail, Sandrine would ring her children at the specified times, but when she went missing these calls abruptly stopped.

For quite some time the children stayed in Western Australia, then Jessie moved back to Queensland to live with her mother. Sam flew to Queensland for a holiday and decided to stay on with his mother and sister, then Nakita came for a holiday and also decided to stay. Sandrine finally had all her children with her again. Sandrine had applied for a Housing

Commission property, so she could have all her children live with her permanently. She was desperate to prove that despite her mental illness, she was fit to have her children live with her, that she was stable and that she was a good mother to them.

In 2010 Sandrine met a man named Mr C when she was camping on Moreton Island with her friend B.[5] Sandrine's car had broken down and B approached Mr C for help, who agreed to try to fix the car. The strange part of the story is sister Christine is certain Mr C and B already knew each other – but they deny this. B had worked on Moreton Island for two years and Mr C owned a shack there, and B's best mate lived two doors down from Mr C. The two men almost certainly had met before, Christine feels. Sandrine and Mr C were immediately attracted to each other and started dating. 'The next thing we know, she moved out of her house and moved in with him,' says Christine.

Sandrine had received a large sum of money from selling her block of land, but much of it had been spent on airfares for the children to fly back and forth from Perth, and when they came to Queensland on holidays Sandrine treated them to camping trips and theme parks. 'Anything she could think of to do with the kids, she did it,' says Christine. 'Camping is one of her favourite things. She bought herself a four-wheel drive and all the camping gear. They never stayed home on weekends, they were always out and about, four-wheel driving, all the swimming-holes around Kilcoy and Woodford.' Sandrine wrote a Facebook post in 2010 saying, 'Looking for a car is proving to be tiresome.' Her friends

---

5 For legal reasons I have only used first initials for some of the people in Sandrine's story.

made some suggestions about what she should buy, and Sandrine replied: 'It needs to be a 4x4 of course!'

'B was the one who introduced her to drumming,' says Christine. 'The drumming group members she became involved with would often go camping and to retreats on weekends, and spend the whole weekend playing the drums.' In February 2012 Sandrine attended a retreat in the Hunter Valley region of NSW. It was to be the start of some changes in Sandrine's life. She broke up with Mr C and was looking for a new place to live, so she could be with her children.

There were still signs that Sandrine was struggling with her mental health. 'Sandrine said she was getting notices for a lot of unpaid tolls that were not from when she was driving,' says Christine. 'We ended up finding a PO box of hers, we found the key in her ute, and all the letters in this PO box were unpaid toll fines, numerous fines.' Did Sandrine genuinely believe that someone else was driving? Or was someone, somehow, racking up fines in her name?

Sandrine then told her sister Christine about something horrific that had happened to her. 'Four weeks before she went missing she said she had made a complaint to the police of a rape. According to her diary, Sandrine had woken one morning and felt groggy; she doesn't even remember going to bed that night. She woke up bleeding from her bowel. Sandrine later told my other sister Diana that she'd had blood tests done which came back positive for her being drugged – our family have searched for these test results but cannot find them. We can't find where she went to get the test.' Christine is sure it was very real to Sandrine, as she wrote in her diary that she'd attended two counselling session at a rape clinic. Sandrine said she was upset at the police response to her complaint, saying they suggested she was a prostitute. However, police say they have no report made by Sandrine of a sexual assault.

Three weeks before she went missing Sandrine had told her family she felt her illness was controlling her, that she was not in control of *it*. So, she did something about it – she went back to the hospital to consult the doctors and alter her treatment plan. She was determined to get better and manage her illness so she could move forward with her life. She was kept in hospital overnight and referred back to her doctor. The day she went missing she had mentioned to her mother that she needed to get some more medication; her last prescription had run out and she needed to visit her doctor for a new one. She had made an appointment for the following Monday. Sandrine's aunt Kathy, who passed away in 2021, told *A Current Affair*: 'Sandrine was on medication, but she didn't like the medication, she felt as though it made her stupid, where she wasn't thinking straight, so she was in the process, through doctors, of coming off those meds.'

Three or four days before Sandrine went missing, she visited Christine at her home. The sisters had been previously arguing, and Sandrine waited outside Christine's house for more than two hours for her to come home. 'When I got home, I told her to just give me time, as I didn't really want to talk to her just then. We'd had a disagreement about money. I told her I was okay and that's all she needed to know, and the rest of it we'd deal with later. I thanked her for giving me her phone number. As she walked away, she said, "It wasn't me, I'm sorry,

I didn't mean to." And I said, "Fine, Sandrine, just give me your bank account details so I can start paying you back." She said, "Don't worry about it, I don't want the money, it was never me who wanted it, I know I did it to help you." I said that I had promised to pay her back, so I told her to just give me her account details. That was the last one-on-one contact that I had with Sandrine,' Christine says sadly.

Sandrine and her drumming friend B were close; he called her often, and Christine says it's possible they were in a relationship. A few days before the day she was last seen Sandrine had had an argument with B about matters concerning some mutual friends. Sandrine felt caught in the middle of the conflict, and B told Sandrine he felt she'd betrayed their friendship. Two days before Sandrine went missing her mother Sylvia overheard a disturbing phone call from B during which he asked Sandrine to make a double suicide pact with him. When later confronted by Sandrine's family, B told them that Sandrine had been 'badgering him about it' and his response was to flippantly say, 'Well, let's both go and kill ourselves, then!' He claims he didn't mean it. Sylvia clearly recalls Sandrine responding on the phone, 'No, no, no!' to B's suggestion, at which point B hung up, and would not take any more of Sandrine's calls for the next two days. She was desperate to contact B, as she was fearful he was going to take his own life, and she tried calling his parents and their other friends, trying to find him. Sylvia and Sandrine sat up until 4 am talking about B the night before Sandrine went missing.

On the day Sandrine went missing, B was speaking to a friend of Sandrine's, P, who was living with Sandrine at the time she went missing. B said to P: 'That's it, I'm going to go and find her, and sort this out with her.' However, he instead went to a friend's home, and stayed there until late afternoon. It is unclear whether he tried to contact Sandrine, and her phone could only receive calls, not make them, so if Sandrine had tried to call B she would have had to find a public phone. Police have extensively interviewed and investigated B and do not believe he was involved in Sandrine's disappearance. 'B said to me that Sandrine was suicidal, that she would have gone and killed herself, and that we'll never find her,' says Christine, clearly upset. The day Sandrine went missing was B's birthday, and he had indicated he wanted to go to Kilcoy to a drumming camp for the weekend. B had apparently intended to go to a Buddhist retreat on the Gold Coast with Sandrine, but changed his mind.

Sandrine went missing on Friday 13 July 2012. Daughter Jessie was in Queensland at the time, staying with her Aunt Diana, and she and her mother had organised to go to the movies together on the Sunday to see a film. A week before, Sandrine had been to the Housing Commission office, pleading with them for a house so she and her children could all be together. Sandrine had also enrolled in another TAFE course. She was in the process of setting up her own website to sell her art and had started to contact art dealers. She had plans and appointments and commitments and goals – she doesn't sound like a woman who was planning to harm herself or run away. She was getting her life back on track. She was desperate for her children to live with her again, and was putting in place plans for that to happen.

Sandrine had told her mother that morning that she was keen to get away for the weekend and 'clear her head', and she was hoping to go to the Buddhist retreat on the Gold Coast. She had taken all her clothes from her mother's home – even the wet ones from the wash. She said she was planning to stay with her friend P the next week, which would explain why she collected all her belongings. P told Christine she'd found a note from Sandrine saying she was coming back to stay with her for a few days if that was okay, so Sandrine had made plans for the following week – more evidence she was not intending to run away.

That morning Sylvia and Sandrine had been driving around Caboolture for some time, going to various places like Centrelink and the bank, where Sandrine withdrew $250, and then to visit friends. By 10 am Sylvia was tired and wanted to stop at her son Phillip's home for a rest. Sandrine didn't want to go to Phillip's, as she thought her brother may try to have her admitted to hospital again, so she asked Sylvia to drive her to R's house – a previous neighbour of Sandrine's. Sylvia drove her to R's, and when they arrived Sylvia asked R if he was able to take Sandrine to the retreat on the Gold Coast. R replied that yes, he could take her later in the day, that it would be no problem. Sandrine bid farewell to her mother and went inside.

I spoke to Sylvia about when she'd dropped Sandrine at R's and she had a haunted look in her eyes, as she told me she'd felt very uneasy leaving Sandrine there, because of a number of people who were there at the time. She told me she'd dropped Sandrine off and driven home, but had such an ominous feeling about leaving her that she'd actually turned around and driven back to R's to try to pick her up again and bring her home.

After Sandrine was dropped at R's house, she asked R to take her to the home of her friend J. Sandrine had previously worked for J in the nursery industry and they remained good friends. When Sandrine needed some money, she knew she could always ask J to give her a few days' work to earn it. No-one is quite sure why she asked to be dropped at J's, and why she didn't simply ask her mother to take her to J's directly instead of to R's. R told police that Sandrine had changed her mind about wanting to go to the Gold Coast retreat. By the time Sylvia got back to R's house, Sandrine had already left to go to J's house. J lived just a five-minute drive from R, on Tomlinson Road in Caboolture.

Sandrine stayed at J's house from 11 am until about 5 pm that afternoon. Along with J, there was also a woman on the property who was living in a caravan, as well as J's 11-year-old son and his son's mate. J told police that Sandrine spent the day with him, and that she had decided not to go to the retreat because she wanted to spend the time with her daughter Jessie instead. She thought people were following her and she had removed the SIM cards from both her phones because she thought she could be tracked that way. Sandrine's paranoia about 'people coming to get her' meant that whenever she sat outside at J's house, she always positioned herself so she could see anyone coming up the driveway. She had previously told J there was a man who she didn't want to find her. Justine Ford's book *Unsolved Australia* also details J's claim that Sandrine was expecting a visit from someone at J's house that day, but she refused to name who that was.

J had planned to go to Caboolture Showground to a motocross gathering that evening, and at about 5 o'clock he started to get ready. He drove an old ambulance so he could transport his son's motorbikes. He suggested that Sandrine could go with them to the showground and he handed her an old jacket, as it was starting to drizzle rain. He also took Sandrine's laptop from the house and went to put it in the van. 'When he did this, Sandrine freaked out,' says Christine. 'Apparently, she'd typed something on there that she didn't want anyone to see. She was yelling at him: 'Why are you taking my laptop?' She got quite upset, so J put the laptop back inside.' The police now have the laptop but have not told the family what was on it. Justine Ford's book also details how Sandrine had told Christine she sent an email to the wrong person and was in trouble. Police have never revealed whether they found this email.

J's son and his mate got into the van. Sandrine said she would meet them at the gate leading out to the road, and she would open the gate for the van. At the time the property was hidden from view of the road by thick bushes so J could not see where Sandrine was waiting. By the time J had put the laptop inside the house and driven down to the gate, Sandrine had vanished, leaving the jacket he had lent her draped over his front fence. J thought perhaps she had double backed to the house and was inside, maybe in the toilet, so he parked the van and walked back up the driveway to the house, calling for her. There was no response. When he could not find her, he decided he would go on to motocross, all the while trying to phone her, but he could not reach her. When J arrived at the showground he discovered motocross had been cancelled, so he started to drive around the local streets looking for Sandrine.

J's son told his dad he thought he had seen Sandrine at a bus stop but at the time J didn't go back to check, as he was unable to turn his vehicle around on the road he was on. There were later possible sightings of a woman matching Sandrine's description at the bus stop, which was located on Beerburrum Road. There are no bus stops close to where Sandrine went missing; she would have had to walk some distance to get to the nearest one near Hasking Street, more than 4 kilometres away, taking her almost an hour – in the rain, and by the time she would have arrived it would have been close to 6 pm and dark. No-one saw her walking at all that afternoon or early evening.

'The police haven't really told us too much,' says Christine. 'All they really said was "a bus stop". We've driven around trying to figure out which bus stop it was and the only one we can think of is Beerburrum Road and Caboolture Road, near Pumicestone Road.'

It's possible Sandrine took a shortcut through bushland behind the house to Beerburrum Road. Tomlinson Road runs parallel to the busy D'Aguilar Highway. The road is mainly residential, with houses behind a long continuous fence until it comes to the bend at the end, where it turns into thick bushland, a strange contrast to the busy highway just a few metres away. There are no houses to be seen along this stretch of the road until the area opens up to a few acreage properties and the large, modern Destiny Church almost opposite where Sandrine was last seen. The church holds a Friday night youth group but it doesn't start until 6.30 pm, more than an hour after Sandrine was last seen. It is thought the other woman at the property that day stayed in her caravan – she didn't stay in the house or leave with the others. Police spoke to her when Sandrine went missing but she did not see anything.

I asked Christine if she thought Sandrine had intended to catch a bus to Kilcoy to join B at the drumming retreat, and Christine said she always felt that could have been the case. One of Sandrine's friends, who had been to the drumming group with her, lives close to the bus stop where the possible sightings of Sandrine had occurred. Christine thinks maybe Sandrine was trying to get to her friend so they could travel together to Kilcoy, as her friend lives in between J's house and the bus stop. Perhaps when she tried, her friend was not home, so she continued walking to the bus stop? Christine also thinks Sandrine might have only paused at the bus stop to take shelter from the rain, but then continued walking.

In the meantime, Sylvia phoned Christine to let her know that she hadn't found Sandrine when she drove back to R's house. Christine told her mum not to worry, that Sandrine would be at one of her friend's houses. She told Sylvia to try to call Sandrine's phone and if she didn't answer, they'd try to find her. At 10.30 pm that evening her brother Phillip received a phone call from J. He told Phillip what had happened that afternoon and how he'd been driving around trying to find Sandrine, but had been unable to. All the clothes she had collected from her mother's home were left at J's. Sandrine had originally taken all the clothes to R's, but made sure she brought them with her to J's. J said he'd left his house unlocked in case Sandrine came back there, but when he returned home nothing had been touched.

Phillip was concerned but not alarmed, and a little confused, as he had never met J before and had no idea who he was. J told Phillip that Sandrine had given him her brother's phone number in case of an emergency. Phillip asked J to please call him back the following morning if Sandrine still could not be found. Christine later asked J why Sandrine had given him Phillip's phone number as an emergency contact. Christine was surprised, as Sandrine had been worried Phillip might try to have her put back into hospital for assessment; Phillip had been noticing signs that Sandrine's illness was worsening. J told Christine that Sandrine thought she was being followed, and wanted him to have Phillip's number in case anything happened to her.

On the Sunday, Christine went to Phillip's house, by now concerned that no-one had heard from their sister in almost two days, and they searched her car, which was waiting to be fixed at Phillip's place. Phillip had spoken to Sandrine on the Thursday night, telling her he was getting the parts he needed for her car and that he'd have it fixed by the weekend for her. On the Friday morning, Sandrine withdrew the money she'd need to pay Phillip for the car parts, so she intended to see him in the next day or so. She told her mother at the time she also needed to pay back two friends who had loaned her money.

Becoming increasingly worried, Christine went onto Facebook and friend-requested all Sandrine's friends, so she could contact them all and let them know Sandrine was missing, and ask if anyone had seen her that weekend. They hadn't yet reported her missing to police; they wanted to check with all her friends in case she'd decided to spend the weekend with one of them, as she often did. By Sunday, all Sandrine's friends had responded that they hadn't heard from her, and the family started to get really worried. That was also the day she had planned to go to the movies with daughter Jessie. In Sandrine's car Christine found her previous month's phone bill, so she and her daughter called every number on it, asking whoever picked up the phone if they'd heard from Sandrine. If the number wasn't answered, they texted a photo of Sandrine with a message asking the person to please call them back if they'd heard from her. She also found Sandrine's phone book in her belongings at Diana's house, and they called even more phone numbers. No-one had heard from her. By the end of the first week, they'd contacted absolutely everyone, and when not even her closest friends and her children had heard a thing, they knew something was very wrong.

'We had police coming to and from my brother's house with paperwork for us, like media releases,' says Christine. 'We signed all of that within the first week, but they still never put out a media release or anything. Any of the media attention we got was from us pushing it. Originally, I think Sandrine was only ever advertised on your missing person page. We didn't know how to get her on anywhere else. I've become quite computer savvy now,' she chuckles.

It was eight days before Queensland Police issued a media release about Sandrine. After the first week the family decided they needed to try to get some media attention on Sandrine's case themselves. 'We emailed everybody,' says Christine. 'The only one who helped us out originally was the local paper, and I think that was because one of the girls who worked there had gone to school with my sisters, so she knew Sandrine, Bernadette and Diana quite well.'

As time went on with no leads, the family set up the first of the Facebook pages to make appeals for information about Sandrine's disappearance. Christine was approached by a woman named Di Williams, who has been a true blessing for Sandrine's cause, working tirelessly to raise awareness and organise appeals, and still does today. Other families of the missing often contact Christine for help and she refers them to Di and her admin team to assist them too. 'Paula does all the banners; my family are so grateful for all their help,' says Christine.

Christine contacted the Buddhist retreat on the Gold Coast where Sandrine was intending to spend the weekend, and even sent them her photo in case she had registered under another name, but they had not seen her. The retreat organisers told Christine that they had run a retreat that weekend but it operated strictly on a bookings-only basis, and people could not just show up and join in. Sandrine had not made a booking so even if she had decided to go that weekend, she would have been turned away. Christine then went on to contact every Buddhist retreat in Australia, in desperation.

Police took a cadaver dog to the property where Sandrine was last seen but nothing was found. They also searched nearby creeks with divers and brought in the SES for a ground search. The family wanted to take another dog over to the property next door, one they had organised themselves, but police refused permission. Christine argued that the property was empty and awaiting demolition, so there should not have been a problem, but her request was denied. Christine was also told that the direct neighbours of the property had never been questioned, despite all other residents of the street being interviewed by police. This neighbour has since been interviewed, but Christine is unhappy it took so long. There is bushland at the back of Tomlinson Road, and a creek that can apparently be crossed via a small bridge. Ironically, the bushland backs onto the Caboolture SES – they would have literally been searching their own backyard.

As the months went on it became clear something terrible had happened. In September, her daughter's birthday came and went with no 'Happy Birthday' from her mother. Her son turned 14, and no phone call or Facebook post from Sandrine. For a mother who was devoted to her children, it was unthinkable for her to miss their birthdays.

Christine says:

We've had a lot of contacts with psychics and the majority are saying she's dead, but there are some who say she's alive, and in a cult. A local one who was recommended to me said she's alive but is being held; she said it was a cult and she can't leave. I was contacted by one of the psychics from the TV show The One and she said she didn't sense her being dead, but being trapped. We've all gone out and searched for Sandrine, the whole family. The areas the psychics told us she was at, or her body was at … we've pretty much searched the whole of Kilcoy, we've gone and checked them all out. My doctors told me off because I was out walking through the bush searching and I hurt my hip, so I had to stop. Under bushes, under rocks, the number of places we looked …

The Department of Housing got in touch to say there was a house available for Sandrine, and the family were then in the very difficult position of having to tell them that she had gone missing and they'd have to give the house to someone else. The house Sandrine had worked so hard to get. By now Christine was sure something very serious had happened to her sister:

My first thought was foul play. I had found out how many plans she'd made for the following couple of weeks, so I thought no, something's not adding up. She wasn't suicidal, and she had written in her diary she would never do that again, she saw how much it had hurt everyone. It's not something I believe Sandrine would do, even though she's attempted it in the past. We just tried to figure out her last movements and dissect her last few days and weeks before she went missing. The whole family thought it was foul play, at first. Then there was a split in their thinking and even though at first I thought she'd passed away, now I've learned about the cults and how they work and I realised hang on, that's a possibility.

The family started to hear rumours that Sandrine may have been sighted in Byron Bay, in northern NSW. A friend of hers contacted Christine to say before she went missing Sandrine had visited Byron Bay and introduced this friend to several other people Sandrine knew from the area, and it was somewhere she loved to visit.

'Sandrine is … was … is … I keep saying "is" … it's so confusing,' says Christine sadly. 'I hold out the highest hope but if that's what she's done, it's put us through hell. We know she's not well but she's also so smart, everything is planned, so I don't know, I don't understand. Yes, she may have had a few financial difficulties but that was nothing, she could have got a job in a heartbeat, that was nothing. I don't understand how she would get up and walk away.'

Several years ago, Sandrine's sister Diana received a missed phone call from a NSW number. Christine decided to call the number back and it was answered by a man who told the sisters that he had not made the call, that no-one had used his phone to make any calls, and at the time of the missed call he had been working on his property nowhere near the house. He said he doesn't lock his house and his property is in the middle of nowhere. Interestingly, the man lives not far from Byron Bay, and that is a location that Sandrine loved, and was also where there were possible sightings of her. Police took the information seriously and investigated this call and the man, but determined that he had no connection at all to Sandrine and was not involved in any way with her disappearance. But, what if? What if Sandrine had sneaked into this man's house to use the phone that day?

'When she went missing, everything stopped. It's like she just vanished, she walked off the edge of the earth, and would no longer … be.' Christine's voice wavers with emotion:

One part of me is saying yes, she could be in one of these cults in Byron Bay, that's my top possibility, but for her to be away for years and not contact anybody … and we have had the odd weird phone call here and there where the phone will ring but the other person doesn't speak when you answer. So, that makes me think that maybe she is trying to contact us.

In those places there's no technology and no way for them to be able to contact anyone. If she's chosen to be there of her own free will and doesn't want to be found, the rest of the group will protect her, even if they know she's a missing person, they won't tell her they've seen a poster or anything.

My sister Bernadette has been to a cult where a guy calls himself Jesus, but there was only part of the complex she was allowed to look at; he did take one of the flyers of Sandrine and told Bernadette that Sandrine was definitely not there. Sandrine was raised Catholic, but she was more into self-healing and Buddhism. I've been told by others that if she's in one of the stricter cults, they make them wait two years before they're allowed to go out at all and go into town.

The family cling to the smallest of hopes every time there's a possible sighting reported. Christine says: 'There was a sighting at Bangalow markets of a woman who looked like Sandrine, but their local police officer was on holidays. So, my sister contacted Byron Bay police directly, only to be told that they didn't have Sandrine in their system as a missing person and they couldn't do anything. My sister argued with him, she told him to look at the database. He said, "I am looking at the database!" She said, "Which database are you looking at?" and he told her the New South Wales one. She told him to look at the national one, that she's a Queensland missing person.

'He finally put us on to his supervisor, we explained the situation to him, he then looked up the database and said, "Oh, yep, there she is." We told him who we believed had been seen with the woman who looked like Sandrine, and the officer said yes, he was known to the police and they could check CCTV footage from the markets. All we knew was that they'd been at the markets in August or September, but some of the footage had been deleted, as they don't keep it for very long. The same thing happened with some footage from Woodford. We thought if she'd tried to get to the drumming camp at Kilcoy she might have tried to get a lift on the D'Aguilar Highway, as that's only just a metre away from Tomlinson Road. There's a gap there where she could have crossed over and waited for a lift from one of her friends.'

Christine was frustrated at what she sees as a lacklustre response from police about Sandrine's disappearance. 'They know her as just a number, they don't know her personally, they don't know her like we do,' she says. Christine was told by police just before Christmas 2013 that they no longer had the resources to be able to work on Sandrine's case, and that she would have to make an application for them to allocate more funds.

'At that point my brother and I lost it with the police,' says Christine. 'They only got a statement from my sister Diana almost two years after Sandrine went missing, and Sandrine lived with Diana until a week before she disappeared! And the girl she left the note for, who she was planning to stay with the next week, they only just got her statement too. They're getting statements from people only now and I'm saying, why wasn't this done at the beginning? Why now? It's ridiculous. It makes me feel like they haven't done their jobs as well as they said they had originally. Everything that's been investigated so far has been because of us giving it to them.'

Christine believes there's another diary that was current at the time she went missing, but she doesn't know where it is, and isn't sure whether police have it. Sandrine might have had it with her when she went missing. It was more than a year before Christine, Phillip and Jessie asked the police about Sandrine's green crochet bag, and realised she must have had it with her. It was not amongst her belongings held by police as evidence, and not among the clothes the family picked up from J's. Strangely, Sandrine's passport is also missing. Police did check whether she'd left the country but she had not.

'The green bag went everywhere with her,' says Christine. 'It's a small, crocheted bag. But it wasn't big enough to fit the diary in. In her car we found the cover for it, but no diary. I hope the police do have it, as that would give me an insight into what was going on up to that date. Me, my brother and Jessie went into the police station to ask about it, and at the end of it we got marched into their office so they could find out what we'd said on SBS.'

In 2013, Christine and Sandrine's daughter Jessie appeared on the SBS TV program *Insight*, on a show about missing persons. The experience was too much for Jessie, who had to leave the floor in tears when the host came to ask the family questions. 'I went on the SBS show, and the police wanted to know what I'd said,' says Christine. 'Ron Iddles had contacted the Queensland Police after the show and told them, "You really need to keep this family informed," so I said to the police, "Well, how about you just watch the program?" What I did say off camera was to a police officer who only deals with missing persons, and I did raise my concerns about the way this case is being handled. We're now getting monthly updates since Ron Iddles got involved.' Ron Iddles is a former Victoria Police homicide detective, very highly respected in the force.

Due to the family, and Di's excellent campaign of awareness about Sandrine there have been possible sightings of her reported to police. 'There was a possible sighting in a shopping centre in Coffs Harbour that was given to us and also Crime Stoppers,' says Christine:

The police officer on Sandrine's case was on holidays, so he didn't get the message until the next day. I called the shopping centre security myself and asked them if they could send me the CCTV footage of this woman who had been spotted, and they said they couldn't give it to anyone except police, so they'd have to request it, but he said he'd pull out the footage, find the woman and have it all ready for when the police did contact them. I sent them Sandrine's photo. The police officer called us in to see the footage once he'd been sent it and said the woman did look like Sandrine. I looked at it and said: 'Nup.' My brother looked at it and said: 'Hmm … I don't know.' I said: 'Phillip, look at the colour of her skin.' Sandrine tans very easily; her father is Maltese, and she has really olive skin, so in summer her skin goes really dark. The woman in the footage had really white skin. And I said also, she's too tall, and her boobs are too small.

Christine laughed at that last statement. 'The police officer started laughing and I said, "Look, I know my sister's cleavage!" The policeman said, "Um, I'm not sure how I'm going to write this into the report! Incorrect cleavage!"' They all dissolved into fits of laughter. It was a much-needed light-hearted moment, after so much pain. The woman in the security footage also had tattoos, and Sandrine wasn't a huge fan of them.

'She did always say she wanted to get one, but she would never have covered all her arms and her chest in them. Another time, my sister Diana had gone to the shopping centre to buy some shoes for her children. She looks very similar to Sandrine. Next thing I know I get a frantic inbox from someone saying, "I just saw Sandrine!" The lady was scrambling to get security footage. I sent her a photo of Sandrine and she said the woman looked similar but with lighter hair. I sent her a photo of Diana and she said, "Yes, that's her!" I had to tell her it was our other sister.'

Diana has also been stopped in the shops by people thinking she is her missing sister. She tries to think positively about her sister's safe return, and remembers the last time she saw Sandrine. 'I gave her a big cuddle and I told her we were going to grow old together,' says Diana.

'Sandrine had lots of close friends that she regularly phoned,' says Christine. 'Every two or three weeks they'd touch base. Sandrine just had to have friends with her. She relied on them as family. Some of her friends were higher on her priority list than her family. If she was in trouble she'd call one of those friends and they'd help her, she knew that. She had car troubles just a week before she went missing; it broke down and she called one of her friends in Sydney to help her pay for the car to get towed to the garage to get fixed. The car ended up being towed to my brother Philip's house, and Sandrine's friend fixed it for her there, no questions asked. He just said, "Pay me back when you can, mate, no problem."

'She had awesome friends. She could go to them and talk to them and stay with them as well, if she didn't want to stay with family. Before her car broke down she was staying with a friend out at Mt Mee, then she came down to stay with Mum, who was on her own. In one way I'd feel hurt if she's gone and not wanting anything to do with us, but I'd understand that's how she had to deal with it. Unless she's with friends she wouldn't be happy, as that's what kept her happy. Unless she went and made all new friends – which isn't impossible for Sandrine – but there's no reason for her to do that.'

I asked Christine what her happiest memory of Sandrine was and she firmly said, 'Camping.' She said as children it was playing soccer but as adults, it was camping. 'In the last two or three years before she went missing, as we were both separated, we'd all go camping or motor bike riding together. She bought motorbikes for my kids too. I remember her never being scared of anything; she'd just pick up a crab, whereas I'd be too scared. She also knew so much about the bush, which plants you could eat and which ones were poisonous, as she'd done courses in that. She was very self-sufficient. She was always telling us which plants did what and which ones we could touch and which ones we couldn't.'

Christine says she's a totally different person since her sister went missing. 'I check and double check things now. I don't take things at face value anymore. If someone says something, I'll go and check it now. I don't take things for granted anymore and I'm not as naïve as I used to be. I don't let people take advantage of me. I stand up and if I've got something to say, I'll say it. Before, I just used to shut my mouth. It's made me a lot stronger – there are some days when I don't know how I keep going, but I just really think about the last words that Sandrine spoke to me.'

In her last conversation with Sandrine Christine told her that she'd 100 per cent support Sandrine if she was in a traumatic situation she felt she needed to tackle. 'It feels like I have to be her voice. If people are saying she was suicidal, or she's this or that, I take it personally and will say no, that's not the case, shut your mouth. If that's how they thought she was then they weren't a true friend and didn't really know her. Sandrine used to say to me, "I don't know how you keep it all together, after all you've been through." She used to come to me for advice in that department. I handled stress in different ways than she did. She was following some of my advice and thinking about confronting people about her past issues. I told her to lock them away in the back of her mind and not stress about it.'

Christine feels she's dealt with Sandrine's disappearance in the same way as she has with the other painful events in her life, but this is by far the worst:

> *I have my moments where I lose it totally. I've had a lot of other things going on in my own personal life too, and it's made me really think about my children and Sandrine's children, so I think I'm doing things for her, too, on her behalf. I know if she was here she'd be with me at every one of those difficult times. I will never stop, until I find her, or her body. Whenever I hear on the news that they've found a bone somewhere I always ask them to test it to see if it's Sandrine. Every time I hear a body has been found I say okay, is it female or male? And if it's male you get that sense of relief, which is bad but it means it's not her, maybe she is out there.*

At the moment I'm always expecting a phone call, I don't know why. I've just been on edge for the last few weeks. Expecting them to say we've found her, or we know where she is. I honestly wouldn't mind if I got a call that said: 'We've found her, we've checked her over, she's fine but she doesn't want to see anyone' … that would hurt in a way but at least I'd know she's okay and I can stop looking, for my mum.

It's mainly for my mum that I'm doing this; Mum was the last one from the family who was with her and she has been really sick because of it all. Our family has become closer and tighter since Sandrine went missing. We are always there and always looking out for each other. I think Diana's had the most trouble in handling it. It's the not knowing.

Everyone copes differently, and however they choose to cope is just fine. Diana holds out hope that her sister will walk through the door one day with quite a story to tell, and I hope beyond hope that she's right.

In 2017, Sandrine's supporters gained permission from the property owner to search the area next door to where Sandrine was last seen in Tomlinson Road. The search team included Sandrine's niece and her friend, and long-time supporter Taz. Taz told me about the search. 'I approached every single resident in the street and found out that the end property, owned by the sawmill and rented out for over 20 years, had never been searched. I asked permission from the tenant to search and she said that was fine. We walked down the back of the property to a paddock where the tenant said she'd previously seen other people. After about half an hour, using a metal detector, I caught a glance of a small piece of material. After digging, documenting and photographing, we called the police. We realised we had found black dress pants, mauve material too deteriorated to state what it was, and a bra along with other items.'

The very first news article on Sandrine's page on my website says Sandrine was last seen wearing 'a light mauve long-sleeved jumper and dark dress pants.'

Di Williams tells me they also found sunglasses that looked very much like the ones Sandrine owned at the time. Di said the searchers stopped when they found the clothing, terrified that if they kept digging they'd actually find Sandrine. The items they found were inside a piece of rolled up carpet. There was another object with the clothing that really caught the searchers' attention: half a large seashell. Sandrine loved shells. Sandrine's daughter actually has the other half of the shell, a clear indication that the carpet and its contents had something to do with Sandrine. Also in the carpet was a hessian-type bag, and the family believe the bag is the one Sandrine had with her at the time she disappeared.

Everything was handed over to police, who then called in the SES to search the rest of the property. They waited, eagerly, for the results of DNA testing – and waited, and waited. Finally, after six months, Christine rang police, and was told the tests had been 'inconclusive'. The items had likely been out in the elements for too long. They did not find any DNA, and they could not prove the items found had belonged to Sandrine. Another blow for the family, who had really got their hopes up that they might have finally found a lead. They still believe, as do I, that the clothing, shell, glasses and bag belong to Sandrine.

Christine says there has been only one police officer, from the Homicide Squad, who has been helpful to the family. 'On one hand we felt a coroner's inquest would be a good thing, which is what he was preparing for, but on the other hand we knew by the way he was speaking that he just wanted it off his desk, and he'd had enough. That's the feeling the family gets. He didn't want to have to worry about it anymore. If we sent him information he did go and look into it. He'd email us and say good work, keep it up, but then turn around and tell us to butt out. That gets a bit confusing. I think I'm his thorn.'

In 2018, the detectives working on Sandrine's case came to the conclusion she had killed herself. They compiled their brief of evidence and handed it all over to Queensland Coroner Christine Clements. The family believed police had requested an inquest.

'The lead officer told us they were waiting on an inquest,' said Christine. 'But the next we knew we'd received the coroner's report, and police had no comment to make on it.' The coroner chose not to hold an inquest, instead making her ruling based on the police brief. The report was never made public; I have not seen it, but somehow members of the media got hold of it. The family asked police for a copy of all the evidence they'd compiled and presented to the coroner, but their request was refused. 'We asked for it to be given to us,' said Christine. 'We even went to Brisbane and filed paperwork for it. We were told we're not entitled to the brief that she based her decision on.'

The family are very unhappy and claim the coroner's report is full of inaccuracies. 'My name is even spelled wrong,' says Christine. 'Some of the information the coroner used was about my childhood, and what she said is false. And there are names in the report that no-one in the family knows. None of us know who they're speaking about, but they're meant to be Sandrine's friends.' The coroner ruled Sandrine's death was likely a suicide, but her family are adamant this is the wrong conclusion. The coroner did concede it was possible Sandrine had been murdered, but there was no evidence of this. The coroner raised concerns about the men in her life that Sandrine was fearful of, but said her previous suicide attempts led her to the conclusion that she had taken her own life.

A strange five-page letter was sent to Sandrine's former partner, Michael, six months after she went missing, from someone calling themselves Rosetta Bunton. The coroner's report states: 'Police established the letter had been sent from Horsham in Victoria. It contained personal accurate information about Sandrine's family including the correct addresses, names of her children, and details of her eldest daughter staying in Sydney. The letter urged Michael to forget about Sandrine and move on with his life. Police forensic examination of the letter was inconclusive – the specimen writer could not be identified or excluded. The name Rosetta Bunton could not be identified or traced.' Christine is certain Sandrine did not write the letter, saying the writer even spelled her mother's name incorrectly. But she does feel the writer must have known Sandrine, to have included so many accurate details about her and her family.

In 2017, *A Current Affair* did a piece on Sandrine, interviewing her brother Phillip, who choked up with emotion as he said: 'I miss her company. I miss the company of her kids, who we used to spend time with, and the family gatherings we used to have. I drive down the road and could swear I've seen her. I've had to stop, turn around, go back and have a look.' At that point of the interview Phillip has to stop; he is overcome with tears.

The program also spoke with J, Mr C and B, all of whom seemed happy to speak to the reporter. J was interviewed by Chris Allen and said that Sandrine had made him promise not to call her brother. He had to break his word to her that he wouldn't. He said Sandrine didn't want anyone to know where she was. He called Phillip as he was worried about her. All three men told the TV show they had told police everything they knew about Sandrine.

Mr C told *A Current Affair*: 'Sandrine was an absolutely beautiful girl, but she had a very troubled mind, as everyone seems to understand.' Although he acknowledged they had been previously living together, he claims to have not seen her for a long time before she went missing, and also to not have known she was missing for some time. 'She had been disappeared for months,' he said. He said he didn't think Sandrine was alive, but he didn't know who would want to harm her as 'she was a beautiful person'. He was asked why Sandrine would have been scared or edgy before she went missing and he said: 'Her troubled mind would have caused that.'

Sandrine's Aunt Kathy was also interviewed on the program, and showed the TV crew where they found the clothing. She showed them a piece of mauve fabric, which is exactly the same colour as the jumper she was last seen wearing. Police declined to speak to *A Current Affair*.

So, what now? Things are at a standstill. Police and the coroner believe Sandrine took her own life, but her family believe she's been murdered. It seems that police are no longer actively investigating Sandrine's disappearance. Christine is upset at the words the police used with her. 'The officer in charge said to me that in ten years or so when they are digging up the ground to build the next Woolworths and her remains are found, then they'll reopen the case, but not before. It's case closed unless new information comes in or she's found. That's when they could reopen the case as foul play.'

In early 2022, the family told the media they were planning to appeal the coroner's decision. In January 2024 there was a major development. Christine received a letter from the Coronial Investigations Officer:

> *The investigation into the death of Ms Jourdan has been reopened. The Deputy State Coroner is considering if an inquest will be held but no decision has been made at this stage.*

Shortly after the announcement, Channel Nine's *Under Investigation* TV program, hosted by Liz Hayes, devoted an episode to Sandrine's case. The show detailed some startling new information that had come to light. A neighbour of J, on Tomlinson Road, told police she heard three gunshots at the time Sandrine went missing. Others heard a woman screaming, both on Tomlinson Road and on Beerburrum Road. A woman living near Beerburrum Road said she saw two males leaving an area of bushland, where the screams were heard. There is also an apparent witness, who was walking her dog, who said she saw a woman she thinks was Sandrine talking to two men in a blue Holden Commodore. She said the men pulled the woman into the car. According to the witness, this happened across the road from J's house, further up past the church. Watching the show was the first time I have heard this information.

The program also talked about how Sandrine's laptop, in the possession of police, was found to have sophisticated encryption programs installed on it, highly unusual for something belonging to a civilian. A second laptop belonging to Sandrine was found to have a search history connected to a human trafficking website. Someone also recently hacked into Sandrine's Facebook account and changed the passwords, meaning her family can no longer access it. When I wrote this chapter, I was able to see it, so I'm glad I copied those quotes from Sandrine, if it is now gone.

These new developments are a major step forward; The inquest is now even more imperative; it MUST be held. Sandrine deserves no less.

On the second anniversary of Sandrine's disappearance, back in July 2014, I was invited to attend a special Queensland Carz rally from Caboolture to Kenilworth in Queensland. I had the honour of meeting Sandrine's beautiful family, including finally meeting Christine, who I interviewed by phone for hours for this book. When I met Sandrine's daughter Jessie, the DJ at the event was playing Rick Springfield's 'Jessie's Girl'. I smiled at Jessie and said: 'They're playing your song.' She smiled back, sadly, and said: 'Yes, that's why Mum named me Jessie, after this song.' She hugged me and said softly, over and over: 'Trying not to cry.' As I was writing this chapter I came across a letter to Sandrine written by Jessie, just over a year after her mum disappeared. It is heart-wrenching:

> Mum,
>
> *I have been writing letters to let you know what has been happening if you do come back, but my honest and gut feeling is that you aren't, I wrote my final letter and oh my god it was really hard. You were the person that gave me my life, a special gift normally overlooked. I need to say goodbye. I honestly believe that you are gone and you're not coming back. I'm not angry with you, please know that, I wish you happiness and hope that you are in no more pain. It has been a painful year and a bit and not just for me but for the family and the people that have been helping raise awareness, thank you much, I think I can speak on behalf of the family by saying thank you for all the support and help you have been giving us. I feel like this is the final step of letting go of the pain and the lost feeling I have been having since your disappearance, I love you beyond words Mum and can't explain enough how much I will miss you and how grateful I was to have you in my life.*

My own teary moment at the Kenilworth gathering came when I met Sandrine's teenaged son Sam. I gave him a hug then he and his girlfriend had a look around the AMPR tent we had set up for the day. I printed out lots of missing persons flyers for those missing in Kenilworth and the Sunshine Coast and, of course, lots of Sandrine. I watched Sam as he looked at the flyers of his mum, looking at her photo, especially the beautiful one chosen by supporter Paula, of Sandrine encased in white soft clouds.

The look on Sam's face is one I will never forget – such sadness and helplessness. He misses her so much. His girlfriend put her arm around him, and I knew he'd be okay; he has a wonderful family looking after him and his sisters, but he will always have that sadness in his heart. When I saw it, I teared up. It is times like that those I am reminded so clearly why I need to help these families.

Sandrine's mother Sylvia is lovely; she gave me a huge hug when I met her, then gave my husband a hug. She then declared: 'I've decided I am going to hug everyone I meet today, as I'm so grateful they're all here for Sandrine.' I spoke to her for a long time; she's been unwell but there's a spark of determination in her – she won't stop looking for her girl. I laminated a photo of Sandrine; she has her head thrown back and a glorious smile on her face, she is wearing a colourful jumper that is so very much her Bohemian style, and I attached the photo to the tent with tape. It came loose in the breeze and I found Sylvia reattaching it, and looking at it wistfully.

'She's so beautiful,' she said. I spoke to her about this book, and she hadn't known I was writing it; Sylvia had been very sick when I interviewed Christine, and she hadn't yet filled her mum in on the project. Sylvia interrupted me as I was talking about it, looking at me in wonder, and she said: 'You're writing a book? You're putting Sandrine in a book?' I said yes, and Sylvia started to cry tears of gratitude. She embraced me and said, 'Oh, thank you, thank you, that's wonderful, thank you!' She was overwhelmed. This family is amazed that people still care about Sandrine, are still looking for her. They almost can't believe that people want to help them.

Sandrine's sister Diana bears a striking resemblance to her, as evidenced by the woman who stopped her in the shop thinking she was Sandrine. She's a cheerful woman, busy with three young children and a husband, and she has a positive outlook on life. She is still hopeful Sandrine has simply chosen to go away for a while and will be back one day. She looked at the printed flyers of Sandrine's photo on the table in the tent and quietly said: 'I hope she comes home soon.'

I have spoken to so many people about Sandrine, and watched interviews with others. Almost every person has told me a different story about her. I believe there are many different versions of Sandrine, and the truth lies somewhere in between.

If you know what happened to Sandrine Jourdan, now is the time to speak up. Call 1800 333 000.

CHAPTER TEN
Stephen Mitchell

Stephen Mitchell was last seen on 20 March 2007 in the Mortdale and
Beverly Hills areas of Sydney. He was 35 at the time he went missing.

Stephen Mitchell has a very close, loving family who would do anything for him, and they have never stopped searching. They still hope he's out there somewhere, and may even read this.

Stephen had lots of older siblings and the family lived in several suburbs of Sydney while he was growing up. The family lived in the Redfern area and moved to a unit in Riverwood until sister Sandra was seven and Stephen was five.

They moved to nearby Peakhurst and stayed until Stephen was 12. When Sandra was 14, she packed her bags and left home due to the violence between her parents. Her older sister, Kathy Romeo, a runaway herself, tracked Sandra down, but the desperate act was enough to make her mother realise she needed to get her children away from their father. Margaret Mitchell packed up her children and left, starting their new life.

'It was one of the bravest things I've ever done in my life,' says Sandra about her desperate act of running away. 'My mother and all of us children were the most settled we'd ever been; we didn't have to walk on eggshells anymore. It was a positive, healthy change, but obviously had repercussions. I was adventurous and somewhat rebellious. Maybe when our parents separated it affected Stephen differently. That's where the rocky road started. For him and me, definitely, as we were the closest. I was a bit of a tomboy, so we got on well.'

Sandra remembers her early childhood with great happiness, and her fondest memory of Stephen comes from this time. 'When we were young we used to run around and laugh and be typical kids,' she says. 'We lived next door to a park and were always in there playing cricket and football, and when other kids would come into the park we'd play with them too. Stephen was always bubbly and smiling. After he disappeared, I bumped into an old friend who I'd had a as a teenager; I told him Stephen was missing and he said, "All I remember about him was this happy, bubbly kid.""

However, as the children grew older both Sandra and Stephen lost their childhood happiness. After Stephen went missing, Sandra and her sisters looked back on his childhood to try to work out at what point Stephen started to change, as they didn't realise it at the time. Stephen had been a very social child who had lots of friends, but this changed dramatically when he started high school.

Sandra and her older sister were not the only children to run away from home – Stephen used to sometimes disappear as a child. Sandra remembers: 'There was one time at Riverwood; it was walking distance to the next house we were to move into so Mum walked there one day to look at the property with Stephen. He didn't want to go inside the house, so she told him to wait outside while she ducked inside for a quick look. When she came outside, he was gone. The police were searching for him … he wasn't even five years old, but he'd walked a 15-minute walk all the way back home, crossed a main road. There was another time, when we lived in the unit, there was a council library out the front and he'd often take off and go and hang out there. He was only four. He was a wanderer.' However, Sandra can't work out how Stephen went from being so fearless when he was a young child to being so fearful of everything as an adult.

Stephen's tendency to wander continued as he grew older. 'He would not go to school, and just disappear, forget what time it was, and come home late,' says Sandra. 'We had to drive around the streets trying to find him. Sometimes he'd be sitting at the shops; he'd lost track of time, because he wasn't at school. He just didn't want to go to school, he didn't fit in. His social life slowly diminished, and often he just stayed at home.'

As Stephen moved further into his teenage years, his personality slowly changed. 'He became a lot quieter and more rebellious,' says Sandra. 'It was hard to see looking back; I wonder if it had something to do with our parents separating and having no father figure. There was never a typical father and son relationship over the years between Dad and Stephen – that aspect of their relationship didn't change when we left. There was never a father and son thing. Stephen was very close to Mum.' Their father used to phone occasionally, but they had very little contact with him after he separated from Margaret. Stephen saw his father rarely as an adult.

The family continued to move around the southern Sydney suburbs, trying to settle in one place. Stephen went to Narwee High School for about a year and Sandra thinks he may have been bullied, but is unsure to what extent he talked about it, or whether anything was done about it, as Stephen's reaction was to just refuse to go to school. Margaret and her children moved from Narwee into a house in Hurstville. At this time, when he was about 14, Stephen chose to not attend school regularly. He told his sister that he would jump on a train and 'go for a ride' instead of going to school.

'The new house was within walking distance of Kingsgrove High, but they wouldn't take Stephen. I don't know why,' says Sandra. It's possible that Stephen's regular lack of attendance affected his chances of enrolment at the school. 'He'd never been expelled, never had a fight or been violent, so I'm not sure why they wouldn't take him,' says Sandra. 'He had to go to Kingsgrove North, which was not our local school, it was about four kilometres away. Mum didn't drive, so it was hard to get there. There's no way he would have walked it. He didn't last long there, and he had to attend counselling organised by the school board because of his lack of attendance. He ended up at a school called Woniora Road School in Hurstville, which was a school for troubled children.'

Woniora School is a New South Wales Government school that caters for secondary students diagnosed with emotional disorders and mental health issues. Their website says the enrolment of a student is based on the appraisal of the student's individual emotional needs and abilities. Stephen stayed at the school until he completed year 10.

After leaving school, Stephen was very keen to enter the workforce. Sandra says he would have tried anything and everything that was offered to him, but he really struggled to find a job. 'He wanted to succeed, and make a future for himself,' says Sandra. He went to plenty of job interviews.' He did briefly work as a delivery boy for the local pharmacy, but the job did not last long. Stephen started spending more time shut away inside his bedroom.

Margaret became very unwell, and she leaned on Sandra for assistance and support. Sandra was the most independent of Margaret's children, as she drove and worked full time. 'I was the one who would oversee things and support the family wherever I could,' says Sandra. She visited Margaret in hospital every day, often taking 19-year-old Stephen and her sisters with her. One of Margaret's final wishes was to be reunited with Peter, a son she had given up for adoption many years before, and as she lay gravely ill in hospital, Peter was given the news about where his birth mother was. He immediately jumped in the car and headed for Sydney. He met his other five siblings for the first time. Sandra remembers them all being very excited to meet him, and it was a positive meeting; they all got on very well. Stephen was very happy to meet his brother, and Peter and his partner Michelle stayed with their new family for several nights. Stephen even happily came out of his room to get to know Peter during his stay.

Margaret was heavily sedated at the hospital, and had a serious heart condition, and the nurses were concerned she wouldn't be strong enough to meet Peter, so they very gradually brought her out of sedation and introduced her to her son. 'It was amazing,' says Sandra tearfully. 'That's all she wanted, to meet him. Even the nurses were a mess. We were all very happy for her. For years prior she would read the Sunday papers, and see the adoption notices and stories of children taken away from their mothers. This caused her ongoing anguish, as she felt she was coerced into signing the adoption paperwork, and she always wanted to meet him.'

After Margaret's death, Peter maintained a close relationship with his sisters and brother and frequently visited them in Sydney. Tragically, Peter passed away from a heart attack in his early forties. Sandra would love to be able to help her nephews and nieces Bianca and Peter-James and Brooke find out more about their father's birth side of the family. Peter's birth name was Steven Folkes Romeo but when he passed he was known as Peter Harry Honeyman, his adopted family's surname. Since losing Stephen, Sandra has a new appreciation for how important family connection is.

Sandra eventually moved out of home, and didn't see her brother as much as she had growing up, but they remained close. Not having a father on the scene made her more aware of the need to look after her brother, and she encouraged him as much as she could in his quest to find work and become independent. Even up until just before he went missing Stephen talked about trying to find a job. 'I always helped him out in any way I could. He was very good with his money; if he ever had a loan from me he always paid it right back. He was very careful with his unemployment money, and never wasted a cent. After he went missing, the police checked his bank account, and he'd only ever taken out the bare minimum of what he needed.' He very rarely drank, and didn't smoke. Stephen would spend money on music, his mobile phone, and he liked clothes. 'He had to have nice clothes, good brands, he'd like his surf brands and good sneakers,' says Sandra. 'He'd saved up and furnished his own bedroom with what he wanted. He was quite level headed in that regard.'

As Stephen moved from his teenage years into his twenties, he became more and more introverted, now spending most of his time in his room. Sandra had a boyfriend by this stage, who got on well with Stephen. Sandra thought that was good for Stephen, who never left the house to pursue his own friendships, as at least he had some male company in his life instead of spending all his time with his mother and sisters. Sandra was often out socialising with her friends, so Stephen spent more time with his family, and they all enjoyed being at home together. 'Whoever came to the house, he'd come out of his room and be fine with, and he'd go out fishing, but other than that he just wouldn't leave the house,' says Sandra.

Stephen was still very keen to find employment. Sandra says, 'He always went by the rule book when it came to his unemployment, he was always looking for a job.' He occasionally had a one or two day trial period at a job, but they never lasted. With his limited education, skills and experience the only places that would hire him tended to be factories.

After years of trying to get a job, Stephen finally started work at a carpet factory at Peakhurst. It was near to Sandra, so she would sometimes pick him up after work, if it was a hot day. Stephen worked there for about 15 months, until the factory closed down. Stephen was in his mid-to-late twenties, and after this he never worked again. 'He lacked confidence,' says Sandra. 'He wasn't handy … he'd mow the lawn, but give him a hammer and nail and he wouldn't be any good with them.'

Even though Sandra had now moved out, she tried to keep an eye on her little brother. 'I'd help him if he needed clothing, I'd take him shopping and make sure he got the clothes he liked,' she says. 'We were always close, but I was working full time, and was spending less time with Stephen. He'd still talk to me about his daily things, but I look back now thinking, could I have seen the signs and helped him more? Sometimes, I'd find the job ads, and give him encouragement about what to say when he phoned them, as he lacked confidence in this area.'

One night, when Stephen was about 24, visitors were invited to the house, but before they arrived Stephen left the house and didn't come home that night. It seemed he could not cope with anyone outside the family coming into the house. 'We were panicking,' says Sandra. 'I called the police the next morning. We didn't go out looking for him, as we had no idea where to look. I'd started ringing all the motels in the area. He ended up staying overnight in a motel at Carss Park. I don't know how he got there, maybe by taxi, as the man at the motel told me he'd left in a taxi.' He eventually returned home the next day, and his family decided not to mention they knew where he had been until Stephen chose to open up and talk about it. 'He just wanted his own space,' says Sandra. 'He didn't think it was a big deal. We didn't want to upset him by showing that we were too worried, as we knew he had depression by this stage. I don't think we ever told him that we did our own investigation and knew he'd gone to the motel.'

Sandra thinks Stephen's extreme lack of confidence in himself deeply affected the way he thought about his social life. All he wanted to do was find a job and become successful. 'Mum probably kept him too close,' says Sandra. 'Was it because he was her only son, and she'd given her first son up for adoption? We'll never know.'

After the death of their mother, the sisters discussed their concerns about Stephen and his extreme withdrawal from the world. Margaret's death seemed to make Stephen withdraw even more. His sister Kathy's friend Sue noticed a big change in Stephen. They hadn't seen him for a while, even though they'd talk to him on the phone. Stephen's sister Kathy Romeo has since tragically passed away; she developed a brain tumour and died in 1997.

Continuing to be concerned about Stephen but not knowing how to help him, Sandra would try to see him as much as she could:

Every time I'd go over there I'd go straight to his room, knock on the door, ask him to come out and have a chat. He was always happy to see me and fine to come out. We'd always be talking rugby league – we follow the Rabbitohs. He would have been over the moon with the premiership in 2014. Stephen would meet other rugby fans, and there was always something to talk about. My son had the experience of the junior development ranks of the St George rugby league club, and Stephen would have been so proud of him, if he was here.

There was an intelligent side to him, and he'd remember a lot of things about sport, especially statistics. He'd go out shopping on his own, and come home and show us what he'd bought. He wouldn't do the full grocery shop, but he'd go and get the things he preferred. He'd spend a lot of time in his room listening to music. He bought the paper every day; he always wanted to know what was going on in the world. He also bought rugby league magazines.

I mention to Sandra that Stephen's habit of reading the newspaper daily would have meant it was likely he'd have seen that he was a missing person, as there were several newspaper articles after his disappearance. Sandra sombrely agrees.

When Sandra married, it was her brother who walked her down the aisle. 'When I asked him, he didn't even hesitate, he said yes,' says Sandra proudly. 'That was a big thing for him, and he must have been in a good space, because if he was an introvert and didn't mix, he wouldn't have coped with that. He stayed at the wedding the whole night; it wasn't an issue.' Stephen loved being an uncle. 'His nephew and nieces brought a lot of joy to him,' says Sandra.

Stephen had always wanted his own place, so eventually he rented a unit from a friend of Sandra's, in Mortdale. 'He only lasted about 15 months there,' says Sandra. 'I remember one time he said to me the unit was too small, like a box. That can be a sign of mental illness, that they feel confined all the time. It was very dark, lots of trees around.' Stephen's name had been on the Department of Housing list for several years. He was given a public housing bedsitter at Brighton Le Sands. They would only allocate him a bedsitter, being a single man. Sandra felt it was a very nice place, near the beach and overlooking an oval but, now looking back, she thinks Stephen's mental illness was worsening at this point in his life.

'He used to say that the men in the flat above him were a bit strange. Stephen felt like they were watching him. We're not sure if Stephen was feeling paranoid, or if people were actually watching him. When he'd come home, they'd be drunk and loitering around, trying to talk to him.' Stephen was only there for six months.

By this stage he had turned 30. He moved into another bedsitter at Narwee and regularly went to Sandra's home to visit and do his washing. Stephen didn't like his new bedsitter, however; he was surrounded by elderly people and he once again felt like the lady next door was watching him. 'We know he was a private kind of person,' says Sandra. 'When you live in public housing, everyone's in everyone's pocket.' Sandra is still unsure whether Stephen's stories about his neighbours watching his movements were true or paranoia.

Stephen again applied for a transfer, and went to see his doctor – he wanted to move into a larger home than just a bedsitter, and his doctor was willing to write a recommendation for this to happen as being necessary for Stephen's mental health. Sandra thinks Stephen may have started taking medication at this time, but she's unsure what type it was, possibly for depression. Sandra never discussed it with her brother; Stephen made the decision to consult his doctor on his own, without being urged or prompted by his sisters. 'After he went missing, I found out which doctor Stephen had been seeing and I went to see him. He told me Stephen had schizophrenia. I was thinking, how can a GP diagnose that?' The doctor did not refer Stephen to any mental health specialists, but instead treated him with medication himself.

Stephen had applied for a disability pension and to qualify for this the Department of Human Services require applicants to have been diagnosed with a mental health condition by a clinical psychologist or psychiatrist, so Stephen did, at some point, see a government-appointed doctor. 'He went missing at the wrong time, when there was a lack of education about mental health, and limited services,' says Sandra. 'If only I'd known that he was unwell, and I was more educated about mental illness. I encourage anyone to gain some courage to have a conversation with someone they love if they have some concerns about their mental wellbeing, however uncomfortable this may feel for you. I know I would if I had my time again with Stephen.'

The Department of Human Services accepted his doctor's recommendation, and in November 2006 Stephen was given a two-bedroom unit at Mortdale. 'It was the best place he'd ever had,' says Sandra. 'Great outlook, great suburb, it was very light, he was on the middle floor so there was no-one peeping in his windows.' Stephen moved into this unit about a year before he went missing. 'He unfortunately had no furniture, as his bedsitters had been too small for much. I gave him some curtains that I had so he could cover his windows, and he wanted to save up to buy some proper window covers, and a lounge and dining setting. He also wanted a screen door.' Covering his windows was very important to Stephen, so people could not look in on him. He was a very private man.

'I told him I'd take him to the furniture shop and we'd buy him a whole package, and he could pay me back whenever. But we never got to go … that was when he went missing,' says Sandra sadly.

Despite being of a larger build in his teenage years, Stephen's appearance changed dramatically around the time of his mother's death. 'I have photos of him then where he looks almost anorexic,' says Sandra, 'But that changed overnight. When he was medicated, he started putting the weight back on. He'd go through health kicks – he'd have some weights in his room, and we'd talk about exercising. I'd go to the gym, but he couldn't afford to. He'd never talk about what he ate, just the exercise.'

Stephen was in weekly contact with his sisters, either face-to-face or by phone. He would get up around 7 am, have breakfast, go for a walk, buy the paper and his food for the day, then head home. He often walked to the homes of his sisters, but they were the only people he would visit. He was polite to his new neighbours at Mortdale but, once again, he told Sandra the lady in the unit below him would watch him.

'Two weeks before he went missing, he came here,' says Sandra. 'He was on top of the world, and that's when we had the talk about the furniture. I told him to give me two weeks and I'd have his whole place decked out, everything would be wonderful, and he'd be a lot more settled. He agreed, he said that would be great. I even ducked up to the shop to get some bread, and he watched my little one, nothing was a drama. He stayed the whole day, did his washing – I still feel guilty to this day that I didn't ask him to stay for dinner. I had to pick my other children up from school at three o'clock, and I asked Stephen if he was ready to go home then. I keep thinking back on that, thinking did I do the right thing? He rarely stayed for dinner, only if we were celebrating something. He'd often come over and help me, he'd clean my house. He was always very motivated, he was keen to help out. I remember telling him just to relax and have a chat to me.

'Anyway, I dropped him home, and from that day on he went downhill. We now know it takes about two weeks for the medication to wear off to the point where you hit a rock-bottom low, so the family now know he'd stopped taking his medication prior to that day. When he'd done his laundry his pillowslip had fallen out of the basket in my car, and I tried several times to call him to tell him I had it. I couldn't get a hold of him. My other sister had spoken to him and it was quite a short conversation. He apparently said he didn't care that he'd left the pillowslip in my car; he was really in a very *I don't give a toss about anything* frame of mind.'

On 19 March 2007, Stephen walked to the local service station, bought his newspaper, and withdrew some money. There are CCTV images of Stephen at the service station.

'He'd paid his rent the day before he went missing,' says Sandra. 'That's why it was odd – he'd made sure everything was all paid.' He'd told family, 'I might go into town and watch the rugby league.' Souths and the Roosters were playing. That night at one of his sister's homes, and the next morning, he declined an offer of breakfast. He said either, 'I'll leave at ten' or 'I've got to leave at ten'.

Stephen left the house, but it is unknown which direction he went in. If Stephen's words were 'got to leave at ten' that would suggest he had an appointment to get to. Stephen left on foot, so they're unsure whether he was trying to catch a particular bus or train. It was 20 March 2007.

'We don't think he made it home,' says Sandra. 'He left with a newspaper, and the clothes he was wearing weren't at his house when we checked later.' As soon as Sandra walked into Stephen's house she knew something was wrong. She says she was actually afraid of what she may find inside, thinking something had happened to Stephen, so she took her husband David with her for support. But when they arrived the lights were switched off and there was no-one home. 'I had a set of keys, and when I went to check his house, after we reported him missing, his bed wasn't made, and the Sunday papers were still on the floor. That was very unlike him, as he was very tidy. His dishes were in the sink, and the milk was off in the fridge. We often thought Stephen had OCD, because he was very tidy. When the police came to look at his flat they thought it looked pretty normal, but we said, 'No, for Stephen, it's very messy.'

'It was nine days before we were able to report him missing,' says Sandra:

We'd all been trying to call him for several days. We started realising he wasn't there. We'd thought maybe he was ignoring the phone, having a bit of time out, as I knew he'd been there when I was trying to call about the pillowslip, but hadn't answered. But no, we were wrong. When he wasn't at the flat, I got together some photos and went to Riverwood police station. They said, 'Sorry, you're at the wrong police station, you need to go to Hurstville.' So, I went to Hurstville police station and they said, 'Oh, they should have taken the enquiry at Riverwood, we shouldn't be doing it here.'

The police were very casual about it; there was just a young fellow on the desk who asked the basic questions. I don't think he even made eye contact with me. I didn't feel like I was being acknowledged. I'm a very relaxed person and can put on a calm façade even when I'm not feeling like that, but I was telling police that this was very unlike Stephen, it's been several days, we've looked at his unit, it was clear he never returned home.

It's a story I unfortunately hear time and again: when people report adult males as missing persons, there's often no sense of urgency on the part of the police to investigate immediately.

'The officer wrote it all down in his black book then told me, "There's nothing we can do until something comes to light,"' says Sandra, clearly disappointed. 'He said, "If he's been hit by a bus or he's in hospital, then go home and we'll call you if we hear anything." That doesn't sit lightly with me.'

Sandra found it very difficult to continue her already busy life with a young family while Stephen was missing. 'It was coming up to the Easter long weekend, and we always went away to Kiama, and Stephen would come and housesit for me. So, from then on, my holidays were never the same. I ended up sending my family away while I stayed at home; every time I drove down there I'd look at the bush and think, is he in there? What's he doing? I just felt like I had to do something 24/7. I did some silly things – I put an ad in the paper with my phone number on it. I had some very strange people call me at strange hours.' Sandra's idea of the newspaper advertisement, although not successful, was a great idea, because Stephen's habit was to buy a newspaper every day.

Sandra called her father and let him know Stephen was missing. He wanted to help search, but he also did not drive, and found it hard to help physically look for his son. Still trying to work out what to do to try to find her brother, Sandra started searching online and found the phone number for NSW Missing Persons Unit. She called them and spoke to Sergeant (now Inspector) Gary Bailey:

He was fantastic; he really got the ball rolling with checking bank accounts and that sort of thing. He called me to say there was someone admitted to Royal Prince Alfred Hospital, but he had a beard, he asked me could Stephen have grown a beard in those six weeks. But it wasn't him. Gary was fabulous, I couldn't fault him, or Mandy [at the Missing Persons Unit]*;*

they were all fabulous. I felt like finally someone was doing something.

I spoke to Hurstville police a few times, but they wouldn't budge, they wouldn't do a thing. I asked them if they could locate some CCTV footage of Stephen at the service station and they said no, they couldn't do that as the service station people wiped it within 24 hours.

I went to the service station myself and asked if there was any chance they still had the footage and they said sure, no problem, and they emailed it to me that day. I asked the police if they could check the footage from Narwee and Mortdale train stations, the two closest lines to where Stephen went missing, but they said they couldn't do that because more than 72 hours had elapsed. I still went to the train stations myself and asked, but they couldn't help me. It was frustrating.

At the end of the day, the only way I managed to get a detective on the case was through a friend of a friend who asked a favour. I didn't want to have to go down that road, but that's just what you have to do in those circumstances.

The police went to Stephen's flat twice to look for clues, but found nothing to explain his disappearance. They took his toothbrush for future DNA comparison but were unsuccessful at obtaining a DNA profile from it. They also took a sample from Sandra.

In the first few weeks after Stephen went missing, the sisters felt that he was probably 'out there somewhere' and that he'd just wanted to get away for a while. Sandra rang all the motels, as she had done the previous time Stephen went missing overnight, but this time she had no success. She called every hospital in the area, and kept calling every few days, for weeks. She and her husband David drove into the city and visited men's hostels, soup kitchens, medical centres that specialise in the homeless, anywhere they could think of.

'It was an eye-opener, it was shocking,' says Sandra:

I felt my mind was racing quicker than my legs could take me. I couldn't sit still, and it was tough because I had three children under ten. I felt my hands were tied; it was so, so frustrating. I did a lot of driving around on my own. I drove the streets, printed flyers, put them up everywhere, put them all into the little plastic sleeves to protect them. I started at Mortdale, where he lived; Olds Park where he walked; the local shops; Jannali, where I knew he'd recently been shopping.

I even went to clairvoyants — one I'd been to many years ago after Mum died, and the things she said had come true. She gave us lots of place names, like a place out at Kurnell that Stephen had been to, near Boat Harbour. We went out there, and I put up signs on the walking tracks, because he loved to walk. One time we stopped in to a shop that said Tarot Card Reader, at Jannali. I was pretty vulnerable at this stage. I went in and showed her a picture of Stephen and she said: 'He's dead.' Straight out. I've been to another medium who told me he's hanging out with the angels. I recently saw David The Medium who told me that Stephen has passed away, but within the next 12 months we will find his remains, in a semi-rural area, under a bridge. The medium told me Stephen knows what I've done to find him and is grateful; he knows the heartache we've been through.

Speaking with the mediums does bring Sandra comfort. 'As a family, we never say he's dead or alive, we say he's *somewhere*. I went to another one and I said over and over to Stephen, "It's okay, if you have crossed over, we just want to know you're okay." They encourage you to speak out loud to the person you're trying to contact, and we didn't give any names or descriptions. Well, she described him as looking very similar to Stephen. She asked me if he had OCD; he was sitting with his back to her and was feeling intimidated. She said we'll know within ten years. I don't know … what do you believe?'

Sandra doesn't know what to believe, but continues to keep an open mind.

There were reported sightings of Stephen around the area after he went missing, thanks to Sandra's excellent flyer campaign. The first of these was a report of Stephen being at the fish shop at Jannali. However, Sandra isn't sure the sighting was of her brother. 'We were out in that area looking and there was a guy who looked a lot like Stephen, walking around the streets, so I think it was him the person saw,' she says. There was another sighting, at Eastern Suburbs Cemetery, in Matraville, that Sandra thinks was much more likely to have been Stephen. The cemetery is where their mother's ashes are interred, and there is an onsite cafe where the sisters left a missing person poster of Stephen. Sandra says:

> *This girl was trying to tell me on the phone what she'd seen, and she was just about hyperventilating; she said she'd just seen him. We'd been out there several times and left a poster in the shop; we'd spoken to the ladies there and they knew us, and that Stephen was missing. It was a Saturday, and this girl*

told me he'd just walked out of the cemetery and got on a bus heading towards Botany or the city.

I immediately rang the police – but they didn't want to know about it. I argued with them, and insisted they get the camera footage from the bus. I said I'd come in and sit down and look through all the footage myself, but they said legally I wasn't allowed to. They finally agreed to check it, but then told me no-one of that description was on the bus at all. I spoke to the girl from the café again and she's sure about what she saw.

The man the girl in the café saw had a chipped front tooth, the same as Stephen.

An intriguing incident at the same cemetery also raises several questions – a blue artificial flower was left on their mother's grave on 21 July 2008, more than a year after Stephen disappeared. Margaret's ashes are in the same area as Sandra's father's family, and it was her father who actually discovered the blue flower when he was visiting his own mother's grave. Their sister Kathy's ashes are also interred in the same area. Her father told Sandra that the flower had not been on Margaret's grave the previous week, as he visited the section often. 'There was no other flower like it on any other grave nearby,' says Sandra, meaning the flower was unlikely to have been put there by chance after falling from another grave. It had been placed inside the vase on the grave, so it could not have blown there by accident. 'We rang around the family and asked everyone, and no-one had been out there and put this flower there.' It's an area Stephen had visited many times in the past, and being so close to his mother, it's somewhere he'd be likely to go.

Another sighting, not long after Stephen went missing, was on a train between Miranda and Hurstville stations. A group of schoolgirls saw a man on their train who looked like Stephen, then when they alighted at Hurstville station they saw Stephen's poster. When they got to their school they alerted their principal about their sighting, who contacted police. 'It was lovely of them,' says Sandra, very grateful that they were so observant. A nurse also contacted the local newspaper to say she had seen a man she believed to be Stephen, also on the same train.

Sandra recalls another sighting, this time at Sutherland Hospital, as the most difficult time of her search. A police officer from Cronulla had been at the hospital and overheard the name Stephen Mitchell being given by a man who walked into the emergency department, who then walked out again. At the time the officer didn't know Stephen was a missing person. Sandra recalls:

> I went to Cronulla police station and had to ask them lots of questions, only to find out the police officer I had to speak to wasn't rostered on, so I had to go back to the next day to speak to him. When I finally got to speak to him, he was very vague. A lead that was so strong became very vague. They had been investigating someone at the hospital for their behaviour, a Stephen Mitchell, but he'd already left the hospital. I went back to the hospital and went to Security, and they were really fantastic. I showed them photos of Stephen and they went back through their CCTV footage and they showed me bits and pieces, but we couldn't see him on the tape. It was all really strange because it didn't match up with what the police officer saw.

Stephen's disappearance continues to take a serious toll on Sandra's health. Two years before we spoke she suffered a seizure due to stress, and it has resulted in some memory loss. She also suffers debilitating migraine headaches. She says:

Every time I got a phone call I'd nearly fall to the ground, which was so out of my character. I'm trying to be this brave, strong woman who can conquer the world and get through anything. I have to be strong. The minute my mother passed on, I became the mother. I was raising a family, trying to support my husband to run his business, I had to stay strong. I'm so fortunate to have my husband, he's just amazing, he's supported me through thick and thin, and never complained once. He's fantastic. He supported me in the search for Stephen in every way he could. We've had friends in the police tell us that they've seen marriages break down due to people going missing, and just to be mindful of that, but David's been so supportive.

I don't know how long I physically searched full time for Stephen ... for several years; I just couldn't sit still. But after that, I had to accept that there was nothing more I could do. I do feel, in a way, that I have let Stephen down, and let myself down. You try and try and just never succeed. Throughout my life I've started things and never completed them, and this was just another thing that didn't get an outcome. My house fell apart, it was never cleaned because I was always out searching for Stephen. I also used to shop, I'd spend a lot of money, I just had to try and fill up my time as I always had to be out. There was one day when I came home and I'd spent close to $500 in *less than an hour, and reality hit. I collapsed and thought, I can't do this anymore.*

I realised I had to be proactive and get back in the saddle, so I started helping out at my kids' schools more often, trying to get my life back to some normality. I had to get my life back, rather than being focused on finding Stephen. I was a changed person after his disappearance, so I had a different outlook on life. What can I do to help the community, to help society become a better place?

Sandra decided to work helping children, and the decision had a very positive impact on her life. She became a teacher's aide. Sandra went on to work in various fields, helping her community, including at a leisure centre, and loved it. 'I wish that centre had been there 40 years ago; my brother would have definitely benefited from it. It would have helped him dramatically, if he'd had somewhere like that to go. The centre offers facilities like a gym, sports and crèche, but also has a special exercise program for those on a mental health program.

The NSW State Coroner held an inquest into Stephen's disappearance on 27 September 2012 – his mother's birthday. It lasted only an hour, with the coroner declaring Stephen to be deceased. After the findings were released Sandra spoke with *The Leader* newspaper and said, 'We are still holding hope he will knock on our door one day.' She has reached out to as many media organisations as possible, eager to tell people about Stephen's case. 'In 2007 I was the guest speaker at the launch of Missing Persons Week in Canberra. I made a speech in front of other families of missing persons, including the Morcombes, and police and media. I also spoke to *Woman's Day* in 2007 and I appeared on *The Today Show* in 2007 and 2008. I've also spoken to local newspapers whenever they've asked.'

In January 2015, Sandra told me about a strange new twist in Stephen's story. Her nephew was visiting a family grave, close to Margaret's resting place at Eastern Suburbs Cemetery. On Margaret's plaque, he found a little plastic sign, the same as you'd put on the top of a cake, saying Happy Mother's Day. Like the mysterious blue flower, it's unlikely to have ended up there by accident. This is the third strange event at the cemetery since Stephen's disappearance – coincidence? Or is Stephen out there, still visiting his mum?

The search for Stephen Mitchell goes on, as does the life of his brave and loving sister Sandra. She will never give up searching for her little brother, until they day he's found. 'I know in my heart, and I have accepted now, that I have done all that I can do,' says Sandra. 'You always think you could have done more, but I have to accept I've done the best I could do. I have a very open mind. I still have to keep an open mind, knowing Stephen is out there somewhere, and I am optimistic that we will hopefully get to reconnect with him in the distant future, however that may look. We love and miss our brother Stephen dearly.'

If you have visited the cemetery and think you've seen Stephen Mitchell please call Crime Stoppers on 1800 333 000 – his family are desperate to know he's okay.

CHAPTER ELEVEN
Shaun Barker

Shaun Barker, aged 33, was last seen at Broadbeach on the Gold Coast,
Queensland on 10 December 2013.

Hi Nic, I'm in a pickle & wanted to please ask your advice. My brother Shaun has been missing for nearly 2 weeks now, I've tried his phone, his Facebook, his friends, his ex partner (they have a child) and no-one has heard from him.

This message was the beginning of one of the biggest Homicide Squad investigations in recent Queensland history. It was sent to my Facebook page by a young woman named Sheridan. I first started speaking to this courageous lady more than two years before her brother went missing; she was a regular follower on my Australian Missing Persons Register Facebook page, but she never imagined she would ever be involved in a missing person case herself, let alone lose her beloved brother Shaun.

In 2011, before her own world was turned upside down, Sheridan sent me a message about another missing person, who she'd spotted in the media being reported as found. She ended her message with, 'You have a good night, and on a final note you are truly an inspiration.' So began a friendship that continues to this day. Over the next couple of years, she often messaged me about missing person cases she'd seen. She sent a message in 2012 about an awful murder, the motive being an argument about a car. I said to her, 'I can't get my head around killing two people over a car!' and Sheridan replied, 'I have seen stranger things happen, very sad how someone can bring themselves to do this! Terrible! And their poor family. Breaks my heart...' These messages are eerie to read when we now know what was about to happen to her own family.

I interviewed Sheridan for this book in late 2017. Our first conversation left me shaken for a long time. It was several months before I could face calling her with extra questions, as her story is just horrific. It was very hard to listen to and to write.

**Warning: this story contains graphic and
distressing content.**

Sheridan and her older brother Shaun grew up in Plumpton in western Sydney. The family moved to Cabarita Beach on Queensland's Gold Coast around 1996 when Sheridan was about 11 and Shaun about 14. I asked Sheridan if it was a happy childhood, and she replied that it was for her, but that Shaun had always experienced difficulties in his life.

'He didn't think that we had the best of everything,' says Sheridan. 'We were a lot better off than a lot of people, but when Shaun told the story it was different. Shaun always wanted more. He needed the best; he was very possession focused. I am not materialistic, but he was always like that.' Sheridan thinks her brother's friends heavily influenced this need for wealth and status. 'He was very popular,' she says. 'He loved school, I think because of his friends; he was very influenced by friends.'

Shaun liked to throw himself headlong into new interests, and had an addictive personality. 'Shaun is one of those types of people who would be addicted to a sport, and he'd live that sport,' says Sheridan. 'Like surfing; he would go every day. Then he started bike riding, and he'd ride from Tweed Heads to Surfers Paradise every day, to work. He was very fit. There were always a lot of girls around. I couldn't determine if they were my friends or if they wanted my brother. He dated a girl from *The Adventures of Skippy the Bush Kangaroo* TV show; she's a model now. He dated a TV journalist. He dated quite a number of people; he had an influence on the girls. He started dating when he was about 15.'

Sheridan pauses to think when I ask her if she and Shaun were close growing up, considering she later devoted her life to firstly trying to help him, then to achieving justice for him. 'We have never been really close,' says Sheridan. 'He always used to pick on me. Now I look back on that and think he wanted the *best* for me, but I didn't see it that way, when it actually happened. We used to fight like cats and dogs; that was just how we were. But in some sense, we were very close, in that he was very protective of me. All through my life I was *Shaun's sister*, I was not myself. As adults, we became closer when he moved home. I was always living at home, so he'd come home, and then he'd move out and we'd drift apart. It depended on where he was at in life.'

Shaun developed a pattern in his life of moving in with a girlfriend, breaking up, and moving back in with his parents. Then doing it again. Sometimes he'd move in with a few mates but always got sick of it, and came home. 'He absolutely adored my mum,' says Sheridan. 'Couldn't not be around her. If anything would happen, he'd call Mum and tell her he needed her to do something for him. They had a very close bond. He was very smart, he did no homework and he just aced it at school. When we were growing up he always wanted to be a pilot, so he'd watch *Top Gun* and that sort of thing. I could really see him going places.'

When Shaun left school, instead of heading to university to study medicine or law, or pursuing his dream of being a pilot, he shocked everyone by getting a job as a window cleaner. 'He did it because his friends were doing it,' says Sheridan. 'They used to clean a lot of upscale high rises. He loved the thrill. He was absolutely a risk taker.' However, Shaun's days of thrill seeking were to come to a shocking halt. When he was about 20 he had an experience that changed him forever.

'Shaun had spent a day out on a boat with his workmate,' says Sheridan. 'His mate had just broken up with his girlfriend, but seemed fine. The next day, he and Shaun both went to work, cleaning windows on a very tall building. Shaun was abseiling down the building, and his mate was above him, on top of the high rise. He said to Shaun, "Mate, I can't do this," and he jumped. Shaun had to watch him. That really affected Shaun.'

After the tragedy, Shaun tried to carry on at work but his concentration was greatly affected. Shortly afterwards, he had an accident at work that ended his career. 'He fell off a three-storey building and nearly died,' says Sheridan. 'He was in hospital for eight weeks and broke his arm in three places. For months he had metal plates in his arm. He was also still badly affected by the suicide of his friend. It took him a while to get over that. He just stayed home, he didn't want to do anything. Shaun used to go out on Friday night, and you wouldn't see him until Sunday morning, but he stopped doing that; it really affected him to a point where he couldn't cope. His boss ended up getting counselling for Shaun. I don't know if it helped, he never talked about it. He ended up resigning from his job; he really had to after his fall. He had a payout from WorkCover, and he bought a car and a boat.' Shaun's personal life was also affected by the two major events at his workplace, and he separated from his partner. The break-up was not amicable.

'He always picked the wrong girls,' says Sheridan.

However, Shaun got himself together and started his life over again, and began a job in computers. He was an IT manager for an internet company. 'He could have done anything he wanted, he was so smart,' says Sheridan. 'He loved that job. After that he became the senior systems administrator for a car yard. That was his last job he had; he was there for many years.'

Shaun still had the urge inside him to have the best lifestyle possible. He needed to find a way to make the sort of money that would impress his friends and buy himself the sort of life he craved. On the Gold Coast, there's an all too obvious and dangerous way of doing that. At the start, Sheridan believes he only wanted to sell drugs, not take them. 'I wouldn't say he was addicted to drugs,' says Sheridan. She believes Shaun became involved in drugs purely to make money. 'He was very materialistic. He longed for more. That was a lot of Shaun's problem. Now I look at it, he had everything he could possibly want, but there was something missing, and I don't know where that came from.'

Shaun's parents did everything they could to guide their children along a safe pathway in life. Sheridan recalls: 'Dad used to sit there and warn us about drugs. He and Shaun argued a lot. Every weekend Dad would say: "If you do drugs, then you want to get out of reality and you want to die. Just talk about it instead." I was never influenced by drugs.' Shaun, however, ignored his father's advice and started to dabble on the dark side. His father had no idea that his words would be unheeded. Learning about his son's decline would have a devastating effect on him.

Shaun found a new girlfriend and they eventually became engaged. 'Sean never wanted kids,' says Sheridan. 'But then he got engaged and settled down, and we were really surprised. I was blown away, because he wasn't the type to settle down. He was a player.' It seemed Shaun was going to become a stable family man, and his parents and sister were very happy for him. 'They were trying for a baby for about two years,' says Sheridan. 'He struggled when she was pregnant; I think he was scared of settling down. As soon as his daughter came into the world, though, he was a changed man. He absolutely adored her. He brought her to the house and he couldn't take his eyes off her.'

But Shaun's idyllic new life with his little family was to be short lived. Sheridan tries to think back to when Shaun's behaviour started to change. 'Shaun's life started to go wrong just after his daughter was born,' says Sheridan. 'He just stopped talking to us. I thought he was busy. People get busy, I understand that; he's got a baby and he's working full time, but I found it very weird when he stopped talking to us. We wouldn't speak every day, but it was weird. I went to his house one day, in late 2012, and he was pacing the kitchen.

'I asked him if he was on drugs. I said, "What are you doing? It's 11 o'clock at night and you're pacing the kitchen. What's going on? Tell me." He said, "I'm doing computer work, Sheridan, for these really bad guys, and I wish I hadn't got involved." He never once told me it was drugs. He was freaking out; I'd never seen him like that before. I asked him what I could do, and he said there was nothing I could do. He said he was doing the computer work to get a bit more money for him and his partner.'

Shaun showered his daughter with gifts. 'On her first birthday, I've never seen a baby get so many things in my life,' says Sheridan. 'They really spoiled her.' Shaun and his fiancée planned a wedding, but Sheridan says it was always on hold, mainly because of their baby. The relationship broke down and they separated when their daughter was about two, and they had been separated for around a year when Shaun went missing.

After the incident where she found Shaun pacing the kitchen, Sheridan was trying to work out what was going on with her brother, and what trouble he'd got himself mixed up in. She gradually realised that ice had taken a hold of Shaun. She did what she could to help. Sheridan says:

When I found out my brother was on drugs, I took his daughter every single weekend. I worked full time, 40 to 50 hours a week, then they'd drop the baby off at my house and I would have her all weekend. Shaun started out on the drugs by doing ice on the weekends. He said he needed it to get through his week. I think he started dealing ice because he wanted to provide the best possible life for his daughter.

Shaun's need to have the best of everything had led to him becoming involved in a very dangerous world.

Sheridan said she found it difficult living in Brisbane while Shaun lived on the Gold Coast, as she couldn't see him in person as frequently as she'd like, so she was not always aware of just how bad the problems were. In fact, they were about to become very serious indeed.

The contact with Shaun stopped, to the point where I was the only one trying to make contact. He wouldn't answer when I called him. In October 2013, his partner called me and said that Shaun had gone missing, that he wasn't answering his phone. I was at work, and I tried to ring him, but it just rang out. I tried for days. He finally answered when I was getting on the train one day, and he said, 'Oh, look, Shez, I'm all right, everything's all right, I've just been busy.'

I ended up finding out later that he'd been abducted and tortured. He'd been held by these people for two or three days and tied to a chair. Shaun never told me that it had happened, I only found out in court during the later trial. After that, I would just call him, and keep calling him. I knew he was on drugs, and I offered for him to come and move in with us, we had a spare room, but he never would.

Most drug addicts feed off their families, they take, take, take, but he never did. He never asked for anything. Sometimes he'd answer my calls, and when he did he'd say he was fine. I told him I loved him and that I'd look after him, but he kept saying no, he'd be all right.

From October to December of 2013 Sheridan continued to reach out to Shaun, offering help, but he always declined.

Sheridan had been very concerned about Shaun in the days before he went missing for the final time. 'On 4 December 2013, I found out Shaun had been at a service station, and was paranoid.' It would seem Shaun had a psychotic episode. 'This was the same service station he'd been abducted from in October. The next week, Shaun went missing from the same service station. Isn't that crazy? The second time he was the same as before, very paranoid.' During the trial the court heard

Shaun had been paranoid that Japanese Yakuza gangs were after him, and he refused to speak around mobile phones because he thought his phone calls were being monitored.

Shaun's life continued to spiral into a dangerous vortex. Sheridan struggled to reconcile the Shaun she'd known all her life as her brother with a man she now barely recognised.

Saturday, 21 December 2013: Sheridan sent me that fateful message about Shaun. The full message read:

> *Hi Nic, I'm in a pickle & wanted to please ask your advice. My brother Shaun has been missing for nearly 2 weeks now, I've tried his phone, his Facebook, his friends, his ex partner (they have a child) and no-one has heard from him. I live in Brisbane & so do our parents & he lives on the Gold Coast. About 1 month ago I found out alot of stuff I never knew about (he's now a drug addict) & he quit his high paying job out of the blue, and he has moved out of his beautiful house to live in his car???? Yes his car ... it just doesn't add up??*
>
> *I have called the police on several occasions & have been told he may not want to be found. Early this week, I have been told, the police were asking for him. So, I assume he may be 'wanted'??? I just don't know what I can do, he has not called his daughter in 2 weeks & that's just not like him. I feel helpless. What I don't understand is he knows right from wrong, no-one has ever taken drugs in our family & we had a fantastic childhood, I don't understand? Sorry about the spill, I just really need advice.*

It was a message that had me worried from the start. Clearly, Shaun had been hiding his drug habit from his family and was in trouble. Sheridan became extremely concerned when Christmas approached and there was no word from her brother. 'When he didn't contact his daughter for Christmas, then I definitely knew something had happened,' she says. As Sheridan's message was sent at Christmas, I was interstate with family and didn't get it until 29 December. I asked her if Shaun was still missing.

Sheridan: Yes, he is but every time I call the police they say he doesn't want to be found, he has a two-year-old daughter that never saw him at Xmas time ... I don't know what to do ...

Me: Okay, so did the police say he 'may not' want to be found or that he 'does not' want to be found, i.e. have they actually located him to ask?

Sheridan: May not, sorry. I assume he is wanted for questioning, it's a tuff one, if I report him as missing I'll be the worst person ever, if I don't my family will never know. My mum's beside herself.

Me: If he hasn't been in trouble before, and from what you've said he's always been a good guy up until this has happened to him, then he won't be in much trouble with police, they'll be very lenient with him, but the longer it goes on the worse it will be. So, even if police locate him on the warrant it's likely to not be as bad as the family thinks it will be. But if he's out there with no contact with family etc. then he's probably in a bad way. My advice would honestly be to report him as a missing person and insist that they take the report. You need to make it clear that he hasn't seen his daughter for Christmas and that's very out of character for him (use that phrase) and that you are really worried about his welfare (use that phrase). If they try to say 'he doesn't want to be found', then be firm and insist that they take the report because he always makes contact with family at Christmas and you're really worried about him.

Sheridan: He hasn't been in trouble before from what I know. He was a manager at a big IT company so I assume he hasn't. I have heard a few things that he may have been found with drugs but once again that's from my unreliable source. I'll let you know how I go.

A couple more weeks went by, and Sheridan checked in with me on 13 January 2014. By this stage, Shaun had been missing for just over a month. Because there was no missing person report made to police about Shaun, I could not add him to the AMPR page, because I add the Crime Stoppers number to every post. If someone called police with information and there was no missing report on the system, the information would go nowhere.

Sheridan: Hey, lovely, my brother is still missing. I have been sharing his photo around but no luck, I will give it until Friday before I go and report him missing. Just thought I would keep you posted.

Sheridan was in a really difficult situation. She had *tried* to go to the police, who kept fobbing her off, and yet she had a terrible feeling that something awful had happened to Shaun. If he'd become involved with drug dealers, would making his disappearance public put him in further danger? She says:

Mum didn't want to think about any of it. She's as soft as soft can be. We thought he was probably trying to escape from people and get away from the 'ice life', but he'd been gone so long with no contact. Although I'd had minimal contact with him, I still thought he'd call. I hung unto that. When I finally called police, they told me there was a warrant out for his arrest. I asked them was he in lock-up. He wasn't. I still don't know what the arrest warrant was for. I can't believe my brother had a warrant. If you knew him … he was so normal.

Sheridan's persistence paid off and she finally convinced the police to list Shaun as a missing person. It was 14 January 2014, more than a month after he was last seen. She says, 'Before that, the only person who would help me was you. When I went to Milton police station, I told them [about Shaun] and the officer got straight onto it. She was fantastic. I spoke to Annie, the police officer, the first day I reported Shaun missing and she said, "We're going to put Shaun's photo up on Police Link, I hope you're okay with that." Then I had to go in for a statement. But I was amazed, and I remember you were amazed too, that it went on Police Link straightaway.' Finally, police were taking Shaun's disappearance seriously.

Journalist Jack Harbour of the *Gold Coast Bulletin* later spoke to Detective Sergeant Steve McBryde, the team leader at Burleigh CIB, who said: 'We got that a day or two later basically as "Do you want to look at this missing person job? It seems a bit odd." Our first port of call was to talk to L, the mother of Shaun Barker's daughter. She reported that she hadn't had contact with him since early December. He hadn't seen his daughter for Christmas, which she thought was unusual. We could find no record of this bloke accessing anything. They basically came back to me and said there's something amiss here. This bloke's dropped off the planet. We treated it as more than a missing person then.'

The case was given to Detective Senior Constables Michael Bradley and Annie Watt, and Sheridan says they were absolutely fantastic, from day one. 'Annie went from the start of Shaun's life to the end. We went through question after question after question. I wanted to give her everything I could possibly give her because I wanted answers.' Sheridan says Mick Bradley was also an outstanding officer. 'He has been there from the start. He has been coming to all the cases; he's someone I absolutely trust with my life.'

Now desperate for answers about what had happened to Shaun, Sheridan reached out to anyone and everyone. 'I even contacted a psychic, and she said he was in Melbourne.' Sheridan laughs at the ridiculousness of this now, but like most of the cases in this book, the families will try anything they can think of to help find their loved one. She says:

> I tried every avenue I could possibly try. Police, hospital, his friends. Everyone kept turning me away. The news people said to me, 'Why didn't you contact the police earlier?' Like, seriously? I tried so many times! I'm not angry at them about that, though. I just got so frustrated. I was begging them to please help me.

On 20 April 2014, two forestry workers in Toolara State Forest, north-east of Gympie, QLD, found a partially burned skull. Initially, police were sure they'd found the skull from a different murder victim. They didn't connect it to Shaun, as the forest was more than 280 kilometres from where he went missing. Sometime around 2 September 2013, 66-year-old George Gerbic's fiancée, Lindy Williams, murdered him and dumped his body on Cedar Pocket Rd, near Gympie. On 19 September 2013, his partially burned torso was found by the side of the road. He had been decapitated, and the skull disposed of at another location, so when the skull was found in Toolara Forest, they immediately thought it belonged to George Gerbic. It did not. It was Shaun Barker. Astonishingly, there were two bodies of murder victims found in the same area, within months of each other. Both had been dismembered. Both had been decapitated. Both had been burned. But they had nothing to do with each other.

Sheridan says: 'There was another killing right near where my brother's body was found. They found a torso, and then they found the skull, and they thought it was the same person. But it was a guy who'd been murdered by his fiancée. I'd like to hope that my brother's case helped that case. I'd really like to think that his death made a difference in another family's life.' Lindy Williams was sentenced to life in prison in July 2018.

Police commenced an intensive search of the forest for more human remains, and on 26 April 2014, they confirmed they had located some smaller bones. Detective Inspector Bruce McNab stated police had also found numerous 'items of interest' located in the forestry. Search crews were working on their hands and knees in what DI McNab called a 'fine tooth comb search' and involved 65 SES volunteers as well as police. At this stage, police did not know who the remains belonged to and were still waiting on forensic testing of the skull. Police appealed to the public 'to think of any males between the ages of 40 and 80 they have not seen since last September'.

On 12 June 2014, police confirmed the skull found in Toolara Forest was Shaun Barker's. It was heartbreaking timing for Sheridan:

Two days before my wedding was when his skull was found. They didn't want to tell me. I found out on my honeymoon that my brother had been killed; I still remember them sitting on my lounge and telling us. My mum's actually quite deaf, so she didn't hear them ... the hardest thing I've ever had to do in my life is tell my mum that my brother had been killed. I actually had to get rid of my lounge; every time I looked at it, I saw the police officer sitting on it, so I gave it away to charity. I couldn't stand it being in my house.

Soon after the confirmation of the identity of the remains, Shaun's blue Kia Rio car was found in thick bushland on corner of Smith St and Hymix Rd in Pacific Pines, on the Gold Coast, on 17 June 2014. It was about 20 kilometres from where he'd been last seen at the service station at Broadbeach. Shaun's body was found almost 300 kilometres from where he was abducted. As Sheridan says, he was never meant to be found. Not only was he found such a distance away, but he had been dismembered, and part of his body had been moved to another location. As we were to later learn, the location of the remains was simply conveniently near where the men involved lived.

Sheridan embarked on a personal crusade to find her brother's killers. She had some information about his previous abduction, and she started to dig into Shaun's secret life. The same names started to come up, the more she probed:

I'd never met any of them. But I knew of them. I knew their names; he had talked about them. I investigated my own brother's killing. I know that sounds stupid, but I did. Once I found out he'd been killed, I kicked in and I went through everything. One guy who got done, I knew it was him, but the father and son I didn't know.

The media reported that police became aware of another case on the Gold Coast that was remarkably similar in circumstance to Shaun's previous abduction, but they didn't mention how they became aware. It was thanks to Sheridan. 'There was a torture case on the Gold Coast,' she says. 'I had a look at it, and one of the statements from the guy was, "Do you want to be another missing person on the Gold Coast?" And I knew in my heart they were talking about Shaun. They also said, "We're going to make you disappear" or something like that. My gut was saying this has got to do with Shaun. I ended up passing it to the police. I said to them, "I know you probably think I'm crazy, but I know, I really know it's got to do with Shaun." And it was. Same guy.'

The case Sheridan is talking about is the assault of Luke Romhegyi in a disused train tunnel at Molendinar in 2014. William Dean was among three men who pleaded guilty in court to this assault.

Sheridan was in regular contact with police, and passed to them everything she had discovered while she was investigating Shaun's case herself:

There have been a lot of stops along the way. I couldn't have done it without our police, they've been amazing. They probably think I'm crazy because I kept ringing them, screaming at them, saying listen to me, this has got to do with Shaun's case. I think they're wonderful. They were investigating it while I was yelling at them, but they couldn't tell me that. They could only tell me so much.

When they had days off, they were still sitting in court. I know they can't give us information continually, but they would ring me and say they didn't have any information; they were just checking up to see how I was holding up. I know they don't do that for everybody.

I've gone to homicide victims meetings where the police haven't been in contact with the family for six months. I've gone in there and listened to people who know who killed their sibling, and they haven't even got justice.

We're extremely lucky that they were so persistent, and they wanted the same outcomes that I did. They didn't have holidays for months, they worked continually. I'm so thankful. They changed my life. I honestly don't know where I'd be without them. I thought I was going to cark it, I was so stressed out.

Meanwhile, police were closing in on Shaun's killers. They managed to link William Dean, the man who pleaded guilty to assault in the Romhegyi case, with father and son Stephen and Matthew Armitage. A clear and terrible picture began to form of what had happened. Police started to locate others connected to the trio, and people were beginning to talk. Police kept the pressure on, and eventually they were confident they had enough witnesses and evidence to lay charges.

On 5 October 2014, Stephen, Matthew and William were arrested and charged with murder, interfering with a corpse, torture and deprivation of liberty. Stephen was arrested at Brisbane Airport as he flew in from Thailand. Former police Superintendent Dave Hutchinson, who at the time was the South Eastern Regional Crime Coordinator, told media that up to 30 detectives had been working on the case. He said, 'It's certainly one of the most horrific ones that have occurred in recent times.

It is certainly a pretty terrible set of circumstances that Mr Barker has been through. It's been very resource intensive. The detectives have been working around the clock on this basically since January when Mr Barker was reported missing.'

Matthew and Stephen Armitage appeared before Brisbane Magistrates Court. Matthew Armitage's defence barrister, Jeff Hunter, said his client didn't intend to kill Shaun. He said in court: 'This is a case where a man's death came as a complete surprise to those involved. It certainly was not intentional.' Hunter went on to call the prosecution case weak and circumstantial, especially in relation to the murder charge. He said there was no evidence Matthew had been violent towards Shaun. However, the three men were remanded in custody, and police continued to gather evidence to present to the court at the committal hearing. Superintendent Hutchinson told the media they were looking for the vehicle they believed was used to transport Shaun from the Gold Coast to Cooloola Cove, an 80-series 1983 Toyota Landcruiser station wagon.

Sheridan's husband, Matthew, spoke to the media about the family's distress and the loss of his brother-in-law. He and Sheridan were distraught about the impact Shaun's death had on their niece:

He was a brother, father, son, a family man. [Our niece] asks for Daddy, but she's too young to understand. My wife and Shaun's parents are all very upset, it's quite hard for us at the moment. We're shocked this has happened.

The committal hearing began on 18 January 2016. For the first time, the court and the public heard exactly what Shaun had endured in the days leading up to his death. The many witnesses who gave evidence at the committal hearing, and then at the trial, painted a violent and distressing picture of what happened to Shaun. The motive, according to evidence presented in court, was to get information from Shaun about something that had happened 'down the coast'. Some witnesses believed it was because of a drug debt, and others said it was because of a woman. The court heard Shaun owed the men tens of thousands of dollars. It's a lot of money for him to owe to some very frightening people. He must have been constantly living in fear.

The three accused men were committed to stand trial for Shaun's murder on 7 March 2016. The court hearings were very difficult for Sheridan to sit through each day, and this was made far more distressing after an incident outside the courtroom. 'This woman approached me at the committal hearing and asked me what I was doing at court. I didn't know who she was. I said, "I'm going to a murder case." She said, "My son did not kill your brother. My son is a good boy."' The woman was the mother of one of the accused.

At the first trial, the jury were unable to reach a verdict. The second trial began 6 March 2017. Stephen Armitage, his son Matthew Armitage and William Dean all pleaded not guilty to the charges. One of the first witnesses to be called was the service station attendant who had been working the night Shaun went missing for the final time, on 10 December 2013. The attendant told the court he saw Shaun pacing back and forth outside the service station until he eventually came inside. The attendant was uneasy, believing Shaun was a drug addict, and he asked him to leave the store. He told the court that Shaun replied, "Won't go out ... they will kill me, they have a gun." The attendant offered to call police, but Shaun said no. Shortly after, two men came into the service station and approached Shaun. They convinced Shaun they didn't have a gun and Shaun eventually left with the men.

The jury was shown photographs of Shaun's remains, but they were so badly burned they were difficult to identify. Some bones could not be identified at all, and the forensic examiner told the court: 'There was what appeared to be a rib ... under the surface of the soil. So, we had to dig away and excavate it.' She stated the remains were 'scattered'. Sheridan also gave evidence in September, telling the court about Shaun's noticeable weight loss in late 2013, leading her to question whether he was using drugs.

The jury deliberated only a couple of days before returning a verdict of guilty. Justice Jackson summed up the horrific case to the courtroom, saying that on 10 December 2013, William Dean met Shaun Barker at Pacific Fair shopping centre on the Gold Coast. Dean confronted Shaun about some missing drugs, and on this day he bashed Shaun before driving him to Cooloola Cove, Stephen Armitage's property. There Shaun was violently assaulted over days, and died. Stephen Armitage, Matthew Leslie Armitage and William Francis Dean were convicted of Shaun Barker's torture, murder and interfering with his corpse. On 21 February 2018 they were sentenced to life in prison. They also received sentences for torture and interfering with a corpse.

Justice Jackson said the behaviour of the three men was 'sadistic and cruel'. He went on to say: '*Shaun Barker was being tortured to provide some kind of information, probably about drugs, that the defendants … thought he had taken. There was evidence he (Mr Barker) cried out for water and food.'* Justice Jackson said exactly how Shaun died is still unknown, as despite the number of people who gave evidence, no-one was able to determine his cause of death. It is clear it was the most horrifying of deaths. Justice Jackson said the men used a hose to 'pipe water' into the esky until Shaun 'almost drowned' and they 'smashed his face, kneecaps and every bone in his left hand'. He may have had fingers cut off as they demanded information. The men tied Shaun to a tree with cable ties, before covering his genitals in honey so ants would attack him.

Justice Jackson said Shaun's body was burnt in a fire pit, and his remains were scattered through the Toolara State Forest.

Sheridan was able to present her victim impact statement to the court when the men were sentenced, in February 2018. She didn't hold back:

My brother Shaun was just 33 years old when you brutally murdered him, just 33 years old. Shaun was a father to a gorgeous two-year-old girl. Shaun was my only sibling and my parents' only son.

When I reported my brother missing, I never would have imagined that I would be standing in front of the men accused of his murder. To find out on my honeymoon that Shaun's partial remains were found was beyond belief, but then to find out how he died was the worst possible nightmare I could have imagined. To think the three of you were so disgustingly inhumane, and had no regard for the suffering of Shaun or the people who loved him, makes me sick. I struggle to understand how grown men, who have children of their own, can brutally kill someone else's child, and not have one ounce of remorse.

Stephen Armitage, I saw your posts on Facebook after murdering my brother, you went on to put a very large post on your fence advertising that you had body parts for sale in large writing, then in very small writing you wrote the car type. Then you went as far to put a profile picture of yourself laying on a bed with your hands tied to the bed and a human skull in front of you, this is well after you brutally murdered my brother, and to me it's your way of showing the world you killed and you're proud of it too.

You all DIDN'T decide to kill Shaun in seconds or minutes or even hours, you decided to kill Shaun over days. You all had a choice, you all had time to let him go, but you decided his life wasn't worth living and you made damn sure he suffered every remaining minute of his life, then when he died you went as far to burn his remains, you wanted him to be forgotten, you never wanted him to be found.

But let me assure you my brother's memory will live on and as long as I know you are all in your jail cells my life will live on too. It's been over four years since you took Shaun's life and I refuse to let you take anything else from us, I will walk out of here today knowing whatever the justice system throws at you will never be enough to justify what you took away from us.

Outside the court, after the sentencing, Sheridan told reporters she felt relieved: 'It's been four years since my brother was killed, and it's one of the best days of my life today, although it was my brother's birthday yesterday … the only gift I've got left is justice. It's been a hard four years. My life stopped. My family's life stopped. It changed our life.'

The media had a field day with the case. One journalist described the killing as 'tantalising'. Another journalist wrote: 'Three men who … burnt the remains of Gold Coast drug dealer Shaun Barker have been sentenced to life behind bars.' Why are they merely referred to as 'men' but Shaun, the victim, is a 'Gold Coast drug dealer'? Why aren't they blaming the right people for this? Why doesn't that sentence read 'beloved father, brother and son Shaun Barker'? It's hard to imagine how Sheridan must have felt, reading her brother's death described as 'tantalising'. She is the first to admit Shaun was no angel, but he was her brother, he was the father of a little girl who will grow up and probably read those headlines, and he was dearly loved by many.

'I tried to stay away from the media, but it was very hard when they chase you down the street,' says Sheridan. 'It was very big news here. They called me on my mobile; I don't know how they got my phone number. Channel 9 called me during the trials. I told them that I didn't want to talk, and I didn't have any comment. It's been a really long road, I can tell you that. I've seen so many disgusting things on social media. I know that my brother was a small time dealer, but they were congratulating the guys for killing him, saying they should be out, saying that he got what he deserved. It was horrible. It nearly broke me.'

Sheridan breaks down at this point, remembering what she went through.

'The media would write headlines like Drug Dealer's Killers Found Guilty. People thought these guys had done the world a favour by killing my brother. It was the hardest time of my life. Going to court, sitting there for two weeks, seeing the media come in for only 20 minutes, grabbing as much information as they possibly could in that time, then writing a story on it. I found it really hard to cope. Sitting there for two weeks, watching his killers. It was horrible. I never want to go through it again.'

In January 2018 Sheridan contacted me, extremely upset, to tell me about a page she'd just found on Facebook. Apparently set up by one of the convicted men, it is a page to attempt to protest their innocence. Sheridan contacted Corrective Services to ask why a convicted killer is allowed to run a Facebook page. Queensland Corrective Services responded by saying: 'QCS has no jurisdiction if a social media account is being operated by a second party to a prisoner. However, QCS intelligence officers monitor prisoner phone calls and mail and can refer a prisoner to QPS if there is evidence of first-hand information being passed on.' This page is using Shaun Barker's photo as their cover picture, a photo they have copied from Shaun's memorial Facebook page.

Sheridan spoke to the *Gympie Times* and said: 'I just don't want him to use my brother's photo. They can start 20 groups claiming their innocence, but when they use a photo of my brother it is too far. I just want them to take the photo down.' When I checked in late 2023 the page is still there, with Shaun's photo still as their cover photo.

In August 2019, the Court of Appeal came back with a decision that has shaken Sheridan's faith in justice. Stephen and Matthew Armitage's convictions were downgraded from murder to manslaughter. They had also been convicted of torture, but these convictions were overturned. I don't know about you, but if tying someone naked to a tree with cable ties and covering their genitals with honey so ants would bite them is not classified as torture, then I am questioning everything I have ever known. If not torture, then what is that? A prank?

The appeal had been lodged with the legal team, arguing the jury had not been properly instructed on the alternative verdict of manslaughter instead of murder. The Court of Appeal's reason for the decision was that the father and son did not intend for Shaun to die. 'I have concluded that their [the jury] verdict cannot stand because it was not open to the jury to conclude that an act or omission, which killed Mr Barker, was done with the required intent,' Justice Philip McMurdo said. 'But I have concluded, it was open to the jury to find Mr Barker was killed by an injury or injuries caused by the mistreatment and violence inflicted upon him.'

This is hard to fathom, when you read the details of exactly what was done to Shaun Barker during the course of the events that ultimately led to his death. The court also found they could not determine exactly how Shaun died, because Shaun's body was decapitated and dismembered, discarded in various locations after being set on fire, and not found for three months. Matthew Armitage was, in 2020, sentenced to eight years in prison and required to serve 80 per cent of his sentence. Stephen Armitage and William Dean were sentenced to 10 years.

All three men appealed their sentences. In August 2021, the three men won their appeal against their sentences, but the result had no effect on their actual time served. An error was made in the sentencing process, which did not take into account time already served in custody before they were sentenced. Justice Flanagan said: 'The sentences to be imposed by this court should commence from February 21, 2018. These sentences will appear to be higher ... however, the fresh sentences do not have the practical effect of imposing a higher sentence given their retrospective commencement date.'

Even in 2023, the case is still not over, with one of the men being convicted of retaliation or intimidation against a jury, witness or family. He has had extra time applied to his sentence. In November 2023 one of the convicted men, Matthew Armitage, won his appeal after the court decided he could not comply with the No Body No Parole laws. Armitage appealed on the grounds that Shaun's remains likely no longer existed and he would be therefore unable to direct authorities as to where they could be found. *The Guardian* reported that:

About 15% of Barker's remains have never been recovered. The court of appeal heard the unrecovered parts of Barker's body would now have been completely destroyed through fire, weather effects, decomposition and animal activity ... the court of appeal ruled that a review of the parole board's decision had incorrectly applied the no body, no parole law and ordered the board to reconsider Armitage's application for release. Justice Peter Flanagan said all of the remains of Barker that still exist, or were capable of being located, had been located. 'No amount of co-operation from the prisoner will change this situation,' Flanagan said.

Armitage has been granted early release and will be out of prison in 2024.

Sheridan has shown amazing courage and strength of character throughout her entire nightmare. She was supposed to be a newlywed, deliriously happy, starting a new life with her husband. Instead, she found out on her honeymoon that her brother had been killed. From that moment on, her life was forever changed. 'I ended up moving because I just didn't feel safe,' she says. 'Even though I was in a three-storey building with security, I was pacing the house every day, I didn't feel safe going out. It changed my life, it changed my marriage. My husband's been amazing. People normally break, but we came together stronger.'

Sheridan was later asked to present lectures to police recruits about what it's like to live through a homicide investigation. 'I went to the Police Academy in Brisbane and trained new detectives on how to deal with homicide. OMG, it was the best therapy! And the officers got a glimpse of what victims of homicide live with. It personally helped me cope, knowing I'm helping others, and other victims I do it with say the same.'

Sadly, Sheridan and her parents have lost their relationship with their niece and granddaughter, who they were once so close to. 'I haven't seen my niece in many years now, since her third birthday when my husband and I took her to Seaworld,' says Sheridan. 'I've spoken to her on the phone once, and she doesn't even know me. It's really sad.' Hopefully one day she will re-establish a connection with her beloved niece again, as she is the only part of Shaun that Sheridan and her parents have left. Sheridan will be able to answer the questions the child must have about what her daddy was like growing up. Before the headlines, before his life took a fatal turn. Before life changed forever.

Sheridan continues to grow from strength to strength, not allowing what happened to destroy her. She has been in therapy to deal with her trauma, but even the trained professionals struggled to cope with the details of what she had to say. 'I actually went to two different counselling sessions, just to release, and after the second one the counsellor said she couldn't see me anymore, because Shaun's story is too horrific. I totally get it.'

In 2011, Sheridan told me I was an inspiration, but I found myself using those exact words about her when I started to interview her. I don't know how she keeps going, with a dogged cheerfulness. In 2022, she said to me, about telling her story for this book: 'I feel like I've healed somewhat from all this, but it's a different kind of healing. It's like I put it all in a mental box and open it when I feel the time is right.'

In 2023 Sheridan moved her family to live beside the ocean. It's a fresh start, and I truly hope it brings them some much needed, and well-deserved peace.

CHAPTER TWELVE
Paul

This story has a very different ending to the others in this book.

Paul went missing frequently. Every time he did, his devoted sister Julie came to me, apologetically, asking me so politely if I would make another appeal. Of course, I said yes to her. No matter how many times he goes, we will always try to find him. 'It could happen again tomorrow,' says Julie. 'Not that I want it to, but there's every likelihood it could. I'm prepared. It's something I've had to learn to live with. You never think you'll have to, but you do. It's not easy. But when you have someone who's mentally ill, you learn to live with the unexpected.'

Paul has schizophrenia, and when something triggers him, he frequently disappears. 'If he doesn't like something, he'll just wander off,' says Julie. 'It's the nature of the illness, about 80 per cent, and I think the other 20 per cent is him being very frustrated with his illness.'

Julie and Paul had two brothers, who have both since passed away. The family grew up in Villawood, in Sydney. Julie sadly tells me it was not a happy childhood. 'Our parents were alcoholics, so in a way I've always had to look after Paul. Mum is still alive, but she doesn't drink at all today. But it was tough, for a lot of years. It makes you grow up a bit quicker. Paul was the baby of the four of us. I took him under my wing when he was little, and nothing's really changed.'

Growing up, Paul was a very normal happy-go-lucky kid. However, tragedy struck, when his brother died. 'Laurie was only 21 when he was killed in a car accident,' says Julie. 'Our eldest brother lost his leg in the same accident.' Horrifically, their father also died in violent circumstances. 'His death was quite sad – he lived in Sydney, and was murdered. That goes back to 1979. The guy who bashed him to death only got about four or five years in prison. So, Paul hasn't had an easy life.'

After he finished school, Paul went to work at a concreting business, staying there for many years. He never married, but did have several girlfriends. Julie felt he never wanted to be tied down. She was always close to her brother, at one stage living just around the corner from him. She would go over and have coffee with Paul every day. She remembers:

My eldest brother passed away, and I believe that triggered the onset of Paul's schizophrenia. That was more than 15 years ago. My eldest brother took on a fatherly role to Paul, because Paul was only young when our father was murdered; he was about 12. Paul looked after our older brother when he was dying, every day, as they lived together with Mum. Paul was really good with him, but it pushed him over the edge when he died, losing the one special person who meant the world to him. Paul was never the same after that. That's when he started drinking. Paul had never been a drinker before.

Julie feels that Paul just didn't want to live after losing his brother, and sees the drinking as Paul trying to destroy himself. 'The drink masked a lot of grief, as the grief was too overwhelming for him,' says Julie. 'So much, that it caused a severe mental illness. And that's understandable, given the life he's had. Everything he's had, he's lost. He became an alcoholic when he was in his forties, but I didn't realise that he was also drinking to mask the symptoms of his mental illness. I've learned since, through support groups and different professionals telling me, that it was self-medicating.

'He would drink every day, which got him into a bit of trouble. He would go around to Mum's place and be a bit of a menace. She's getting on in years, so she was scared, and put an AVO (apprehended violence order) on him. Paul broke that, and went to gaol for six months. But I was always there in the courtroom, standing up for him, and I maintained to the judge that there was something wrong with Paul. He needed some mental assessment.

'I didn't know the first thing about schizophrenia or any mental illness, but I knew something was not right, it was out of character. I went and explained that to every judge. The last time I had to go to court for Paul, the judge released him, saying he needed to be assessed mentally. Someone finally listened. So, we did all that, but Paul would say, *"I'm okay."* How do you know if you have a mental illness if you're that sick? And these days it's really hard to get help for them, it's hard to get someone to listen.

'I phoned so many people in the mental health department, and they said, "Paul has to want the help." I would argue with them – how does he know that he needs the help when he's that sick? He can't make that decision for himself. I'm his sister; I know him, and I know it's not right. It got to the stage where he came and lived with me for quite a while. He started seeing things. He once looked in the mirror and said, "I've got blood coming out of my eyes." I told him everything would be all right, to just sit down and calm down. I ended up having to call an ambulance. They took him to hospital and I asked the mental health team to assess him. They took him straight through to the hospital. They called me and said he was refusing treatment. I told them they'd have to treat him somehow, because if he came out of hospital, he'd be straight back into an ambulance and back to hospital. They finally listened to me and started treating him, and he responded. The hospital started to really take notice, which was great, after so many long conversations and meetings with doctors. They finally diagnosed him with schizophrenia. That was all new to me; I had to learn about schizophrenia and what it did, and it all made sense. The puzzle just fitted together.'

But the journey was only just beginning for Paul and his sister. Paul would take his medication for a while, and when he started to feel better, decided he no longer needed to keep taking it. He started to disappear for days at a time. He would call Julie to tell her he was fine, and there was nothing wrong with him.

Julie thinks Paul felt quite ashamed to admit he had a mental illness:

He was never like that, he was quite normal growing up. His illness developed when he was in his late thirties. I look at it like I've had two brothers — the one that was quite normal and could carry on a conversation, and lived an everyday life, able to cope and do things for himself to someone who cannot anymore. It was a hard transition. It was like a grief process. You grieve for the person you knew, and you get used to the one you have now. He is the way he is, for as long as he lives. He's as good as he can be. But when he goes off, he goes off his medication, which means he deteriorates.

As Paul's mental illness progressed, he would go missing for longer periods of time, and would usually be very unwell when finally found. He would sometimes go and sleep near his brother's grave. 'Our father's memorial is up there too,' says Julie. 'He'd take off to anywhere. They'd find him in caves, the cemetery – everywhere. Lots of different places. It's always a real worry, to have a family member like that.'

Paul has previously been found in a cave at Bens Walk, a picturesque track leading around the shoreline of the Shoalhaven River. Julie says quite a few homeless people from the Nowra area take shelter in the caves.

'That's the thing I get concerned about. Nowra, being the way it is … you get a lot of undesirables, put it that way. Sometimes I fear for his safety, because he's too vulnerable. He's also been found in the bushes near the war memorial in Bomaderry. The conditions are often cold and wet, and he's been found in a terrible condition. But the time he's found, he's been off his medication too long to grasp the seriousness of what's happened. That's what worries me; if he's off his medication for more than three or four days he becomes incoherent. He doesn't realise he needs to eat and drink, and to be under shelter, and not exposed to the elements. He's filthy, his clothes are filthy, and by the time he's found he always has to go to hospital and spend at least

24 hours on the drip replacing his fluids. Every day that goes past, it's worse for him. This last time, we didn't even know if he'd come back from it mentally. He's not as good as before, but he has come back. But each time this happens he's doing more damage to himself.'

When Paul went missing just before I wrote this chapter, he was found by two young men who helped him, and got him home safely. They found Paul sleeping rough behind some bushes. They took him to a nearby motel and gave him a shower and a meal, and contacted authorities to let them know Paul was safe. Julie is full of praise for these good Samaritans: 'I thought it was the kindest thing I'd heard for a long time. It was really wonderful. When they found him he was very dirty. I think they even went out and found some clothing for him. Instead of someone taking advantage, they were giving.' Julie is very grateful for the help she receives when Paul goes missing. 'The public are really good,' she says. 'The people on your Facebook page, and the people around town have got to know Paul, or know of him, and they're more than willing to get in touch with me if they sight him. They've been marvellous.'

If people contact Julie directly about sightings of Paul, she contacts police, who do go and check, but usually Paul has moved on by the time police get there. It's very frustrating. Julie also often drives around the streets herself looking for her brother:

'I've handed out so many flyers to people,' she says. 'I'm so used to him going missing. It becomes second nature. He's been missing at least five or six times. But I've really lost count. Sometimes I feel so awful getting in touch with you and asking you to put up Paul's photo again, I think you must think I'm a mental case.' I assure Julie that of course I don't. I will always make appeals for Paul, no matter how many times he goes missing. Julie tells me the posts do help her a great deal, especially making the public aware when Paul is missing again:

The community understand Paul is not well, and that he needs help, and needs his medication, and they've been so helpful. That's helped me, to know there are more eyes out there when I can't be there, and when they spot him, that gives me hope. While you've got hope, you've got everything. It's been wonderful.

Julie feels just as worried each time Paul goes missing now as she did the first time he disappeared. No matter how many times Paul is found safe, Julie can never be sure that the next time something terrible won't happen. 'There's always that element of doubt,' she says. 'When I go to my warm bed at night, I always look out the window and think of him. Even when I've been out all day looking for him, I come home disappointed that I haven't been able to do more, or that I haven't found him. I wake up in the night and think of him, out there. Is he okay, what's the weather like, is it raining, is it too cold? You never lose that worry. Even though he does this so very often, the level of concern never changes.'

Julie wishes the police shared her level of concern, as she gets the feeling they become complacent about Paul's disappearances the more they happen. As Paul is always located safely, police tend not to respond with urgency anymore. 'I can't allow myself to think that way,' says Julie. 'Because anything could happen to him. He could walk out in front of a car. He's been found staggering on the road, because he's deteriorating mentally. He's just not aware of the dangers, or where he is and what he's doing. It's like when very young children go missing, who can't fend for themselves. With Paul, it's not so bad on the first or second day, because I know the medication will still be in his system, but after that it becomes no different to having a missing child. He's very vulnerable. When I see someone has a missing child, my heart goes out to them, because I know the level of worry they must be carrying. I can relate to them.'

When Paul isn't missing, and has been stable for a while, Julie can start to relax. 'Especially when he's first been found, because it usually takes about two months of intensive therapy and medication for him to stabilise. Proper diet, being looked after, back on his feet. After three months, I start to think that he's on top of things, and that's more likely the time that he *could* go missing again, because he thinks he okay. I'm coming up to that time very shortly, actually. There's a pattern. But you just go with the flow. It's not a case of *if* Paul goes missing again, it's *when*. I'm 100 per cent sure it will happen again. I think, finally, between the doctors and the hospital we finally got through to the police that it is quite an urgent situation when he goes missing because of his mental health deterioration. In time, he may not come back mentally, so that's always very concerning too. The longer it is, the worse it is.'

Julie sometimes asks Paul about what happens to him when he's been missing, about where he's been and what he's been through, but he's reluctant to talk about it. Julie isn't sure why. 'I talk to him in a roundabout way,' she says. 'There's ways you have to approach someone with schizophrenia. I might say to him, How did you feel when you went missing? But not ask him why, because then he backs off. You have to find the way of talking to them that gets the best out of them. But he's never really opened up about being out there, which I'm quite surprised about. Whether he's ashamed of it, I don't know.'

I suggested to Julie that perhaps Paul is so sick of being poked and prodded by doctors and psychologists and monitored so much that, when he's missing, that's his private time that no-one gets to know about, and Julie feels that's spot-on. 'He sees psychiatrists, he goes to group meetings where they put their feelings out on the table, and I think there are times in his life that he wants to keep to himself. And I have to respect that little bit of privacy that he wants.'

It's difficult to know what will trigger Paul to go missing. Sometimes it is the feeling of being so well he thinks he no longer needs medication. Sometimes something in his living arrangements may upset him. Paul's way of expressing being upset is to go missing and forget about the real world.

It's easy to forget that all the family tragedy that has affected Paul so badly also happened to Julie, yet she is a strong and serene woman who seems like she can cope with anything you can throw at her. She says:

I'm a teetotaller – I do not drink at all. I've seen enough of it to not want to drink. I have accepted this is the way my life is now, with Paul. If I didn't accept it, it would become very unhealthy for me. I had to learn to accept the things I can't change. It is what it is. I can't change it. I wish I could, but I can only do what I can do to look after him, and find him when he goes missing. I would never leave him out there. If you get a phone call to say Paul's gone missing, then you deal with it. It's an ongoing saga.

I don't know how other people cope with it. It's taken me a long time to get to where I am now, though. I used to be stressed out all the time with the worry of him, but I realised that was quite unhealthy. I can't change Paul's illness, and I can't change what could happen; all I can do is accept it and do what I can to help him. Everybody needs to find their way of coping with these situations. I never thought I would accept him being schizophrenic, but I've had to learn.

I've got a great husband, Richard, he's very supportive, he's excellent. We all need our support, and mine is my husband. You can't do it without a support network. He comes out with me to search for him, sometimes in the dark. You have to be very careful yourself, too. You can't go out looking around on your own, so we go together. We go into the shops and medical centres and hand out flyers and it's so good when someone says yes, I saw him today. It lifts you. Richard has helped me so much. There's not a thing he wouldn't do to help me. He's done so much for Paul over the years, but we realised we needed to leave it to the professionals. We just need to know he's getting the appropriate care that he deserves. I do make sure he has it. You've got to draw a happy medium for yourself, though.

Julie knows that she has to look after Paul for her mother's sake, also. 'Mum is over 80 now, and she's very limited in what she can do. She does worry about Paul, though.' Julie tells her mother when Paul goes missing but Julie takes on the responsibility of dealing with it. She lets her mum know about any sightings of Paul when he's missing and it keeps her mother's spirits up during those anxious days. 'At the moment they're trying to find accommodation for him, in a group home type of hostel. They have nurses in attendance who give them their medication, meals, do their washing because they're not capable of looking after themselves. It's a really big job. It's something I've thought about doing, but I soon realised I don't think I could do it. It's a 24-hour-a-day job. But I need to know he's placed in the right accommodation with the right care, as every human being deserves, and that's all I ask for.

'It's been a bit of a battle with him, but he's stable at the moment, and he's going along quite okay. That's a relief. He's very open to going to the supported accommodation. He gets on well with anyone. He's a polite, well-mannered man. He's not violent whatsoever. Everyone who meets him likes him. He's a very gentle man, wouldn't hurt a fly. He'd be the first one to help you, he's a gentleman. Maybe the supported accommodation will be the key to him not going missing again. We'll see how it turns out.'

I asked Julie if she can see a day where Paul will need to live in secure accommodation, to prevent him going missing, and she sadly agrees that's likely. 'It's hard to talk to him about that,' she says. 'And I don't like that idea. I think I'm coping with what's happening with him now, and he can come and go as he pleases. But the day will come when he can't. That will be like losing someone. The psychiatrists have told Paul if he takes off one more time that he will be sent to Sydney, to a secure facility. He will be sectioned, for his own safety. Do I think that's enough to stop him running again? No. I'm pretty sure they mean what they say. I'm disappointed that they have not spoken to me about this, as it was Paul who told me that's what they've said. I was quite shocked. A phone call to me to discuss this would have been more appropriate. It was not helpful for Paul at all. I'm going to ask them why they said it to him. You have to be on top of these things.'

Since my interview with Julie, I am delighted to say that Paul has not been missing again. He's living in supported accommodation, and Julie says: 'He's very happy and contented there. He loves the nature side of living ... he walks down the property every morning and sits near the bush where the kangaroos eat, he simply loves it! There is hope for people like Paul, he is living the best life he can, and that's all I can ask for him. He's very happy.'

CONCLUSION
Thanks for reading.

I know it isn't easy to look into the lives of people in such pain. But on behalf of all the people whose stories you have just read, they want you to know that it helps them. Without exception, they all feel like they can never truly do enough to find their missing loved ones. When do they stop looking?

By reading their stories, you are helping them know that they did one giant thing to look that little bit further. You're helping them shine that spotlight. And to know that you all care means the world to them. As a community, to care about one another is the greatest thing we can do as human beings.

Not long after my first book was published, I was deeply honoured to receive the 2023 Mitchell Ferrario Compassion in Media award at the Queensland Homicide Victims' Support Group gala dinner. This was especially important to me, because showing compassion when I write about victims is of such paramount importance to me.

Shaun Barker's case and how he was described in the media (see Chapter 11) illustrates perfectly how vital it is that we put compassion first when talking about those who have lost their lives. That same night I met Queensland Police Commissioner Katarina Carroll. She congratulated me on the award, and said she thinks it's great that I'm able to make such a connection with victims. I said that as a society, it's something we should all be doing, all the time. She said, 'Yes, actually that's true.'

If we start making little changes in the way we treat other people, with compassion, then that's how we change the world.

ACKNOWLEDGEMENTS

A huge thanks to the families of the missing who shared their stories with me for this book, as well as their extended families and supporters, and police officers:

Sonia, Sylvia, Brenda, Gloria Lockey; Jodie and Samantha; Damien and Fiona; Rick, Roger and Tammy.

Barry and Rachel Butterfield, the late Belinda Butterfield, Thorne and Skye, Lucy.

Stephenie Fielding.

Peter and Catt King and Detective Sergeant Tanya Mason.

Mark, Brian and Tim Jones and the extended Jones family.

Dylan Redman.

Barbara Anderson.

Judy, Adrian, Vernon, Elaine, Dorothy, Greg and John Howe and the extended Howe family.

Christine, Fabienne, Phillip, Bernadette, Diana, Zach and Sylvia Jourdan, Jessie, Sam and Nikita. Di Williams and Taz Millar.

Sandra Mitchell.

Sheridan Mollenhauer and her family.

Paul's sister Julie J.

Also thank you to authors Emma Healey, Dave Warner and Debi Marshall, and especially Duncan McNab, who always messages me back immediately, allays all my fears and is a wealth of knowledge about the Sydney underworld.

To the amazing Kate Kyriacou, who I will always be a bit in awe of, no matter how long we've known each other, and who did a sterling job of introducing me at my Brisbane book launch. Once again, the lovely Justine Ford, for always being an inspiration.

Thank you to my team at Big Sky Publishing, Diane, Jodee, Alison and Denny, and a special thanks to the hardest working publicist in the business, Sharon Evans, who seems to work 24/7 and is my absolute champion. Also the team at Simon and Schuster; I knew I was in very safe hands.

To Julie Hand, for her unwavering support and friendship, and for introducing me at the Highfields book launch, as well as writing the foreword for this book and nominating me for the Compassion in Media award.

Thank you to Rowan MacDonald for being the most enthusiastic book reviewer, who went above and beyond in his support and interest in *Vanished*. He was one of the first to review it and his overwhelming positivity really made me believe I had created a winner. Thanks also to all the other wonderful Instagram book reviewers who happily agreed to read and review a book on a topic they mostly hadn't read about before; to hear their praise for the book was incredible. Not to mention I am in awe of how they posed the book in pretty locations and took amazing photos, something I am hopeless at; despite actually taking the book on holiday to Japan with me I failed to take a single iconic photo of it.

Thank you to Andy, the most amazing friend, who just understands me, and is always there to be my voice of reason and perspective. Your sunrise and ocean photo texts every day help me more than you know.

Thank you to my friends and work colleagues who have all been so incredibly supportive of *Vanished*, and my local community who trekked to my house in droves to buy signed copies. Thank you, Dakota, Kel and Barry at my local newsagency and post office. Barry stocked the book before anyone else after I gave his wife an early copy, and she loved it. Dakota and Kel do not bat an eye when I dump 30 books on the counter for mailing out to readers.

As always, my family are everything to me: Thanks to my parents and sister, as well as Jan and David, and extended family, for being my cheer squad. To Steve, your love and humour keeps me sane. Rowan, Scarlett and Lachy, you bring me joy every day. Last, but not ever least, my constant companion and writing supervisor, Bolt the Samoyed, the greatest dog who ever lived.

ABOUT THE AUTHOR

Nicole Morris is the Director of the Australian Missing Persons Register, which she founded in 2005. In June 2023, Nicole was honoured with the Compassion in Media award by the Queensland Homicide Victims' Support Group. In 2012, she received the Queensland Pride of Australia award for Community Spirit, followed by a National gold medal in the same year. Twice nominated for Australian of the Year, Nicole has made numerous appearances on radio, television, and in newsprint. She serves as a voice for voiceless missing persons, tirelessly advocating for them and raising awareness. Providing comfort and guidance to countless families and friends of missing persons, she supports them on their journeys to find their lost loved ones. With hundreds of thousands of followers on her Facebook page, Nicole has earned the respect of law enforcement and government agencies both in Australia and internationally. Her debut book, "Vanished" (2023), shares the stories of families of Australian missing persons.

Connect with Nicole:
Instagram: nicole_morris_author
Facebook: austmissingpersons
X: AMPRegister
Website: www.australianmissingpersonsregister.com
LinkedIn: nicole-morris-93410575

If this book has raised concerns for you or someone you know please contact Lifeline on 13 11 14 or Beyond Blue 1300 22 4636 or Mensline 1300 789 978, or the National Alcohol and Other Drug Hotline on 1800 250 015 or Family Drug Support on 1300 368 186.

If you have any information about a missing person you can contact Crime Stoppers on 1800 333 000 or go to www.crimestoppers.com.au You don't have to say who you are or get involved.

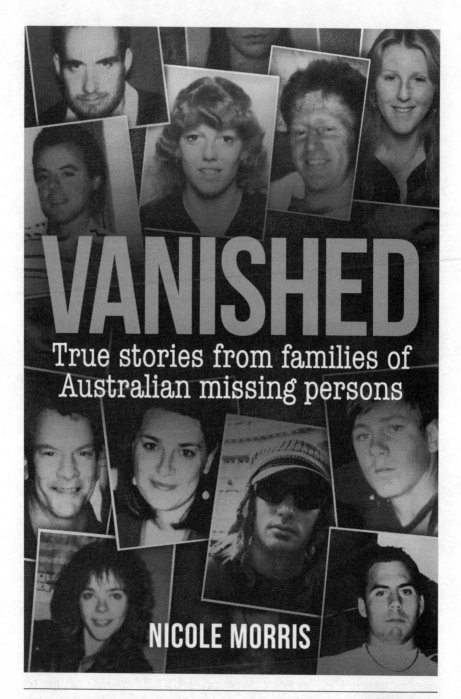

VANISHED

True stories from families of Australian missing persons

NICOLE MORRIS

BIG SKY PUBLISHING

Praise for Vanished:

I saw the cover and it just broke my heart, opened
and read the first page and knew I had to read it,
the writing already had me hooked. I am extremely
sad to read these stories and I can only hope the
families and loved ones find peace.

_____

Thoroughly enjoyed reading this extremely sad book.
Nicole Morris has done a wonderful job relaying
these missing people and their families' stories,
with sincerity and honour.

_____

Just a quick message to let you know your book
is amazing. I cried a lot throughout and looked
at the photos of the beautiful missing men and
women you included in your book.

_____

A deeply moving and insightful exploration
of missing people. Nothing goes unnoticed
in this thought-provoking true crime novel
that will enlighten and enthral.

_____

Nicole Morris touched on a HARD subject
on this book, and she did it with so much
compassion and understanding.

_____

A fantastic and informative exploration into
these individual's stories. Nicole does a great
service and I know her work will continue to help,
inform and advocate for those who need it.

For more great titles visit

www.bigskypublishing.com.au